ARGUING FUNDAMENTAL RIGHTS

ARGUING FUNDAMENTAL RIGHTS

Edited by

AGUSTÍN JOSÉ MENÉNDEZ
University of León, Spain
and University of Oslo, Norway

ERIK ODDVAR ERIKSEN
University of Oslo, Norway

Springer

A C.I.P. Catalogue record for this book is available from the Library of Congress.

ISBN-10: 1-4020-4918-8 (HB)
ISBN-13: 978-1-4020-4918-7 (HB)
ISBN-10: 1-4020-4919-4 (e-book)
ISBN-13: 978-1-4020-4919-6 (e-book)

Published by Springer,
P.O. Box 17, 3300 AA Dordrecht, The Netherlands.

www.springer.com

Printed on acid-free paper

CONTENTS

LIST OF CONTRIBUTORS

Robert Alexy is Professor of Public Law and Legal Philosophy at the Christian-Albrechts University of Kiel. He is the author of the classics *A Theory of Legal Argumentation* (1989), *A Theory of Constitutional Rights* (2002) and *The Argument from Injustice* (2002).

Carlos Bernal is Professor of Legal Theory at the Universidad Externado de Colombia and researcher at the Institute of Constitutional Studies Carlos Restrepo at the same University. He is the author of *El principio de proporcionalidad y los derechos fundamentales* (2003).

Erik Oddvar Eriksen is Professor of Political Theory at ARENA and at the Center for Professional Studies at the University of Oslo. He is the author of *Demokratiets sorte hull* (2001) and *Understanding Habermas* (2003).

Mattias Kumm is Professor of Law at the New York University School of Law. He is the author of *Who is the final arbiter of constitutionality in Europe* (1999) and *The Jurisprudence of Constitutional Conflict* (2005).

Massimo La Torre is Professor of Legal Philosophy at the University Magna Grecia of Catanzaro. He is the author of *Disavventure del Diritto Soggetivo* (1996) and *La Crisi del Novecento. Giuristi e filosofi del crepuscolo di Weimar* (2006).

Agustín José Menéndez is Senior Researcher at the University of León (Spain) and research fellow of the RECON network at the University of Oslo. He is the author of *Justifying Taxes* (2001).

Julian Rivers is Lecturer at the Faculty of Social Sciences and Law at the University of Bristol. He is the author of *Blasphemy Law in the Secular State* (2000) and editor and translator of *A Theory of Constitutional Rights* (2002).

Kaarlo Tuori is Professor of Jurisprudence, Departament of Public Law, at the University of Helsinki. He is also member of the Venice Commission. He is the author of *Law and Power: Critical and Socio-Legal Essays* (1997) and *Critical Legal Positivism* (2002).

A. J. Menéndez and E. O. Eriksen (eds.), Arguing Fundamental Rights, vii–viii.

AGUSTÍN JOSÉ MENÉNDEZ AND ERIK ODDVAR ERIKSEN

INTRODUCTION

I do take law very seriously, deeply seriously, because fragile as reason is, and limited as law is as the expression of the institutionalised medium of reason, that's all we have standing between us and the tyranny of mere will and the cruelty of unbridled, undisciplined feeling.

Felix Frankfurter

This book is an exploration of one of the outstanding works in contemporary legal and constitutional theory, Robert Alexy's *A Theory of Constitutional Rights*, (hereinafter *A Theory*).[1] This is done by means of a critical analysis[2] of the structural elements of Alexy's theory, an appraisal of its substantial implications, and an assessment of its applied relevance. For different reasons and on different grounds, the contributors to this volume conclude that *A Theory* is a chief theoretical achievement, which has made a major contribution to the development of a normatively grounded, post-positivistic analysis of constitutional law.[3] It has not only played a major role in the transcendence of the characterisation of legal reasoning (and very especially, constitutional legal reasoning) as a mere exercise in hermeneutics or else in judicial legislation.[4] It also constitutes a superior alternative to black-letter legal dogmatics, critical legal studies, economic analysis of law and originalism, all of which end up disconnecting law and justice.[5]

I. WHY ARGUING FUNDAMENTAL RIGHTS

In addition to numerous book chapters and journal articles (which are listed in the bibliography which closes this volume), Robert Alexy is author of three major works of legal theory. In 1978 he published the first edition of his ground-breaking *Theorie der Juristischen Argumentation*,[6] perhaps the book which has been and keeps on being more influential in the flourishing of studies on legal argumentation and legal reasoning in the last two decades of the twentieth century.[7] Here discourse theory is applied to law and the constitutional state,[8] which leads to the characterisation of legal reasoning as a reason-giving practice which allows for the rational assessments of norms. In 1992 he published *Begriff und Geltung des Rechts*,[9] which has brought clarity in the

A. J. Menéndez and E. O. Eriksen (eds.), Arguing Fundamental Rights, 1–12.

muddled question of the relationship between law and morality, or more precisely, between moral, ethical, prudential and legal reasoning. Law is described as a system of legal norms that claims to be right or just. The correctness of legal norms is thus internally related to justice. Extremely unjust norms are not only dubiously legitimate in *normative terms*, but they are also *legally invalid*.[10] Between these two works, Alexy published *A Theory*, which, as will be considered in more detail in the remaining of this introduction, has been recognised as a major contribution to both structural and substantive theories on fundamental rights, and as a master general exposition of German constitutional law. Given the breadth and depth of his work, it is hard not to conclude that Alexy is one of the major modern legal philosophers, on a par with Hans Kelsen, H.L.A. Hart, Ota Weinberger, Ronald Dworkin, Neil MacCormick and Joseph Raz.

There are four main reasons why this volume focuses on *A Theory*. It seems to us that Alexy has managed to develop a structural and substantial general theory of fundamental rights, the applied relevance of which goes clearly beyond the interpretation of the fundamental rights provision of the 1949 German Constitution (as tested in the fourth part of the book). We are further convinced that the theory and application of fundamental rights is one of the key questions, if not *the key question*, in democratic, constitutional states.

First, *A Theory* is above all a sophisticated and exact structural theory of fundamental rights, which enhances analytical clarity in legal reasoning. Alexy's characterisation of the scope of rights and rights limits, his examination of the question of the inalienable core of fundamental rights, and his three-fold distinction between *rights to something, liberties and powers* are among the many analytical contributions of the book. All of them are closely related to the central insight of *A Theory*, namely, that fundamental rights are mainly and foremostly principles, not rules (the latter being characterised by not allowing exceptions to their application).[11] Principles are depicted as optimisation commands to be weighed and balanced according to the proportionality principle in a particular situation, and not as deontological levers. This is due to the fact that most reasoning on fundamental rights revolves around the solving of conflicts *between* norms that call for balancing and accommodation of different principles, and not the unconditional application of rules. In this regard, his reconstruction of the principle of proportionality has proved a lasting contribution to the literature, regarded as such even by Alexy's critics (the second section of the book is indeed representative of such criticisms).

Second, *A Theory* also contains elements of a *substantive theory* of fundamental rights. This is so on two different (but related) accounts.

On the one hand, analytical sophistication allows Alexy to draw conclusions which are relevant to a substantive theory of fundamental rights. To put it differently, one could say that analytical clarity contributes to clear-minded substantive theory. Consider the following two examples:

- *A Theory* makes a clear distinction between fundamental rights positions and subjective fundamental rights. Although the *standard* fundamental rights position is a subjective right, fundamental rights comprise not only subjective individual positions, but also collective goods. This entails that a conflict between a subjective fundamental right (e.g., a civic right), and a public policy aimed at rendering effective some collective good (e.g., one closely attached to socio-economic rights, such as full employment) cannot be sorted out by the simple expedient of affirming that the *subjective fundamental right* should prevail. If the collective good also has a fundamental status, we are confronted with a fundamental rights conflict, which requires weighing and balancing the conflicting fundamental rights positions at stake. Thus, a proper dissection of fundamental rights norms shows that fundamental rights positions comprise not only subjective rights, but also collective goods. And further, if the collective good also has a fundamental status, we are confronted with a fundamental rights collision, which requires weighing and balancing the conflicting fundamental rights positions at stake. This helps us avoiding the *unexplicited* endorsement of a liberist or libertarian substantive conception of fundamental rights, which is a common connotation of fundamental rights (and one contested in the fourth section of the book by Mattias Kumm). This theoretical setup renders possible assessing the merits of fundamental rights in substantive terms, and not simply endorsing them on the basis of their plain appearance as fundamental human principles. Or, to say it with not so many words, a proper structural theory of fundamental rights helps us avoiding unintended or ill grounded substantive choices.
- It is usually claimed that it is pretty unproblematic to grant fundamental status and full justiciability to civic and political rights because they are defensive or negative rights, viz., because they only require the state to *refrain from doing something*, and thus can be judicially enforced without the judiciary exceeding its proper and legitimate role in a democratic legal order. On the contrary, the justiciability of socio-economic rights should be ruled out, given that they are protective or positive rights, entitling right-holders to *positive state action*. Judicial review based on socio-economic rights would come at the price of undermining the proper division of labour between legislature, executive and judiciary, as judges would be forced to *second-guess* what it would be appropriate that the legislature should do. However, Alexy's analytical dissection of fundamental rights shows that this argument is only half true. On the basis of a proper analysis of fundamental rights we can summarise that most fundamental rights,

including civic and political ones, are bundles of both *defensive* and *protective fundamental rights positions*. This implies that the justiciability argument should cut across a much less neat line than that pretending to separate civic and political from socio-economic rights.[12]

On the other hand, *A Theory* contains elements of a substantive theory of fundamental rights proper. This is not surprising, given that in his *Theory of Legal Argumentation*, Alexy had already formulated his *special case thesis* (*die Sonderfallthese*), according to which legal reasoning is a special case of general practical reasoning, viz., a variant of moral reasoning.[13] The special case thesis leads quite naturally to the characterisation of fundamental rights as carriers of the practical morality which underpins the legal system. This invites the exploration of the substantive content of fundamental rights, and more specifically, the principles of liberty, equality and solidarity underscoring the postwar *Rechtsstaat*. It is important to notice that Alexy considers *all three* principles, and not merely the former two. Indeed, chapter 9 of *A Theory* contains a case for the constitutional protection of *rights to entitlements in a narrow sense*, which are generally referred as *socio-economic* in the legal orders of *modern welfare states*.

Third, *A Theory* is not only of relevance for (what practioners might find) narrow theoretical reasons. The book is also one of the most authoritative general expositions of German fundamental rights law. Despite Alexy's modest claim to be writing a theory of fundamental rights of "the [German] Basic Law,"[14] that is, a theory circumscribed to German positive law, it seems to us that *A Theory* can and should be applied to other positive legal orders. In general terms, the book contains elements of a structural and a substantive theory of fundamental rights which should be helpful to practitioners and legal operators dealing with the basic legal structure of any modern society. More concretely, we would argue that German constitutional law has exerted a pervasive influence, directly and indirectly, over the constitutional law of many states, and very particularly, European ones. On the one hand, it may not be exaggerated to claim that German constitutional dogmatics has provided the constitutional grammar according to which many European constitutions have either been written, rewritten or interpreted. The German postwar tradition of constructing fundamental rights is indeed likely to leave its imprint even on the common law, once fundamental rights have been *brought home*, so to say, by the UK Human Rights Act 1998,[15] as Rivers highlights in his contribution to this volume. On the other hand, the constitutional law of the European Union is the result of a process of *progressive constitutional integration*, framed by the core constitutional principles common to the Member States of the Union.[16] One of the national constitutions which has exerted a decisive influence upon the common constitutional assets is, without doubts, the German one. This was indeed recently proven again with the solemn proclamation of the Charter of Fundamental Rights of the European Union,[17] whose structure and content is heavily influenced by German fundamental law (from the opening and key role assigned to the right to dignity to the reinforced protection of the right to private property). Menéndez explores this question in chapter 8 by assessing the potential of Alexy's theory when it comes to fundamental rights reasoning in Europe. For these two sets of reasons, Alexy's theory is relevant to most, if not all, European legal orders. Europeanisation through integration into the European Union and through the discipline imposed by the European Convention of Human Rights had an impact upon national fundamental rights norms. Even if the concrete fundamental rights rules which result from the weighing and balancing of fundamental rights norms in specific cases are in some cases divergent, such differences are in most cases so that the solution affirmed in one legal system would have been a plausible alternative in any other legal order (and indeed it is not unconceivable that it may come to be *also the fundamental right rule* in the other legal orders).

Fourth, Alexy's theory constitutes a seminal contribution to the analysis of how legal reasoning on fundamental rights is intimately connected to the very foundations of democracy. On the one hand, democratic legitimacy presupposes the mutual acknowledgment of fundamental rights, a necessary but not sufficient condition for those subject to law also being capable of recognising themselves (at least, that they *could* recognise themselves) as its authors. They must be able to see themselves as rights-bearers as well as subjects – as the ones who give themselves the rights they are to live by, so to say. On the other hand, the subjection of *democratic law* to review on the basis of its compliance with fundamental rights raises complicated institutional questions, which cannot be reduced to technical constitutional engineering. Is fundamental rights proofing better left to public debate? Is it more appropriate to trust judges to review? Who are judges to quash democratically made law? Moreover, what is left of public autonomy, if law is interpreted as the mere concretisation of a thick and wide constitutional program? On the other hand, who are law-makers to disregard constitutionally enshrined fundamental rights? Alexy might be read as holding justice to be a more important value than democracy, which gives rise to problems that Eriksen addresses in chapter 4. Indeed, the centrality of fundamental rights reflects their condition as positive carriers of moral principles, which in their turn contribute to morality by undertaking many coordinative functions.[18] Law reduces transactions costs and information problems as it establishes what is the right thing to do in practical contexts. This explains both the centrality of fundamental rights in democratic debate, and the complexity of the issues involved. But not all issues, we might be allow to add, are equally complex. Although many tend regularly to characterise fundamental rights as a luxury which can only be afforded by those who need them less, namely rich and democratic Western societies,[19] we are periodically confronted with dramatic facts which prove that the very survival of open democratic societies depends on taking fundamental rights seriously. Indeed, the conception of law which underpins a good deal of the law and practice in the so-called war on terror, not only in the United States, but also in Europe, is a dramatic reminder of the practical implications of going from the characterisation of law as a special case of practical reasoning[20] back to a thick ethical conception of law which renders possible its unilateral instrumentalisation by power. When we are confronted with arguments in favour of the juridification of torture,[21] the repudiation of international human rights law[22] and the constitutionalisation of full-range presidential power,[23] there are plenty of reasons why fundamental rights protection remains a burning issue. Indeed, it is sad that events since this volume was first conceived have dramatically revealed the utmost importance of *structural* and *substantial* conceptions of fundamental rights.

In editing this book, we have homogeneised the English translation of the core concepts of Alexy's constitutional theory, essentially following the standard set by Julian Rivers in the masterful English version of *A Theory*. Having said that, we have departed in two instances from Rivers' usage. All through the book, we have rendered "Grundrechte" as *fundamental rights*, not as *constitutional rights*. It seems to us that such a choice is mandated by the strong connotations which the term has in the post-war constitutional practice of continental nation-states. On different but related grounds, we have rendered "Optimierungsgebote" as *optimisation commands*, and not as *optimization requirements*. In both cases, we followed the standard translation approved by Alexy before 2002.

II. CONTENTS OF THE VOLUME

The *three-fold character* of *A Theory* – as structural, substantial and applied theory of fundamental rights – explains the wide breadth and scope of the contributions to this volume.

The *first section* situates and revisits *A Theory*. In the first chapter, *Alexy* revisits *A Theory* and further develops some of its leading themes. He expands on the relation between fundamental rights and human rights, and renders more precise his reply to Habermas' criticisms, more specifically, his well-known firewall and irrationality allegations. In addition, Alexy (1) elucidates the concept of fundamental rights, and distinguishes three different conceptions of fundamental rights (formal, substantial and procedural); (2) differentiates eight potential foundations of fundamental rights: religious, intuitionist, consensual, socio-biological, instrumental, cultural, explicative and existential. The German legal philosopher further claims that a *deliberative-democratic conception* of fundamental rights domesticates the two latter justifications, as it is based on rendering explicit the pragmatic assumptions we make when we make assertions, and also on the characterisation of *assertion* as the most basic human experience; (3) shows that the *rationality* of balancing is a way of solving conflicts between principles; this is done by means of explicating the *rational insights* which underlies the *Law of Balancing* with the help of the *Weight Formula*.

The *second section* focuses on the structural elements of Alexy's theory of fundamental rights. *Eriksen* claims that Alexy's constitutional theory might be descriptively correct, but is *normatively unacceptable*. In democratic societies, legal procedures are to ensure legally correct and rationally acceptable decisions, that is, decisions that can be defended both in relation to legal statutes and in relation to public criticism. But can the legal system via the discretion of the judges itself really autonomously settle normative questions? The problem is whether the substantial factors are legitimate, and whether the judges' interpretations of the situations are correct. Alexy's conception of the legal discourse as a special variant of general practical reason blurs the distinction between legislation and application. There is a danger of assimilating law and morality and of overburdening the legal medium itself. Moral and legal questions point to different audiences, raise different validity claims and require different procedures for resolving conflicts. Further, by characterising *judicial application* as a combination of justification and application discourses, Alexy is bound to shift the authorship of legal norms from democratic legislatures to judges and courts. His theory leads to a relativistic conception of correctness, as at the end of the day what is correct is to be determined by the judges. The author, who shares Alexy's preference for deliberative democracy, favours a variant of *constitutional proceduralism* hinged on discursive proceduralism which sets the terms for a fair procedure of reason giving. This standard for correctness is imperfect but ensures that the substantial, "pre-political" principles – such as conceptions of justice – entrenched in modern constitutions as basic rights are subjected to discursive testing in a deliberative process. *Tuori* contrasts Alexy's and Dworkin's conception of legal principles. While both offer a rather similar characterisation of the distinction between rules and principles, Alexy fails to establish a further distinction between principles and policies. This is problematic as it implies downplaying the deontological character of principles (as also La Torre and Eriksen claim). This is so because his *analytical approach* to fundamental rights blinds Alexy to the central paradox of the modern conception of fundamental rights as limits to state power *which are established by state* power and limits to law *that are legal in* themselves. This paradox cannot be tackled merely analytically, but requires deconstructing the very idea of modern law. Tuori proposes to distinguish between the surface level of law, the legal culture and the deep structure of law. Fundamental rights only act as *limits of state* power and of *positive law* if they are sufficiently sedimented in subsurface levels. *La Torre* puts forward nine challenges to Alexy's legal and constitutional theory. First, is not the *purely semantic conception of norm* put forward by Alexy incompatible with a *substantive* idea of a rule of recognition, and therefore, (and second), with the very idea of a legal system? Third, La Torre contends that a proper distinction between rules and principles will be precisely just the reverse of the one put forward by Alexy, because only then the *deontological character* of principles will be properly acknowledged. His fourth and fifth critique pertain to whether fundamental rights are to be considered as a matter of principle, given that this entails their characterisation as optimisation commands, and consequently, their "prescriptivisation." He further wonders whether Alexy's three-stage theory of rights really does do away the difference between interest or will-theories of rights (sixth); whether his rejection of a neat distinction between discourses of justification and application might not be descriptively accepted (seventh), but normatively unpalatable (echoing one of Eriksen's central criticisms), and whether the nature of law should not be immediately derived from the characterisation of legal discourses (eighth). La Torre dwells at some length with one of the recurrent themes of the book, namely, whether *the law of balancing* actually ensures the rationality of judicial decisions, or, whether it is just a mask which hides the *discretionality of judges*. *Bernal* offers a critical reconstruction of a key element of Alexy's constitutional theory, namely the principle of proportionality in a narrow sense, that is, the balancing between competing principles, in light the recent publications of Alexy. By means of a detailed analysis of the law of balancing, the weight formula, and the allocation of the burden of argumentation, Bernal shows the transformation of Alexy's understanding of the *law of balancing* and of the *burden of argumentation* in the *Postscript* to the English translation of *A Theory*. He claims that the weight formula contributes to the clarification of the structure of argumentation, even if it cannot point to the one right answer in each and every case. If only because there are several steps at which *discretion* is bound to creep in, such as the assessment of the abstract weight of the competing principles, or the empirical facts which determine the graduation of the competing principles.

The *third section* is devoted to a structural component of Alexy's theory with manifold substantial implications, namely, his theory of the horizontal effect of fundamental rights, that is, the binding effect of rights in relationships among individuals. *Kumm* rehearses a critical confrontation between Alexy's fundamental rights theory and Carl Schmitt's characterisation of constitutional states as total states. Kumm starts by challenging the widely expanded characterisation of subjective fundamental rights as claims *exclusively* against public authorities, as shields against public action, but not against private action. He builds upon Alexy's structural theory of fundamental rights, and more precisely, upon the proportionality principle as a frame for legal argumentation, to claim that the *radiating force* of fundamental rights entails the constitutionalisation of all legal norms, including private law norms. And that, consequently, *fundamental rights* do have horizontal effects. Indeed, Kumm affirms that, substantially speaking, the consequences of affirming that fundamental rights have direct *or* merely indirect horizontal effect are not many. To accept one or the other conception has merely an impact upon the way in which constitutional legal reasoning is structured. He finds that Schmitt's characterisation rightly points to the need of transcending the formalistic differentiation between public and private law, quite clearly anchored in a liberal, but not necessarily democratic, political conception. But still, Schmitt's terminology obscures the real implications of the constitutionalisation of law and the affirmation of judicial review on constitutional grounds. Constitutionalised legal orders are, at the end of the day, *complete legal orders*, where the characterisation of legal reasoning as a special case of general practical reasoning reveals a commitment to political justice.

The *fourth section* explores the extent to which Alexy's theory of fundamental rights can be fruitfully applied to constitutional orders other than the German one. *Rivers* aims at a double target; first, testing whether the first 2 years of case law on the UK Human Rights Act 1998 can be reconstructed *rationally*, and if so, whether they tally with Alexy's theory; second, assessing whether Alexy's fundamental rights theory is as *structural* as the German philosopher claims it to be; by means of applying the theory to the British fundamental rights practice, Rivers is able to detect the hidden *institutional assumptions* implicit in many elements of Alexy's fundamental rights theory. The formal recognition of fundamental rights plays a central role in any theory of fundamental rights. While the Human Rights Act 1998 does not introduce a catalogue of fundamental rights proper, but the obligation to interpret British law *in line with (some of) the rights acknowledged in the European Convention of Human Rights*, British courts have derived fundamental rights from the Act in a similar way as the German, Italian or Spanish constitutional courts derive fundamental rights norms from their national constitutional provisions. Similar points are raised on what concerns the horizontal effect of fundamental rights and on the relationship between legislature and courts under the principle of proportionality, and more specifically, the second law of balancing as defined in the *Postscript* to the English translation. Rivers notices that Alexy's assignment to Courts of the critical decision whether to review or not the knowledge basis on which administrative or state action is based, actually presupposes that the only alternative deciding body is a majoritarian legislature and that the rights at stake are typical individual rights against state action. But both presuppositions might not fit the facts of the case. *Menéndez* aims at testing the extent to which Alexy's theory can bring clarity to fundamental rights reasoning in the European Union. First, it is very helpful in understanding the validity basis of European constitutional law. While the validity of fundamental rights norms in national constitutions tends to be *positive*, that is, based on their enactment by the *pouvoir constituent*, this is not exactly the case in Union law. Fundamental rights norms stem from the constitutional traditions common to the Member States (and as such they have a positive basis); but what is common is something to be determined through a critical comparative approach. On such a basis, the validity basis of fundamental rights norms in Union law is better approached from the standpoint of a theory such as Alexy's. Thus, it is not only the case that the interpretation of fundamental rights norms in Union law renders explicit the connection between law and general practical reasoning, but the very individuation of the fundamental rights norms in the Union points to the *practical reconstruction* of the constitutional traditions of the Member States, and thus, to a connection to *general practical reasoning*. Second, it is claimed that Alexy's distinction between fundamental rights and ordinary rights, and between individual subjective rights and collective goods establish the right angle from which to systematise the fundamental rights provisions of the Charter of Fundamental Rights of the European Union. Third, it also provides an adequate theoretical perspective from which to analyse and adjudicate conflicts between the basic economic freedoms enshrined in the founding Treaties of the Union and the fundamental rights consolidated into the Charter of Fundamental Rights. Fourth, and rather paradoxically, it reveals the *egalitarian potential* of the case law of the Court on the principle of non-discrimination on grounds of nationality.

The *fifth section* holds the bibliography of Robert Alexy.

NOTES

[1] *A Theory of Constitutional Rights*, Oxford: Oxford University Press, 2002 (hereafter, TCR).

[2] Critical understood in a rather Kantian sense, as reason-giving examination, and thus eluding both scepticism and dogmatism.

[3] Cf. in general Neil MacCormick and Ota Weinberger, *An Institutional Theory of Law, New Approaches to Legal Positivism*, Dordrecht: Kluwer, 1997.

[4] Cf. the path-breaking contribution of Jerzy Wróblewski in this book series, *The Judicial Application of Law*, Dordrecht: Kluwer, 1992.

[5] On critical legal studies and law and economics, see Owen Fiss, "The Death of Law," 72 (1986) *Cornell Law Review*, pp. 1–16. On originalism, Cf. Dennis J. Goldford, *The American Constitution and the Debate on Originalism*, Cambridge: Cambridge University Press, 2005.

[6] *A Theory of Legal Argumentation*, Oxford: Oxford University Press, 1989.

[7] Cf. Massimo La Torre, "Theories of Legal Argumentation and Concepts of Law. An Approximation," 15 (2002) *Ratio Juris*, pp. 377–402.

[8] Alexy and Habermas have mutually influenced each other. *A Theory of Legal Argumentation* draws on Habermas' "Wahrheitstheorien," while *Between Facts and Norms* was in a way heavily influenced by Alexy's theory. This is allowed by Habermas himself in "Reply to symposium participants," 17 (1996b) *Cardozo Law Review,* pp. 1477–1557, at p. 1529. Quite obviously, differences remain, very especially on judicial application of law, where Habermas sides with Klaus Günther's appropriateness thesis for application discourses (as distinct from discourses of justification). Cf. *The sense of appropriateness: application discourses in morality and law*, Albany: State University of New York Press, 1993.

[9] *The Argument from Injustice. A reply to legal positivism*, Oxford: Oxford University Press, 2002b.

[10] This is influenced by the famous Radbruch's formula saying that the legal character of a norm is forfeited when the injustice reaches "intolerable degree."

[11] Alexy claims that a structural theory of fundamental rights must be ecumenical on the question of whether fundamental rights should be depicted as principles and principles only, or whether some fundamental rights positions are properly characterised as rules. He also seems to claim that a substantial theory of fundamental rights would settle the issue normatively. Thus, one could find very good reasons why some fundamental rights positions should be characterised as rules, and thus, weighing and balancing should not apply to them *qua rules*. This could be the case of the prohibition of the death penalty, or the prohibition of torture, part of the *complete fundamental rights to life and dignity*.

[12] This argument is similar to the central thesis of Stephen Holmes and Cass Sunstein, *The Cost of Rights. Why Liberty depends on taxes*, New York: Norton, 1999.

[13] See *Theory of Legal Argumentation,* pp. 211–220 and "The Special Case Thesis," 12 (1999b) *Ratio Juris*, pp. 374–384 and "Law and Correctness," in Michael Freeman (ed.), *Legal Theory at the End of the Millennium*, Oxford: Oxford University Press, 1998a, pp. 205–222.

[14] TCR, pp. 5 and 30.

[15] The official text of the Act is available at http://www.hmso.gov.uk/acts/acts1998/19980042.htm. Among the many monographs and articles, see Connor Gearty, *Principles of Human Rights Adjudication*, Oxford: Oxford University Press, 2003. Although Gearty uses a terminology quite apart from Alexy's, one is tempted to conclude that there are many commonalities in the attempt to distil the main *principles* underlying the Act, and in considering how they provide an interpretative key to leading cases. See also the "canonical" exposition of David Feldamn, *Civil Liberties and Human Rights in England and Wales,* Oxford: Oxford University Press, 2002. For critical approaches, see Noel Whitty, Thérèse Murphy, and Stephen Livingstone, *Civil Liberties Law: The Human Rights Act Era*, Oxford: Oxford University Press, 2001; and Jeffrey Jowell and Jonathan Cooper, *Delivering Rights: How the Human Rights Act is Working and for Whom*, Oxford: Hart Publishers, 2003.

[16] Case 29/69, *Stauder* [1969] ECR 419, paragraph 7: "Interpreted in this way, the provision at issue contains nothing capable of prejudicing the fundamental rights enshrined in the general principles of Community law protected by the Court;" Case 11/70, *Internationale*,

[1970] ECR 1125. The reasoning of the Court may have been influenced by one of his (then) judges. See Pierre Pescatore, "Les droits de l'homme et l'intégration européenne," 4 (1968) *Cahiers du Droit Européen*, pp. 629–670. A shorter English version, which already refers to Stauder, can be found in "Fundamental Rights and Freedoms in the System of the European Communities," 18 (1970) *American Journal of Comparative Law*, pp. 343–351. A classical account of the jurisprudence of the European Court of Justice can be found in Joseph Weiler, "Eurocracy and Distrust: some questions concerning the role of the European Court of Justice in the protection of fundamental human rights within the legal order of the European Communities," 61 (1986) *Washington Law Review*, pp. 1103–1142.

[17] On the Charter, see among others, Erik Oddvar Eriksen, John Erik Fossum and Agustín José Menéndez (eds.), *The Chartering of Europe*, Baden-Baden: Nomos, 2003; Steve Peers and Angela Ward (eds.), *The EU Charter of Fundamental Rights*, Oxford: Hart Publishers, 2004; Tamara Hervey and Jeff Kenner (eds.), *Economic and Social Rights under the EU Charter*, Oxford: Hart Publishers, 2003.

[18] On this, see the key contributions of Tony Honoré, "The Dependence of Morality on Law", 13 (1993) *Oxford Journal of Legal Studies*, pp. 1–17 and "The Necessary Connection between law and morality", 22 (2002) *Oxford Journal of Legal Studies*, pp. 489–495.

[19] Cf. for example, Robert Barro, *Determinants of Economic Growth*, Cambridge: The MIT Press, 1997.

[20] At least if the practical reasoning is understood in a Kantian sense, as the gatekeeper and not the maiden of thick ethical conceptions.

[21] On the academic front, the pioneer is Alan Dershowitz, see his *Why Terrorism Works*, New Haven: Yale University Press, 2002, pp. 131–164, and "The Torture Warrant: A rejoinder to professor Strauss", 48 (2004) *New York School Law Review*, pp. 275–294. His argument is essentially a consequentialist one, but he oscillates between melioristic defense and plain endorsement. Indeed, his case for judicially reviewed torture is not new. Cf. his "Is it necessary to apply physical pressure to terrorists – and to lie about it," 23 (1989) *Israel Law Review*, pp. 192–200. Dershowitz's argument is xeroxed by other authors, such as Andrew Moher, "The Lesser of Two evils. An argument for judicially sanctioned torture in a post-9/11 world," 26 (2004) *Thomas Jefferson Law Review*, pp. 469–489. It is interesting to notice that the latter explicitly resorts to the weighing and balancing language at pp. 485ff. On the official front, see John Yoo, "Letter regarding the 'views of our Office concerning the legality under international law of interrogation methods to be used on captured al Qaeda operatives'," in Karen J. Greenberg and Joshua L. Dratel (eds.), *The Torture Papers*, New York: Cambridge University Press, 2005a, pp. 218–222. Three major (critical) anthologies on the issue are Sanford Levison (ed.), *Torture: A Collection*, Oxford: Oxford University Press, 2004; Karen J. Greenberg (ed.), *The Torture Debate in America*, Cambridge: Cambridge University Press, 2005 and Kenneth Roth. Minky Worden and Amy D. Bernstein (eds.), *Torture. Does it make us safer? Is it ever OK? A Human Rights Perspective*, New York: New Press, 2005.

[22] Cf. John Yoo, "The Status of Soldiers and Terrorists under the Geneva Convention," 3 (2004a) *Chinese Journal of International Law*, pp. 135–150; "Transferring Terrorists," 79 (2004b) *Notre Dame Law Review*, pp. 1183–1236.

[23] Cf. John Yoo, *The Powers of War and Peace*, Chicago: Chicago University Press, 2005b.

PART I

A THEORY OF CONSTITUTIONAL RIGHTS REVISITED

ROBERT ALEXY

1. DISCOURSE THEORY AND FUNDAMENTAL RIGHTS

The relation between discourse theory and fundamental rights is close, deep, and complex. It comprises three dimensions, which are intrinsically connected.

I. THREE DIMENSIONS

The first dimension concerns the foundation or substantiation of fundamental rights. One might call this the "*philosophical*" dimension of fundamental rights. The second concerns the institutionalization of fundamental rights. In order to distinguish this problem from the first, one might call it "*political*." The third dimension concerns the interpretation of fundamental rights. This problem might be classified as "*juridical*." I will concentrate on the philosophical and juridical problems.

II. THREE CONCEPTS OF FUNDAMENTAL RIGHTS: FORMAL, SUBSTANTIAL AND PROCEDURAL

It is difficult to say how something can be substantiated, institutionalized, and interpreted without having an idea about what it is that is to be buttressed by reasons, transformed into reality, and made vivid by way of an interpretive practice. The question of what fundamental rights are is the question of the concept of fundamental rights. Where fundamental rights are concerned, there are three kinds of concept: formal, substantial, and procedural.

A *formal concept* is employed if fundamental rights are defined as rights contained in a constitution or in a certain part of it, or if the rights in question are classified by a constitution as fundamental rights, or if they are endowed by the constitution with special protection, for example, a constitutional complaint brought before a Constitutional Court. Without any doubt, formal concepts are useful, but they are not enough if one wants to understand the nature of fundamental rights. Such an understanding is necessary not only for reasons theoretical in nature, but also for reasons that concern the practice of applying the law. An example that illustrates this is Article 93(1) (no. 4*a*), Basic Law of the Federal Republic of Germany, which provides that a constitutional

A. J. Menéndez and E. O. Eriksen (eds.), Arguing Fundamental Rights, 15–30.

complaint can be raised by anyone on the ground that his or her fundamental rights *qua* rights, listed in the first part of the Basic Law under the heading "Grundrechte," or rights contained in Articles 20(4), 33, 38, 101, 103, and 104, have been infringed by a public authority. The second group contains, *inter alia*, the classical *habeas corpus* rights. It seems, on the face of it, to be quite natural to conceive of all rights named in Article 93(1) (no. 4*a*) of the Basic Law as fundamental rights. On closer inspection, however, this first impression proves to be mistaken. This decidedly literal reading of Article 93(1) (no. 4*a*) would include too much. One item in the list is Article 38, Basic Law. Article 38 not only grants – in the first sentence of its first paragraph – the right of the citizen to vote, which can without difficulty be conceived of as a fundamental right, but – in the second sentence of its first paragraph – also grants rights that define the basic position of a representative, that is, a member of the *Bundestag*. These rights, however, are fundamentally different from the rights of the citizen against the state. They are rights that determine the status of the representative not *qua* private person but as an element of the organization of public power. The Federal Constitutional Court has therefore decided that these rights cannot be defended by means of a constitutional complaint, but only by an action between state organs, which is regulated in Article 93(1) (no. 1).[1] The reason for this decision, which is a decision against the wording of the constitution, is that the rights of representatives – notwithstanding the fact that they are rights granted by the constitution – are not fundamental rights in the proper sense of the word.

Such a claim, however, is only possible if there also exists a *substantial concept* of a fundamental right, one that serves to revise results stemming from the application of the formal concept. Thus understood, a substantial concept of a fundamental right must include criteria that go above and beyond the fact that a right is mentioned, listed, or guaranteed in a constitution. A classical example of such a substantial concept has been presented by Carl Schmitt and Ernst Forsthoff.[2] They claim that the only genuine fundamental rights are defensive rights of the citizen against the state. To follow Schmitt and Forsthoff here would be to accept an exclusively libertarian understanding of fundamental rights. To be sure, there are good reasons to include libertarian rights in a substantial concept of fundamental rights. There are, however, also good reasons not to restrict this concept to these rights. Protective rights, rights to organization and procedure, and social rights ought not to be excluded from the club of genuine fundamental rights merely because a concept follows the tradition. If one then decides to expand the concept of a fundamental right, only one criterion seems to be adequate to define a substantial concept of fundamental rights. It is the concept of human rights. Again, there is a difference between the initial impression and what one arrives at upon reflection. On first glance it seems that a substantial concept of fundamental rights is possible which simply defines fundamental rights as human rights transformed into positive constitutional law. On this basis, human and fundamental rights would become extensionally equivalent. This, however, would count both as over- and under-inclusive. Constitutions may contain rights that are not to be classified as human rights and there may well be human rights that have not found entry into a certain constitution. Still, one can, on closer inspection, take account both of these two possible directions of divergence, and of an intrinsic relation between human and fundamental rights if one holds that fundamental rights are rights incorporated into a constitution with the intention of transforming human rights into positive law.[3] This intention theory makes it possible to conceive of the catalogues of fundamental rights of different constitutions as different attempts to transform human rights into positive law. As with attempts generally, attempts to transform human rights into positive law can be successful to a greater or lesser extent. The intention theory has far-reaching consequences for the philosophical problem of the foundation or substantiation of fundamental rights. The foundation of fundamental rights is essentially a foundation of human rights. By this means, a critical dimension is brought into the concept of fundamental rights. If human rights *qua* rights that ought to be constitutionally protected can be substantiated and if a constitution does not contain these rights, then the foundation becomes a critique. This critique can lead to constitutional reform or to a change in the constitution through constitutional review. The latter shows that there is an intrinsic connection between the philosophical and juridical problems. In any case, one point seems to be clear: one cannot raise the question of the substantiation or foundation of fundamental rights without raising the question of the substantiation or foundation of human rights.

The third concept of fundamental rights is *procedural* in character. This concept mirrors the institutional problems of transforming human rights into positive law. Incorporating human rights into a constitution and granting a court the power of judicial review with respect to all state authority is to limit the power of parliament. In this respect, fundamental rights are an expression of distrust in the democratic process. They are, at the same time, both the basis and the boundary of democracy. Corresponding to this, there is a procedural concept of fundamental rights holding that fundamental rights are rights which are so important that the decision to protect them cannot be left to simple parliamentary majorities.[4] The three concepts are closely connected. An adequate theory of fundamental rights has to address not only all three concepts but also the relations in which they stand to each other.

III. THE FOUNDATION OF FUNDAMENTAL RIGHTS

As already mentioned above, the intrinsic relation between constitutional and human rights, which is expressed by the substantial concept of fundamental rights, answers the question of why the problem of the foundation of fundamental rights is basically a problem of the foundation of human rights. That is, if human rights can be substantiated, fundamental rights can, too, whereas if human rights cannot be substantiated, then fundamental rights, too, must remain without foundation. This state of affairs would have far-reaching consequences for the legitimacy and interpretation of fundamental rights. The insight that there is no foundation of fundamental rights without a foundation of human rights makes it possible for us to treat the question of the foundation of human rights as a part of the question of the foundation of fundamental rights.

The concept of human rights is highly contested for reasons both philosophical and political in nature. It is not possible to take up this debate here, and, happily, it is not necessary to do so either. The answer to the question of whether a foundation of human rights is possible requires only a general idea of what human rights are. The required general idea can be expressed by means of a definition that employs five properties that serve to explain what human rights are. According to this definition, human rights are, first, universal, second, fundamental, third, abstract, and, fourth, moral rights that are, fifth, established with priority over all other kinds of rights.[5]

On the basis of this definition, the question of how to substantiate human rights can now be formulated as the question of how moral norms or rules that grant, with priority, universal, fundamental, and abstract rights may be substantiated. This shows that the problem of the substantiation or justification of human rights is nothing other than a special case of the general problem of the justification of moral norms.

In order to be able to assess whether and to what degree discourse theory is able to provide for a justification of human rights, it is necessary to have considered other attempts at providing such a foundation. No attempt is perfect. Thus, the comparative concepts of being better and being good enough play a pivotal role in the context of the foundation of human rights.

The theories about the justifiability of moral norms in general as well as those theories that refer only to the justifiability of human rights can be classified in many different ways. The most fundamental distinction is that between approaches that generally deny the possibility of any such justification and approaches claiming that some kind of justification is possible. The general denial may have its roots in radical forms of emotivism, decisionism, subjectivism, relativism, naturalism, or deconstructivism. The general assumption of the possibility of a justification may well include one or more of these sceptical elements, but it insists that there exist the possibility of giving reasons for human rights, reasons that can raise a claim to objectivity, correctness, or truth.

The approaches reflecting this latter view differ greatly. This does not, however, preclude various combinations. Eight approaches shall be distinguished here.

The first is the *religious* model. A religious substantiation of human rights provides for a very strong foundation. Whoever believes that human beings are created by God in his own image has a good reason for considering human beings as having value or dignity. This value or dignity is a good basis for human rights. These strong reasons serve, however, as reasons only for those persons who believe in God and his creation of man in his own image. The same applies to all other kinds of religious arguments.

The second approach is the *intuitionistic* one. Human rights are justified according to the intuitionistic model if it is claimed that they are self-evident. Self-evidence, however, does not count as a reason if it is possible not to share the self-evidence without thereby exposing oneself to any reproach other than that one does not share this form of self-evidence. If intuitionism is not embedded in reasoning, it boils down to emotivism. If it is embedded in arguments, it is no longer intuitionism. Self-evidence can be the result of argument, but it is not a substitute for argument.

The third approach is the *consensual* one. If a consensus is nothing more than a mere congruence of beliefs, then consensualism is nothing other than collective intuitionism. Its only source of objectivity is the fact of congruence. If this congruence embraces all human beings and if it is stable, then it ought not to be underestimated. Even then, however, reasons for the concurrent beliefs can be demanded. Once consensus is connected with argument, the approach is more than a merely consensual approach. It moves in the direction of discourse theory. If the consensus is not complete, the role of reasons counts more than mere majorities, which might well be based on bad arguments.

The intuitionistic and the consensual models are based on beliefs or claims without argument. The forth approach dismisses even beliefs and claims, substituting them for behaviour. It is the *biological* or, more precisely, the *socio-biological* approach. According to this model, morality is a species of altruism. Certain forms of altruistic behaviour, such as, in particular, caring for one's own children and helping relatives but also reciprocal altruism generating mutual help, are said to be better for the survival of the genetic pool of individuals than is mutual indifference or even aggressiveness. The tendency to maximize one's reproductive success may in some cases lead to respect and help *vis-à-vis* some persons, but it is a pattern of behaviour "often accompanied by indifference and even hostility towards outsiders."[6] This is incompatible with the universalistic character of human rights. If human rights can be justified, then it is not by means of any observations of empirical facts about the biological nature of human beings, but only by means of an explication of their cultural nature. This is the path of discourse theory.

The fifth approach is the *instrumentalistic* one. A justification of human rights is instrumentalistic if it is argued that the acceptance of human rights is indispensable to the maximization of individual utility. This approach appears in decidedly primitive forms as well as in highly sophisticated models. An example of the primitive version is the argument: "If you do not want to be killed, you must respect others' right to life." Highly sophisticated models have been developed, for instance, by James Buchanan and David Gauthier. If it is possible for some people to increase their utility by violating the human rights of others, then the primitive argument breaks down. History shows that this possibility cannot be ruled out, not at any rate as long as human rights have not been transformed into positive law backed by effectively organized sanctions. The sophisticated models must either work with provisos that exclude unacceptable outcomes, as Gauthier does when he says that "(r)ights provide the starting point for, and not the outcome of, agreement,"[7] or their proponents must be willing to accept outcomes that, to put it in Buchanan's words, "may be something similar to the slave contract, in which the 'weak' agree to produce goods for the 'strong' in exchange for being allowed to retain something over and above bare subsistence, which they may be unable to secure in the anarchistic setting."[8] Buchanan's model is a purely instrumental model, but the possibility of a slave contract shows that it is not compatible with human rights. Gauthier's model may be compatible, but this is entirely owing to reasons addressing elements that can be justified only within a non-instrumentalistic approach. All of this does not mean that the instrumentalistic approach has no value with respect to human rights. In so far as it can provide reasons for respecting human rights, it should be incorporated in a more comprehensive model. This model, however, must be governed by principles that purely instrumentalistic reasoning cannot generate.

The sixth approach is the *cultural* one. It maintains that the public conviction that there are human rights is an achievement of the history of human culture. Radbruch presents a combination of this argument with a consensual one: "To be sure, their details remain somewhat doubtful, but the work of centuries has established a solid core of them and they have come to enjoy such a far-reaching consensus in the declarations of human and civil rights that only the deliberate sceptic can still entertain doubts about some of them."[9] The cultural model, too, is useful but not sufficient. Human rights are not the result of the history of all cultures. The mere fact that they have been worked out in one or more cultures is not enough to justify their universal validity, which is included in their very concept. Cultural history can only have significance in justification as a process that connects experience and argument. Universal validity cannot be established by tradition but only by reasoning.

Our consideration of the six approaches has shown that if anything can establish the universal validity of human rights, that is reasoning that establishes it. Discourse theory is a theory centred on the concept of reasoning. That is the most general ground for the view that discourse theory can contribute to the foundation of human rights. The discourse-theoretical approach might be called "*explicative*," for it attempts to give a foundation of human rights by making explicit what is necessarily implicit in human practice. Making explicit what is necessarily implicit in a practice follows the lines of Kant's transcendental philosophy. The discourse-theoretical argument is not only complex, it is also in need of support by means of other arguments. I attempted to elaborate this some time ago,[10] and my arguments are doubtlessly in need of improvement. This cannot, however, be done here. I will confine myself to a handful of considerations that may perhaps suggest how it is that discourse theory can serve to justify human rights.

The argument proceeds in three steps or at three levels. At the first level, it attempts to show that the practice of asserting, asking, and arguing presupposes rules of discourse that express the ideas of freedom and equality as necessarily connected with reasoning. This first step concerns what Robert Brandom calls the "practices of giving and asking for reasons."[11] The assumption that discourse necessarily presupposes freedom and equality as rules of reasoning is, however, by no means sufficient to justify human rights. It implies neither that these practices as such are necessary nor that the ideas of freedom and equality presupposed by them as rules of reasoning imply human rights which are not only rules of discourse but also rules of action. Thus, a second and a third step must follow the first step.

The second step concerns the necessity of discursive practices. I have attempted to argue that someone who in his life has never participated in any moves of any discursive practice has not taken part in the most general form of life of human beings.[12] Human beings are "discursive creatures."[13] It is not easy for them to forbear from participating in any discourse whatever. One possibility here would be to abolish the factual ability to do so, but this would be a akin to self-destruction. Another possibility would be systematically to substitute for any practice of giving and asking for reasons for a practice of expressing desires, uttering imperatives, and exercising power. The choice of such a farewell to reason, objectivity, and truth is an existential choice. This will be the topic of our last approach, the eighth.

Before we can proceed to this last model, however, we have to take the third step of the explicative justification of human rights. This step concerns the transition from discourse to action. In order to bring about this transition, additional premises are necessary. The first is the autonomy argument. It says that whoever takes part in discourse seriously, presupposes the autonomy of his partners.[14] This excludes the denial of autonomy as the source of the system of human rights. The second additional premise is established by the argument of consensus. It says that the equality of human rights is a necessary result of an ideal discourse.[15] The third additional premise connects the ideas of discourse, democracy, and human rights.

By means of this third premise, the philosophical dimension of human rights is connected with the political problem. This connection expresses the fact that the discourse-theoretical justification of human rights is holistic in character. It consists of the construction of a system that expresses as a whole the discursive nature of human beings.

By these means, the explicative approach of discourse theory is connected with an eighth approach, which might be called "*existential*." It concerns the necessity of the discursive nature of human beings. Is it really impossible to give up this discursive nature? It seems, on the contrary, to be possible to do so, at least to a certain degree and in certain respects. This means that the degree of discursivity depends on decisions concerning the acceptance of our discursive nature and thereby, of ourselves.

IV. THE INSTITUTIONALIZATION OF FUNDAMENTAL RIGHTS

Human rights are institutionalized by means of their transformation into positive law. If this takes place at a level in the hierarchy of the legal system that can be called "constitutional," human rights become fundamental rights. The incorporation of a catalogue of human rights at as high a level in the legal system as possible is not the only demand discourse theory makes with respect to the constitution. The second constitutional requirement is the organization of a form of democracy that expresses the ideal of discourse in reality. This form of democracy is deliberative democracy. Instead of "deliberative democracy" one could also speak of "discursive democracy."

One might think that the institutionalization of human rights *qua* fundamental rights would be perfect once they were connected with discursive democracy. This, however, would mean that the parliamentary legislature would be controlled only by itself and by public argument. In the world as it is, this could not rule out violations of fundamental rights by just the public power that ought to protect and realize them, namely the legislature. To avoid this as far as possible, constitutional review has to be institutionalised.

This, however, not only resolves problems, but also gives rise to new ones. Discourse theory is compatible with constitutional review in a deliberative, that is, discursive democracy only if constitutional review for its part is discursive in character. Constitutional review has a discursive character if the interpretation of the constitution, and especially of the fundamental rights contained in it, can be conceived of as a discourse that can be linked to general democratic discourse in a way that comes closer to discursive ideals than general democratic discourse is able to arrive at alone. This criterion leads to a cluster of problems. Here only the question of whether and under what conditions the interpretation of human rights can be conceived as a rational discourse shall be of interest.

V. THE INTERPRETATION OF FUNDAMENTAL RIGHTS

A. *The Principle of Proportionality*

One of the main topics in the current debate about the interpretation of fundamental rights is the role of balancing or weighing. In the actual practice of many constitutional courts, balancing plays a central role. In German constitutional law balancing is one part of what is required by a more comprehensive principle. The more comprehensive principle is the principle of proportionality (*Verhältnismäßigkeitsgrundsatz*). The principle of proportionality consists of three sub-principles: the principles of suitability, of necessity, and of proportionality in its narrow sense. All these principles express the idea of optimization. Interpreting fundamental rights in the light of the principle of proportionality means to treat fundamental rights as optimization commands, that is, as principles, not simply as rules. As optimization commands, principles are norms requiring that something be realized to the greatest extent possible, given the legal and factual possibilities.[16]

The principles of suitability and necessity concern optimization relative to what is factually possible. They thereby express the idea of Pareto-optimality. The third sub-principle, the principle of proportionality in its narrow sense, concerns optimization relative to the legal possibilities. The legal possibilities are essentially defined by competing principles. Balancing consists in nothing other than optimization relative to competing principles. The third sub-principle can therefore be expressed by a rule that states:

> The greater the degree of non-satisfaction of, or detriment to, one principle, the greater the importance of satisfying the other.

This rule might be called "Law of Balancing."[17]

B. *Habermas's Critique of the Balancing Approach*

The phenomenon of balancing in constitutional law leads to so many problems that even a list of them is not possible here, much less a discussion. I will confine myself to two objections raised by Jürgen Habermas.

Habermas's first objection is that the balancing approach deprives fundamental rights of their normative power. By means of balancing, he claims, rights are downgraded to the level of goals, policies, and values. They thereby lose the "strict *priority*" that is characteristic of "normative points of view."[18] Thus, as he puts it, a "fire wall" comes tumbling down:

For if in cases of collision all reasons can assume the character of policy arguments, then the fire wall erected in legal discourse by a deontological understanding of legal norms and principles collapses.[19]

This danger of watering down fundamental rights is said to be accompanied by "the danger of irrational rulings."[20] According to Habermas, there are no rational standards for balancing:

Because there are no rational standards here, weighing takes place either arbitrarily or unreflectively, according to customary standards and hierarchies.[21]

This first objection speaks, then, to two supposed substantive effects or consequences of the balancing approach: watering down and irrationality. The second objection concerns a conceptual problem. Habermas maintains that the balancing approach takes legal rulings out of the realm defined by concepts like right and wrong, correctness and incorrectness, and justification, and into a realm defined by concepts like adequate and inadequate, and discretion. "Weighing of values" is said to be able to yield a judgment as to its "*result*" but is not able to "*justify*" that result:

The court's judgment is then *itself* a value judgment that more or less adequately reflects a form of life articulating itself in the framework of a concrete order of values. But this judgment is no longer related to the alternatives of a right or wrong decision.[22]

This second objection is at least as serious as the first one. It amounts to the thesis that the loss of the category of correctness is the price to be paid for balancing or weighing.

If this were true, then, to be sure, the balancing approach would have suffered a fatal blow. Law is necessarily connected with a claim to correctness.[23] If balancing or weighing were incompatible with correctness and justification, they should have no place in legal argumentation.

Is balancing intrinsically irrational? Is the balancing approach unable to prevent the sacrifice of individual rights? Does balancing really mean that we are compelled to bid farewell to correctness and justification and, thus, to reason, too?

C. *The Triadic Scale*

It is difficult to answer these questions without knowing what balancing is. To know what balancing is presupposes insight into its structure. The *Law of Balancing* shows that balancing can be broken down into three stages. The first stage involves establishing the degree of non-satisfaction of or detriment to the first principle. This is followed by a second stage in which the importance of satisfying the competing principle is established. Finally, in the third stage it is established whether the importance of satisfying the latter principle justifies the detriment to or non-satisfaction of the former. If it were not possible to make rational judgments about, first, intensity of interference, secondly, degrees of importance, and, thirdly, their relationship to each other, then the objection raised by Habermas would be justified. Everything turns, then, on the possibility of making such judgments.

How can one show that rational judgments about intensity of interference and degrees of importance are possible, such that an outcome can be rationally established by way of balancing? One possible method is the analysis of examples, an analysis that aims at bringing to light what we presuppose when we decide cases by balancing. As an example, I shall take up a decision of the German Federal Constitutional Court on health warnings (The *Tobacco* judgment).[24] The Court qualifies the duty of tobacco producers to place health warnings respecting the dangers of smoking on their products as a relatively minor or *light* interference with freedom to pursue one's profession (*Berufsausübungsfreiheit*). By contrast, a total ban on all tobacco products would count as a *serious* interference. Between such minor and serious cases, others of *moderate* intensity of interference can be found. In this way, a scale can be developed with the stages "*light*," "*moderate*," and "*serious*." Our example shows that valid assignments following this scale are possible.

The same is possible on the side of the competing reasons. The health risks resulting from smoking are great. The reasons justifying the interference therefore weigh heavily. If in this way the intensity of interference is established as minor, and the degree of importance of the reasons for the interference as high, then the outcome of examining proportionality in the narrow sense can well be described – as the Federal Constitutional Court in fact described it – as "obvious."[25]

The conclusions drawn from the *Tobacco* Judgment are confirmed if one looks at other cases. A rather different one is the *Titanic* Judgment. The widely-published satirical magazine, Titanic, described a paraplegic reserve officer first as a "born murderer" and then, in a later edition, as a "cripple." A German court ruled against Titanic and ordered the magazine to pay damages to the officer in the amount of DM 12,000. Titanic brought a constitutional complaint. The Federal Constitutional Court undertook a "case-specific balancing"[26] between the freedom of expression of the magazine [Article 5(1) (1) Basic Law] and the officer's general right to personality [Article 2(1) in connection with Article 1(1) Basic Law]. In the Postscript of *A Theory of*

Constitutional Rights I tried to show that this case, too, can be reconstructed by means of the triadic scale "light," "moderate," and "serious."

D. *The Idea of an Inferential System*

The triadic structure as such is, however, not enough for a showing that balancing is rational. For this it is necessary that an inferential system is implicit in balancing, which, in turn, is intrinsically connected with the concept of correctness. In the case of subsumption under a rule such an inferential system can be expressed by means of a deductive scheme called "internal justification," which is constructed with the help of propositional, predicate, and deontic logic. It is of central importance for the theory of legal discourse that in the case of the balancing of principles, a counterpart to this deductive scheme exists. It shall be called "Weight Formula."

E. *The Weight Formula*

The most simple form of the Weight Formula goes as follows:

$$W_{i,j} = \frac{I_i}{I_j}$$

"I_i" stands for the intensity of interference with the principle P_i, say, the principle granting the freedom of expression of Titanic. "I_j" stands for the importance of satisfying the competing principle P_j, in our case the principle granting the personality right of the paraplegic officer. "$W_{i,j}$" stands for the concrete weight of P_i. The Weight Formula makes the point that the concrete weight of a principle is a relative weight. It does this by making the concrete weight the quotient of the intensity of interference with this principle (P_i) and the concrete importance of the competing principle (P_j).

Now, the objection is clear that one can only talk about quotients in the presence of numbers, and that numbers are not used in the balancings carried out in constitutional law. The reply to this objection can start with the observation that the logical vocabulary we use in order to express the structure of subsumption is not used in judicial reasoning, and that it is nevertheless the best means to make explicit the inferential structure of rules. The same applies to the expression of the inferential structure of principles by numbers that are substituted for the variables of the Weight Formula.

F. *Geometric Sequence*

The three values of our triadic model, light, moderate, and serious, shall be represented by "*l*," "*m*," and "*s*." There are various possibilities for allocating numbers to *l*, *m*, and *s*. A rather simple and at the same time highly instructive one consists in taking the geometric sequence 2^0, 2^1, and 2^2, that is, 1, 2, and 4. On this basis, *l* has the value 1, *m* the value 2, and *s* the value 4. The Federal Constitutional Court considered the intensity of infringement (I_i) with the freedom of expression (P_i) in the *Titanic* Judgment as serious (*s*), and the importance of satisfying the right to personality (P_j) of the officer (I_j) in case of describing him as a "born murderer" because of the highly satirical context as only moderate (*m*), perhaps even as light (*l*). If we insert the corresponding values of our geometric sequence for *s* and *m*, the concrete weight of P_i ($W_{i,j}$) is in this case 4/2, that is, 2. If I_i were *m* and I_j were *s*, the value would be 2/4, that is, 1/2. In all stalemate cases this value is 1. The precedence of P_i is expressed by a concrete weight greater than 1, the precedence of P_j by a concrete weight smaller than 1. The description of the officer as "cripple" was considered as serious. This gave rise to a stalemate, with the consequence that Titanic's constitutional complaint was not successful in so far as it related to damages for the description "cripple."

G. *Transfer of Correctness*

The rationality of an inferential structure essentially depends on the question of whether it connects premises that, again, can be justified in a rational way. The structure expressed by the *Weight Formula* would not be a structure of rational reasoning if its input had a character that excluded it from the realm of rationality. This, however, is not the case. The input that is represented by numbers is judgment. An example is the judgment that the public description of a severely disabled person as "cripple" is a "serious breach"[27] of that person's personality right. This judgment raises a claim to correctness and it can be justified as a conclusion of another inferential scheme in a discourse. The Federal Constitutional Court does so by presenting the argument that the description of the paraplegic as a "cripple" was humiliating and disrespectful. The *Weight Formula* transfers the correctness of this argument, together with the correctness of arguments that concern the intensity of the interference with the freedom of expression, to the judgment about the weight of Titanic's right in the concrete case, which, again, implies – together with further premises – the judgment expressing the ruling of the court. This is a rational structure for establishing the correctness of a legal judgment in a discourse.

H. *Fire Wall and Over-proportional Growth of Resistance*

The Weight Formula is presented here in its most simplest form. This simplification is sufficient in order to express that part of the inferential structure of the *Tobacco* and the *Titanic* Judgment which has been of interest up to now. Often, however, refinements are necessary. They run in any of four directions. The first concerns the inclusion of the abstract weights of the principles, what becomes necessary where they are different; the second refers to the reliability of the empirical assumptions incorporated into the inferential structure; the third concerns the inclusion of more than one principle on one side or the other, or on both sides of balancing; the forth aims at a refinement of the scale. Only this last refinement is of interest here, for the possibility of refining the scale is necessary in order to render complete the rejection of Habermas's fire wall objection.

It cannot be ruled out that there could be cases in which not even the rather rough triadic scale is applicable. These are cases in which it is only possible to distinguish two grades, say, light and serious. There, a dual scale must be used. This would be enough for balancing. Balancing is excluded only if no graduation at all is possible, which is the case when everything has an equal value. Of much greater practical importance is the possibility of refining the scale. A method that seems to correspond well to our practice of balancing consists in an iteration of the triadic scale. By this, a double-triadic scale is produced, which looks like this: (1) *ll*, (2) *lm*, (3) *ls*, (4) *ml*, (5) *mm*, (6) *ms*, (7) *sl*, (8) *sm*, (9) *ss*. This scale comports well with expressions like "very light" (*ll*), "already medium" (*ml*), "already serious"(*sl*), "really serious" (*sm*), or 'extremely serious'(*ss*). The decisive point is that the application of a geometric sequence makes it possible, unlike an arithmetic sequence, to express the over-proportional growth of resistance of fundamental rights against infringements. This is not very easy to recognize in the case of the simple triadic scale. Here, 2^0, 2^1, 2^2 only expresses rather small differences, namely, those between 1, 2, and 4. This is completely different from the case in which one uses a double-triadic scale. The geometric scale $2^0, \ldots, 2^8$ ranges from 1 to 256. The distance between *sm* and *ss* is 128.

This provides for a more subtle reconstruction of the *Titanic* Judgment. The humiliation and the disrespect expressed by the public designation of a severely disabled person as a "cripple" violates his dignity. Violations of dignity are, at any rate often, not only simply (*s*) or already serious (*sl*) infringements, but really (*sm*) of even extremely serious (*ss*) infringements. That makes it difficult to find counter-reasons that come up to this level. It is exactly this structure which erects something like a fire wall, precisely where Habermas thinks the balancing approach is bound to fail.

NOTES

[1] BVerfGE 43, 142 (148–149); 64, 301 (312); 99, 19 (29).

[2] Carl Schmitt, *Verfassungslehre* (1928), quoted from the 1970 reprint, Berlin: Duncker and Humblot, at pp. 163–165; Ernst Forsthoff, Article: "Grundrechte," in Joachim Ritter (ed.), *Historisches Wörterbuch der Philosophie*, vol. 3, Basel and Stuttgart: Schwabe, 1974, at pp. 922–923.

[3] See Robert Alexy, "Grundrechte," in Hans Jörg Sandkühler (ed.), *Enzyklopädie Philosophie*, vol. 1, Hamburg: Felix Meiner, 1999a, pp. 525–529, at p. 526.

[4] Robert Alexy, *A Theory of Constitutional Rights*, trans. Julian Rivers, Oxford: Oxford University Press, 2002a, p. 297 (hereafter, TCR).

[5] See Robert Alexy, "Die Institutionalisierung der Menschenrechte im demokratischen Verfassungsstaat", in Stefan Gosepath and Georg Lohmann (eds.), *Philosophie der Menschenrechte*, Frankfurt: Suhrkamp, 1998b, pp. 246–254.

[6] Günther Patzig, "Can Moral Norms be Rationally Justified?," 41 (2002) *Angewandte Chemie. International Edition*, pp. 3553–3558, at p. 3355.

[7] David Gauthier, *Morals by Agreement*, Oxford: Oxford University Press, 1986, p. 222.

[8] James M. Buchanan, *The Limits of Liberty*, Chicago and London: Chicago University Press, 1975, p. 60.

[9] Gustav Radbruch, "Five Minutes of Legal Philosophy," trans. Stanley L. Paulson, in Joel Feinberg and Hyman Gross (eds.), *Philosophy of Law*, Belmont, California: Wadsworth, 1980, at p. 90.

[10] See Robert Alexy, "A Discourse-Theoretical Conception of Practical Reason" 5 (1992a) *Ratio Juris*, pp. 231–251; "Discourse Theory and Human Rights" 9 (1996) *Ratio Juris*, pp. 209–235.

[11] Robert B. Brandom, *Articulating Reasons*, Cambridge, Mass. and London: Harvard University Press, 2000, p. 11.

[12] Alexy, *supra*, fn. 10 (1996b), at p. 217.

[13] Brandom, *supra*, fn. 11, at p. 26.

[14] Alexy, *supra*, fn. 10 (1996b), p. 222.

[15] Ibid.

[16] TCR, 47.

[17] TCR, 102.

[18] Jürgen Habermas, *Between Facts and Norms*, trans. by William Rehg, Cambridge: The MIT Press, 1996a, at p. 256.

[19] Ibid., at p. 258.

[20] Ibid., at p. 259.

[21] Ibid., at p. 259, (translation edited).

[22] Jürgen Habermas, "Reply to Symposium Participants," in Michel Rosenfeld and Andrew Arato (eds.) *Habermas on Law and Democracy*, Berkeley, Los Angeles, and London: California University Press, 1998, pp. 381–452, at p. 430.

[23] Robert Alexy, "Law and Correctness," in M. D. A. Freeman (ed.), *Legal Theory at the End of the Millennium*, Oxford: Oxford University Press, 1998a, pp. 205–221, at pp. 209–214.

[24] BVerfGE 95, 173.

[25] BVerfGE 95, 173 (187).

[26] VerfGE 86, 1 (11).

[27] BVerfGE 86, 1 (13).

PART II

STRUCTURAL PERSPECTIVES

KAARLO TUORI

2. FUNDAMENTAL RIGHTS PRINCIPLES: DISCIPLINING THE INSTRUMENTALISM OF POLICIES

I. INTRODUCTION

The following chapter has two main themes: first, the distinction between principles and policies, and, secondly, the problem of the limits of law in the age of modern, positive law. I shall examine the distinction between principles and policies by comparing the views of two central participants in recent legal theoretical debates: Ronald Dworkin and Robert Alexy. I shall argue that in order to account for the solution to the problem of the law's limits – and, in fact, even to pose the problem – we have to keep the distinction between principles and policies in the way suggested by Dworkin. This argument also establishes the connecting link between my two themes. When discussing the issue of the law's limits, I shall also try to dissolve two paradoxes which I call the paradox of the *Rechtsstaat* and the paradox of fundamental rights. Both of these paradoxes result from the essential positivity of modern law.

Fundamental-rights principles play a crucial role in determining the law's limits in our era of positive law. Protecting fundamental rights also means protecting these limits. At least in established constitutional democracies, which meet the criteria of a democratic *Rechtsstaat*, the emphasis in this protection still lies at the level of the nation-state; monitoring mechanisms established by international human-rights treaties, such as the European Convention on Human Rights (hereafter, ECHR), play only a complementary, although growing role.[1] This may justify the by-passing of the international aspect, especially in a paper which focuses more on issues of legal theory questions than on issues of legal doctrine.

II. PRINCIPLES AND POLICIES: THE POSITIONS OF ALEXY AND DWORKIN

In his *Theorie der Grundrechte*[2] (hereafter, TGR), Alexy is very careful in specifying the object and the level of his discussions. He characterises his book[3] as presenting a general juristic theory of the fundamental rights of the

A. J. Menéndez and E. O. Eriksen (eds.), Arguing Fundamental Rights, 33–52.

German Basic Law; put in another way, it deals with the general part of the fundamental-rights doctrine of the Basic Law.

According to Alexy,[4] legal doctrine (*Rechtsdogmatik*) includes three dimensions: an analytical, an empirical and a normative one. At issue in the analytical dimension is the conceptual-systematic elaboration (*Durchdringung*) of positive law; the empirical dimension of legal doctrine deals with the contents of the positively valid law; and, finally, the normative dimension includes normative or value-based positions on the interpretation and application of positively valid law. The main focus of Alexy's book lies on the analytical dimension; its primary aim is to develop a structural theory of the fundamental rights of the Basic Law.[5] The distinction between rules and principles and the possible significance of the distinction between principles and policies are clearly issues which pertain to the first, conceptual-systematic dimension. In fact, it seems that for Alexy, they are legal theoretical issues whose bearing cuts across the borders of the various fields of positive law and which by no means concern only the general theory of the fundamental rights of the Basic Law. Thus, Alexy has also analysed these distinctions as general legal theoretical issues, that is, detached from their links to the fundamental-rights doctrine of the German Basic Law.[6]

Alexy's analysis of rules and principles often has been compared to that of Dworkin, and when elaborating on the characteristics of these types of legal norms, Alexy explicitly refers to Dworkin.[7] And, indeed, their analyses have much in common. They both link the defining features of rules and principles to situations of norm conflict. The conflict between legal rules is solved either by subsuming one of the rules under the other one as an exception to it or by declaring one of them invalid. The collision between two principles, by contrast, is to be solved in a process of weighing; neither of the colliding principles loses its validity, but the losing principle is considered merely to have less significance in the situation at hand than its counter-principle.[8] It is true, though, that Alexy's understanding of the concept of principle is not wholly identical to that of Dworkin. Dworkin's principles are of a deontological nature, whereas Alexy, by defining principles as optimisation commands, takes a decisive step in an axiological direction. In accordance with their character as optimisation commands, "principles can be fulfilled to different degrees and the required measure of their realisation depends not only on factual but also on legal possibilities." The scope of what is legally possible, in turn, is determined by counter-principles and counter-rules.[9] The divergence of Dworkin's and Alexy's conceptions of principles has important consequences, but I shall not dwell on them here. My interest lies in another, though related, difference in the views of the two theorists.

Dworkin introduces another distinction which complements that between rules and principles and which is of equal importance for his argument.

Principles in the broad sense of the term may be of two kinds: principles in the strict sense and policies. Policies are standards which determine ends concerning the economic, political or social state of the community. Principles in the strict sense are not attached to such states but express moral demands, such as the demand for justice; they are characterised by their ties to morality. Principles, in contrast to policies, justify individual rights: "Arguments from principle are arguments which are supposed to justify a right; arguments from policy are arguments which are supposed to justify some collective end. Principles are propositions describing rights; policies are propositions describing ends."[10] The goods protected by rights are distributive in nature, whereas policies concern non-distributive collective goods.

Alexy[11] has conceded that distributive rights and non-distributive collective goods are conceptually distinct, and he has also analysed possible relations between them. Collective goods and individual rights may, for example, be connected by a relation of justification: collective goods may justify individual rights and individual rights, in turn, collective goods. What is, however, important for our present topic is that Alexy does not see any need for complementing the division between rules and principles with an additional analytical distinction between principles and policies; he argues that Dworkin's principles and policies behave in the same way in legal decision-making.

Alexy's argument may be seen as a consequence of his axiological definition of principles as optimisation commands: if even principles in Dworkin's strict sense are characterised by scale-like, gradual realisation, they indeed behave in the same way as policies aiming at collective goods. However, Dworkin's and Alexy's differing views on the importance of the distinction between principles and policies also reflect different views of the characteristics of jurisprudential research. For Alexy, norm-theoretical distinctions belong to the analytical dimension of legal doctrine. At the same time, he stresses the connections between the analytical, the empirical and the normative dimension: they constitute a whole, the doctrine of a certain field of positive law. In this whole, the task of the analytical approach is to create conceptual clarity for both the empirical exposition of positive law and normative argumentation concerning its interpretation and application. Thus, the distinction between rules and principles, as presented within a general theory of the fundamental rights of the Basic Law, supports normative fundamental-rights argumentation by enhancing its rationality.

In spite of the existence of such relations between the analytical and the normative dimension, conceptual-systematic distinctions, like the one between rules and principles, are supposed to be normatively uncontaminated; according to Alexy, they do not involve or imply any normative position with regard to the interpretation or application of positive law. The specific perspective of legal doctrine is that of the judges, and the distinction between rules and principles is based on the different behaviour of the two types of norms in legal decision-making, especially in situations of norm conflict. This is the only relevant difference; the distinction abstracts from all further variances in the contents of norms. In Alexy's view, a principle functions in the same way in legal decision-making irrespective of whether it is related to individual rights or collective goods; therefore, at least in an analytical, conceptual-systematic exposition, Dworkin's distinction between principles and policies must be abandoned.

I have already noted that for Dworkin, the distinction between principles (in the strict sense) and policies is (at least) as important as that between rules and principles (in the large sense). The purport of the very title of his breakthrough-work, *Taking Rights Seriously*, would be impossible to grasp without this distinction; what taking-rights-seriously means is that in hard cases, principles justifying and protecting individual rights trump policies related to common goods. For Dworkin, there is no point of making analytical distinctions independently of normative concerns. The purpose of the distinctions he introduces is not merely to increase the analytical clarity of normative argumentation and to raise the level of its rationality; these distinctions are part and parcel of normative argumentation. The very idea of a distinction between analytic, empirical and normative dimensions is foreign to Dworkin's style of jurisprudence.

Dworkin too introduces his distinctions from the perspective of the judges. However, his primary normative concern is not with legal decision-making in courts, but with the law or the legal system as a whole; as a full-blooded philosophical and political liberal, he is worried about the threat that the increasing policy-orientation of legislation poses to individual rights. Dworkin needs the distinction between principles and policies in order to be able to conceptualise the menace created by instrumentalist legal regulation and to explicate how the courts should try to fend it off. With respect to his main normative point, the first distinction (between rules and principles), is of a merely preparatory nature; what really matters for his argument is the second distinction (between principles and policies).

Although taken in the analytical dimension, Alexy's decision to discard the distinction between principles and policies has obvious normative-doctrinal implications in the interpretation and application of constitutional provisions on fundamental rights. In German debates, he has been criticised for locating standards related both to individual rights and to collective goods at the same level and, thus, according them equal initial argumentative weight. As an example of balancing between principles,[12] he has used a case of the German Federal Constitutional Court (hereafter, FCC) where the central issue was whether legal proceedings could be launched against a defendant whose health, and even life, could be endangered if he were obligated to appear in court. According to Alexy (and the FCC), the solution depends on which of the two principles of equal rank was assigned greater weight in this specific case: the principle of the efficiency of criminal justice or the principle establishing the right to life and personal integrity. Let me present a rather lengthy citation from Ingeborg Maus' critique of Alexy (and the Constitutional Court):

> Alexy accommodates the constitutional jurisdiction … by combining rights and common goods as equal objects of principles. This extension of the concept of principles … extends the limit of what prevailing constitutional law is, whilst, at the same time, subjecting constitutionally guaranteed individual rights to greater restrictions. If, for example, the "common good" of the efficiency of criminal justice is declared to be a constitutional principle – although the text of the Basic Law does not give the slightest indication for this – only then can it be introduced as an equal point of view into a constitutional "weighing up" in which, for example, it is opposed to the basic rights to life and physical integrity enjoyed by an accused person unfit to stand trial and in danger of suffering a heart attack. … (T)his artificially induced collision of principles in individual cases … owes its existence to a concept of constitution which is diametrically opposed to the liberal constitutional concept asserted in the 18th/19th centuries. The constitution in the classical sense of the rule of law (the *Rechtsstaat* – KT) always presupposed as a fact the functional efficacy of the organs of the state and criminal prosecution and determined their limitations. This functional efficacy itself need not be guaranteed by a constitution, but is greatest without any constitutional regulation whatsoever. The classical constitutional concept of the state of emergency clearly indicates the contradiction of the state's functional efficacy and constitutional law; in order to increase efficiency, the constitution (or part of the constitution) is temporarily revoked. Therefore, the efficiency of constitutional organs of the state cannot itself be the content of a constitutional principle, because the *ratio essendi* of the constitution consists precisely in restricting this efficiency. … This approach … jeopardizes freedom when common goods can also be regarded as principles. In this case, constitutional guarantees of freedom compete with principles which are opposite not only in terms of their content, but also in terms of their entire structure, such as the efficiency of criminal justice, the "efficiency of the Bundeswehr" or the "efficiency of national defence" (BVerfGE 28, 243, 261; 48, 127, 159f.), the "efficiency of the enterprise and the economy as a whole" (BVerfGE 50, 290, 332). … Not only the basic rights guaranteeing freedom, but also the freedom-limiting state functions themselves are a measure of judicial review. It is precisely in this way that the constitution loses its function of limiting the spread of government powers.[13]

The significance of the distinction between principles and policies can be tackled at different levels or – to use Alexy's vocabulary – in different dimensions of legal doctrine (legal dogmatics), although at the same time bearing in mind the interdependencies between these levels or dimensions. First, the discussion can be focused on the deontological/axiological character of principles; here we can point to Habermas' critique of Alexy in his *Faktizität und Geltung*.[14] Another possibility is to concentrate on a legal doctrinal assessment of the implications the alternative analytical positions have in the interpretation of constitutional fundamental-rights provisions. Indeed, at the end of my article, I will take up some such legal doctrinal issues, concerning the

Finnish Constitution and the ECHR. However, the main thrust of my argument will be of neither an analytical nor an immediate normative doctrinal nature. I shall discuss a topic which is rather hard to locate in the standard divisions of legal scholarship: the problem of the law's limits. This problem is of great importance to both the philosophy and the (macro) sociology of modern law, and it also underlies Dworkin's treatment of principles and policies. Alexy's approach, by contrast, runs the risk of ignoring it.

III. THE PARADOX OF THE *RECHTSSTAAT*

Let us return for a moment to Maus' criticism of Alexy. The criticism is related to the interpretation of the German Basic Law and, thus, is legal doctrinal in its orientation. However, she also outlines a more general background to her critical point.

In agreement with Dworkin, Maus emphasises the limiting task of individual (fundamental) rights, a task which is easily ignored, if principles (individual rights) and policies (collective goods) are regarded as equal in the way suggested by Alexy. However, in a significant respect, Maus' approach differs from that of Dworkin. Maus anchors her argument in the function the law – especially the constitution – of a *Rechtsstaat* fulfils with regard to politics; in her analysis, what law – here fundamental-rights norms – restricts is located outside the law. Dworkin, by contrast, is interested in what can be termed an intra-legal relation of limitation. Before elaborating on Dworkin's theme, let us follow for a moment the path of argumentation opened up by Maus. This path leads to a dilemma, which is related to a vital problem we will confront when examining the intra-legal issue of limitation.

The constitution has a double domicile. It is both a legal and a political phenomenon; it fulfils important functions not only in the legal, but also in the political sub-system of modern society. However, as Niklas Luhmann,[15] for example, has stressed, the constitution's main societal function consists of mediating the mutual relations between these two sub-systems: the constitution channels the influences of the legal into the political system and, correspondingly, those of the political into the legal system. The constitution confers on the organisation of political power its legal form, and contributes to its stability and legitimacy. In addition, as the German *Rechtsstaat* theory as well as the Anglo-American constitutionalist doctrine have stressed, the constitution draws the legal boundaries to the exercise of this power; it is this very function that constitutes the kernel of Maus' argument against Alexy. On the other hand, through its provisions on legislative power, the constitution opens the channels through which political actors can influence the formation and development of the legal order.

After the positivisation of the law, the *Rechtsstaat* solution to the disciplining of political power runs into a difficulty which can be termed the paradox of the *Rechtsstaat*.

When the concept of the *Rechtsstaat* is – as is the case in Maus' criticism of Alexy – applied to the relations between the law and political power, the central requirement of the concept can be formulated as follows: political power (state power) can only be exercised on the basis of authorisation conferred, and in the forms defined and the limits drawn by the law. In Germany, the concept of the *Rechtsstaat* was introduced by the early constitutionalist school of the first half of the nineteenth century. However, for this school the law which was supposed to impose restrictions on political power was not yet identified with positive, enacted law; the law was essentially conceived of as a supra-positive ethical order. It was only the late constitutionalist school, which dominated German state-law doctrine after the unification and the proclamation of the Constitution of 1871, that accomplished the turn to statutory positivism and reduced all law to enacted norms. In line with their predecessors, the representatives of the late constitutionalist school retained the *Rechtsstaat* as a key doctrinal concept. But their positivistic understanding of the law gave rise to a new problem. According to the idea of the *Rechtsstaat*, the law is supposed to impose restrictions on state power but, at the same time, after the positivistic turn, all law is said to spring from this very same public power. The circle seems to close: state power is supposed to limit state power. The late constitutionalist school proposed to dissolve the paradox with the doctrine of the self-limitation of the state: in analogy with the Kantian moral subject, the state imposes limitations on itself through its own laws.[16] But this analogy does not really solve the problem; at the most, it only provides it with a new formulation.

I shall leave the paradox of the *Rechtsstaat* and take up again Dworkin's intra-legal perspective on principles and policies. From this perspective, the question is no longer how the law can discipline extra-legal power but how it can limit itself.

IV. THE PARADOX OF FUNDAMENTAL RIGHTS

The problem of the law's limits is a perennial one, accompanying the law throughout its history and the different forms it has assumed in the course of this history. Attached to the law is the possibility of external coercion which ultimately resorts to physical force. Hence the issue of the limits of law: *not all coercion in the name of law can be justifiable*.

In the Western legal tradition, the question about the boundaries of the powers of human law enactment, application and enforcement, up to the era of modern law, had been posed and answered in terms of natural law. However, cultural modernisation has destroyed the basis of a natural law which could limit the reach of positive law. Not only objective nature as a cosmic world order but even the subjective nature of human beings has lost its credibility as a point of reference for the law: we no longer believe in an immutable human nature, defined as universal attributes of human beings, their ever identical rationality and/or their structure of needs and instincts. Natural law can no longer fulfil the function of natural law, that is, the task of being the critical and reflexive instance of the law, to use expressions coined by François Ewald.[17]

Modern law is positive law, which is based on conscious human action and which is continuously amendable. Never before has such a plethora of regulations called law been issued as in the modern welfare state. It is to the credit of F. A. Hayek[18] to have drawn our attention to the at least implicit danger of totalitarianism that has been entailed by the law's positivisation. Hayek's analysis cannot be overlooked by simply pointing to his extreme liberal – or even libertarian – premises.

If modern law is characterised by a fundamental positivity, the traditional way of posing and solving the problem of the law's limits is no longer available. The positivity of the law means that only positive norms are accorded legal validity in legal practices, such as adjudication. The requirement of positivity obviously also concerns the criteria by which the law's limits are determined; otherwise these criteria would not be respected in the practices of modern law. If this is the case, the limits of modern law should be determined within its very positivity.

Above, in the context of the *Rechtsstaat*, we examined the functions of the constitution with regard to the political system. Now we can continue our examination by turning to the specific functions that the constitution accomplishes within the legal system of a modern democratic *Rechtsstaat*. First, through its provisions on the use of legislative power, the constitution creates the very possibility of modern law's positivity: the constitution lays down the intra-legal validity criteria of positive law. This could perhaps be called its Kelsenian function. But particularly through the provisions on fundamental rights and constitutional review, the constitution of a modern democratic *Rechtsstaat* fulfils also another essential task. It appears to provide a solution to the problem of the law's limits through arrangements which respect modern law's positivity.

However, this solution appears to be plagued by a dilemma akin to the paradox of the *Rechtsstaat*. This paradox concerned the law's limiting function with regard to political power: how can the law impose restrictions on state power, if it itself is – as positive law – created by that very power? In order to capture Hayek's (and Dworkin's) concern, the dilemma must be reformulated from the law's internal perspective: the totalitarianism that Hayek was worried about does not result from illegal or extra-legal use of state power but from legal regulation which takes advantage of the opportunities offered by modern law's positivity. One possible re-formulation of the paradox of the *Rechtsstaat* would be the following: *how can the law fend off the menace of totalitarianism, if it itself is a vehicle of this menace?*

We can try to specify the self-limiting function and attribute it to fundamental rights, guaranteed by a system of constitutional review: the fundamental rights draw the boundaries to legal regulation. But this specification does not yet rid us of our dilemma. The positivity of modern law entails that even fundamental rights must be understood as being based on positive norms, such as constitutional provisions; otherwise, the legal practices of modern law would not recognize them as legally relevant at all. Unlike in the natural-law thinking of the early modern age – say, from Hobbes to Kant – fundamental rights can no longer be grounded in universal moral principles, independent of time and place. But if the norms establishing fundamental rights must be conceived of as norms of positive law, are they not exposed to the possibility of amendments and even annulment which is a central characteristic of the very notion of positivity? If this is the case, how can they accomplish their task of guaranteeing the self-limitation of modern law? Obviously, a mere appeal to fundamental rights is not enough to account for the solution of the problem of the law's limits. The paradox of the *Rechtsstaat* has now been developed into what might be termed the paradox of fundamental rights.

V. THE DISSOLUTION OF THE PARADOXES

In his solution to the paradox of the *Rechtsstaat*, Habermas indicates a way out of the dilemma in power-theoretical terms, by "deconstructing" the concept of political or state power. He argues that the *Rechtsstaat* is possible only as a democratic *Rechtsstaat*. According to Habermas, what Jellinek called the self-limitation of the state can function only because the limiting power, in fact, is not exactly of the same nature as the power to be limited. In state power, Habermas distinguishes between communicative and administrative power. Communicative power is the power of common convictions and public opinion, power of influence rooted in discourses within the civil society and its public sphere. Democratic law-making procedures, which involve such unofficial discourses, engender communicative power, which is distilled into legitimate laws. In a *Rechtsstaat*, these laws bind the coercion-backed administrative power, wielded by administrative and judicial authorities. In power-theoretical terms, the idea of the *Rechtsstaat* consists in the subjection of administrative to communicative power.[19]

The present context does not allow for commenting at length on Habermas' conception of the democratic *Rechtsstaat*. Let me only re-state that the mere *Rechtsstaat* requirement of binding the exercise of state power to law cannot by itself provide a sufficient guarantee against the threat of totalitarianism which Hayek was concerned about, and which also motivated Dworkin's discussion of policies and principles. What engenders this threat is not illegal or extra-legal power, but power exercised through positive law; *power in a legal guise*. If Habermas' solution to the paradox of the *Rechtsstaat* is based on a deconstruction of the concept of state power, my proposal for dissolving the intra-legal paradox of fundamental rights proceeds through a deconstruction of the concept of (positive) law. I would like to stress that I will be discussing what I call a "mature" modern legal system; a legal system which has fully realised the potentials of modern law; which, to put it in a Hegelian way, corresponds to its concept. The "mature" modern legal system is an idealisation, a Weberian ideal type, of the same type as, say, John Rawls' "well-ordered society" or H. L. A. Hart's "healthy society."

The kernel of my solution lies in recognising modern law's multi-layered nature.[20] Law, as a symbolic normative phenomenon, does not consist merely of the surface level of explicit, discursively formulated normative material, such as statutes and other legal regulations, and court decisions; it also includes "deeper," sub-surface layers, for which I have proposed the terms "the legal culture" and "the deep structure of law." The different levels of the law – the surface level, the legal culture and the deep structure – follow different paces of change: the surface is the level of incessant movement, caused by ever new regulations and decisions; the legal culture also evolves, but according to a slower rhythm; and finally, even the deep structure, although constituting the most stable layer in law, is not immune to change. If we are justified in talking about different historical types of law, such as our own modern law or the preceding type of law, called somewhat vaguely "traditional law," this is because they are distinguished by the specificities of their respective deep structures.

According to my interpretation, the deep structure of modern law involves three kinds of elements: conceptual, normative and methodological. By conceptual deep-structural elements, I allude to the basic legal categories which open up the conceptual space of law and, thus, constitute the very possibility of legal thinking and legal argumentation in our era of modern law; categories such as "legal subject" or "subjective right." Normative elements consist of the most fundamental principles characterising modern law, and by methodological elements, I refer to the basic form of rationality distinctive of modern law and its practices. What is crucial to my argument now are the normative elements in modern law's deep structure.

At this point, I would like to resort again to Habermas' *Faktizität und Geltung*. Its legal philosophical chapters can be read as a reconstruction (and an interpretation) of modern law's normative deep structure. If we accept his reconstruction, the main elements in the normative deep structure of modern law would consist of fundamental rights as general normative ideas, as well as certain (other) fundamental *Rechtsstaat* principles, such as the separation of powers and the legality of administration. In different legal cultures and at different stages of modern law's evolution, these principles are interpreted in somewhat divergent ways; for example, the US legal culture assigns greater weight to liberty rights than European legal culture(s), and the status of a "super" right accorded to freedom of expression in the USA has no counterpart in Europe, to take two conspicuous examples. At the level of legal cultures, Habermas[21] examines legal paradigms, that is, different interpretations of how fundamental rights should be specified and realised in varying historical circumstances. Reference can also be made to the material or substantive fundamental-rights theories which, according to Alexy,[22] have guided the interpretation of the German Basic Law's provisions on fundamental rights. Finally, when we reach the law's surface level, fundamental-rights principles find their most precise expression in individual constitutional provisions and court decisions.

Now, I would like to argue that fundamental-rights principles can only fulfil their restrictive role in virtue of their being sedimented into the sub-surface layers of the law, that is, into the legal culture and into the law's deep structure. The multi-layered view of modern law also holds the key to the solution to what I have called the paradox of fundamental rights. In order to make my point, let me turn to the relations prevailing between the law's levels in a "mature" modern legal system.

The sub-surface layers of the legal culture and the deep structure constitute the very possibility of the legal practices which continuously bring new material to the law's surface in the form of legal regulations and court decisions: the sub-surface levels provide the conceptual, normative and methodological means without which the legislature could not make its laws or the judge formulate her decisions, or – we may add – the legal scholar write her learned treatises or articles. In quasi-Kantian terms, we can speak here of a constitutive relation. But the reverse side of this constitutive relation consists of a relation of (self-)limitation. This relation can, first, be examined in the functioning of the conceptual elements of the sub-surface levels; thus, the most basic legal categories do not only open the space for legal thinking and argumentation, they also close this space from fundamentally alternative ways of thinking and arguing legally. However, what is of primary interest for our present topic is the relation of limitation working through the normative principles established in the legal culture and the law's deep structure.

The normative self-limitation of the law is realised through a kind of censorship which the sub-surface principles exercise with respect to surface-level material, such as individual statutes and other legal regulations. The relations between the law's levels are maintained and channelled through legal practices, primarily through law-making, adjudication and legal scholarship; the relations are not realized automatically through an internal movement within a closed normative sphere of the legal order. This also holds for the relation of limitation which can only be brought into fruition through legal practices. The totalitarian threat is posed by the instrumentalism of a purposive rational legislator, by policy-oriented legislation. The main responsibility in securing the self-limitation of the law, in turn, falls to other legal practices, to adjudication in particular.

Legal practices are social practices whose main agents are professional lawyers. In legal practices, lawyers employ two kinds of knowledge: discursive and practical. Discursive knowledge is knowledge of which the actor is immediately aware. In every kind of social action, a major part of the actor's knowledge is embedded in her action in its practical state. Practical knowledge is implicit and self-evident, something which the actor does not question, at least not in routine action; it is openly thematised only in problematic situations. Correspondingly, a major part of the legal knowledge that legal actors rely on is in a practical state. This concerns especially the knowledge they have of the law's sub-surface layers. In every criminal case, *nulla poena sine lege* is applied, and in every case of contract law, *pacta sunt servanda* plays an integral role. However, these principles are not usually spelled out in the decisions; in routine cases, the judges may not even be immediately aware of employing them. They are expressly taken into examination only when their bearing in an individual case appears to be problematic. The analysis of legal cases in terms of the knowledge required for their solution allows for the following definition of a hard case: in hard cases, judges must openly thematise sub-surface elements of the law, transform part of their knowledge of the law's sub-surface layers from a practical into a discursive shape.

In a "mature," well-functioning modern legal system, the normative self-limitation of the law – the censorship to which sub-surface principles submit instrumentalist, policy-oriented legislation – works primarily through the practical knowledge of legal actors; already during their university education, they have internalised the central principles of modern law, as these have been interpreted in the relevant legal culture. The normative censorship which guarantees the law's self-limitation is operative every time when, for example, a judge interprets in the light of morally- and/or ethically-laden legal principles, statutes which the law-giver has issued from its mainly instrumentalist, purposive rational perspective. Conceived of in this way, the law's self-limitation is a daily phenomenon, accomplished through routine legal practices.

Constitutions contain provisions on institutional practices which have been expressly specialised in the task of the law's self-limitation. Although these practices constitute the most conspicuous aspect of this auto-censorship, in a well-functioning modern legal system their role is only complementary; the major responsibility in the law's self-limitation falls to routine legal practices, where it is realised through the practical knowledge of legal actors. Of course, even in such a legal system, it is conceivable that, for instance, the legislator issues a statute violating human-rights principles and that we encounter at the law's surface level formally valid norms which stand in contradiction to sub-surface legal principles. If such a case should arise in our idealised "mature" modern legal system, the floor would now belong to the specific institutional arrangements which have been created through constitutional provisions to ensure the functioning of the law's self-limitation. These arrangements include constitutional review either in ordinary courts or in a specific Constitutional Court. We can also point to examples of *ex ante* control of constitutionality, such as the scrutiny of government bills by the Constitutional Committee of the Parliament of Finland.[23]

VI. MEETING SOME OBJECTIONS

There are obvious objections to my account of the law's self-limitation. As regards constitutional review or other institutional arrangements expressly fashioned for such a purpose, do they not operate at the surface level of law Is it not a question of assessing the mutual relations between norms which all are located at the law's discursively formulated surface: sub-constitutional legal regulations are appraised in the light of constitutional provisions? My answer is yes and no. Constitutional provisions, including those affirming fundamental rights or *Rechtsstaat* principles, belong to surface-level normative material. But they are specific among such normative material, not only because of their formal hierarchical status, but also because of their intimate links to the deep-structural normative principles on which they confer an explicit discursive formulation. Therefore, it can be argued that constitutional review, where the fundamental-rights provisions of the Constitution are used as a criterion for assessing a statute's validity, also manifests the law's self-limitation, as exposed in the framework of the law's multi-layered nature. Another counter-argument can be built on the hard-case nature of cases brought before constitutional review. In private and criminal law justice, routine cases make up a clear majority of the cases before ordinary courts. In constitutional justice, the reverse holds: most of the cases in constitutional justice are hard cases whose adjudication requires the opening up of the sub-surface layers. These cases cannot be decided merely on the basis of discursive knowledge about surface-level constitutional provisions but call for probing into the sub-surface foundations of these provisions.

Another probable objection challenges the positivism of my account of how modern law can, in the absence of natural-law yardsticks, meet the persistent problem of the law's limits. Have I not, with my assumption of sub-surface layers in the law, drifted into a contradiction with the positivity of modern law and taken a step in the direction of natural law?

Let us continuously keep in mind that we are discussing a "mature" modern legal system, where, for instance, constitutional provisions giving explicit expression to the principles of a democratic *Rechtsstaat* are supported by an established legal culture and a legal deep structure which include these principles as integral normative elements. But how do such sub-surface layers arise? What can we say about the formation of a "mature" modern legal system? One of the relations connecting the law's layers is that of sedimentation: the sub-surface layers result from processes of sedimentation with their origins in the normative material with which legal practices continuously enrich the law's surface. Through this relation of sedimentation, the sub-surface levels also partake in the positivity of modern law; positivity is not a characteristic only of the surface of modern law but reaches out to the levels of the legal culture and the deep structure.

The position in modern law of such fundamental normative ideas as human-rights principles should also be approached through the relation of sedimentation. These principles can be justified with moral arguments, but this is not enough to make them into elements of the law's deep structure. In the rationalist natural-law thinking of the early modern age, these principles were seen as universal norms, whose justification was supposed to lie in an immutable human nature. They have established themselves as elements of the deep structure of modern law only as a result of a long process of sedimentation. The early steps of this process can be traced back – in addition to the debates of natural-law theorists – to the American and French constitutional documents of the late eighteenth century. In the twentieth century, the process continued through new constitutional documents, international human-rights treaties, decisions by national and international monitoring bodies, as well as publications by legal dogmaticians, theorists and philosophers. Seen from a legal point of view, this process has signified the positivisation of human-rights principles, their transformation from moral-philosophically justified natural-law principles into elements of modern, positive law.

Now, I believe, we have dissolved the paradox of fundamental rights. Fundamental-rights norms can play a crucial role in the self-limitation of modern law, not only despite, but expressly in virtue of their positivity. However, the positivity of modern law has to be understood in a larger and profounder sense than is common in positivistic legal theory. Positivity is not a property only of surface-level legal norms; through the relation of sedimentation, it extends to the law's sub-surface layers, including human-rights-related principles as integral normative elements of the legal culture and the deep structure of a "mature" modern legal order.

VII. FUNDAMENTAL RIGHTS AND THE GROUNDS FOR THEIR LIMITATION

I have tried to show that discussing the problem of the law's limits in the context of modern, positive law necessitates something resembling Dworkin's distinction between principles and policies. This, of course, is not the same discussion in which Alexy engages when he, from the perspective of an analytical, legal-theoretical examination of legal decision-making, rejects this distinction. Yet another context is provided by the legal doctrinal task of interpreting and systematising the fundamental-rights provisions of a specific constitution or international human-rights instrument. We may recall that the criticism to which Ingeborg Maus subjected Alexy's fundamental-rights theory, although building on an exposition of the general *Rechtsstaat* background of fundamental rights, focused on the doctrine of the German Basic Law. In the final part of this article, I shall briefly comment on two other legal doctrinal issues where it appears to be important to conceive of fundamental rights as individual rights and to maintain their separation from collective goods.

These issues concern Finnish constitutional law and the ECHR. In 1995, a new Chapter on fundamental rights was inserted into the Finnish Constitution. The Chapter includes the right to security which, according to the governmental bill, was modelled after Article 5 of the ECHR. Article 7(1) of the Finnish Constitution states that "everyone has the right to life, personal liberty, integrity and security." Correspondingly, Article 5(1) of the ECHR lays down that "everyone has the right to liberty and security of person."

"Security" is a tricky concept; it can be interpreted as connoting either a collective good – in the sense of "national security" or "public safety and order" – or an individual right, the right to personal security. In its praxis, the Human Rights Court has adopted the latter alternative when interpreting Article 5(1) of the ECHR. This interpretation, which has been shared by most legal commentators, entails that the right to security has in general been treated as a non-independent, auxiliary right. By contrast, in the praxis of the Constitutional Committee of the Finnish Parliament, one can notice a tendency to raise security as a collective good to the rank of fundamental rights. Such a reading of the Constitution's fundamental-rights provisions has been propped up by three argumentative steps.

First, the right to security has been detached from the rights to personal liberty and integrity, and assigned independent legal relevance. This already points to the direction of a common good: it is hard to see what independent legal meaning, not included in the rights to liberty and integrity, could be attributed to an individual right to personal security. The second step in the argument consists of an appeal to the horizontal effect or *Drittwirkung* of fundamental-rights norms: these norms not only regulate the relations between public power and private individuals, but extend their effects to the mutual relations of the latter.[24] Thirdly, the argument refers to Article 23 of the Finnish Constitution which establishes a general obligation for public power to secure the realization of fundamental and human rights; this obligation corresponds to what in German fundamental-rights doctrine is called the *Schutzpflicht* of the state. Taken together, these arguments – the independent nature of the right to security, the horizontal effect of fundamental rights and the *Schutzpflicht* of public power – lead to the conclusion that the state (public power) is obliged to ensure the realization of the independent right to security in the horizontal relations between private individuals. Public safety and order as a collective good has been transformed into a fundamental right with a rank equal to that of individual liberty rights, such as the rights to personal liberty and integrity. With the same move, the Dworkinian distinction between policies aiming at collective goods and principles focusing on individual rights has been obliterated from constitutional doctrine.

Now the doctrine allows for justifying, say, new powers requested by police authorities in terms of fundamental rights: the powers can be said to be necessary for the fulfilment of the state's obligation to guarantee the fundamental right to security. If and when the powers encroach on individual fundamental rights, such as the rights to personal integrity, privacy and the confidentiality of correspondence, their constitutional acceptability is said to depend on the mutual weighing of fundamental-rights principles of equal rank. What according to the liberal understanding of the constitution and the *Rechtsstaat* was to be restricted through the system of fundamental rights has itself been absorbed into this system; there is an evident parallelism to that interpretation of the German Basic Law which constituted the object for Ingeborg Maus' criticism.

The constitutional doctrine of the *Rechtsstaat* involves a peculiar dialectic between collective goods and individual fundamental rights. On the one hand, the main thrust of fundamental rights – here I am alluding to the first-generation liberty rights – is said to be the creation of a sphere of private autonomy, secured against infringements from the side of public power in the name of collective goods, such as public safety and order or national security.

However, the guarantees that fundamental rights offer are not – with certain important exceptions – absolute: limitations to these rights can be adopted, with appeal to the same collective goods whose purport the rights are supposed to restrict. This might seem paradoxical, but the solution to the paradox is quite simple: the limitations may not touch upon the core (the *Wesensgehalt* of the German doctrine[25]) of the right in question. Thus, Dworkinian policies (re-)enter the constitutional doctrine in the form of grounds for limitations to fundamental rights. The determination of the relevance that these grounds can be accorded certainly involves weighing and balancing, for example when applying the principle of proportionality. However, at issue is not a weighing within the system of fundamental-rights principles but between such a principle and an external factor of a policy nature. Such a view of the relation between fundamental rights and the grounds for their limitation also corresponds to the structure of the ECHR.

The ECHR includes references to policy standpoints, but these references are included in the provisions laying down the grounds for limitation, and not in the provisions confirming the rights to be protected. Some of the provisions also mention "security" in the sense of a collective good as a ground for limiting a right. In Article 8(1), everyone is guaranteed the right to respect for his private and family life, his home and his correspondence. According to par. 2 of the same article "there shall be no interference by a public authority with the exercise of this right except such as is in accordance with the law and is necessary in a democratic society in the interests of national security, public safety or the economic well-being of the country, for the prevention of disorder or crime, for the protection of health or morals, or for the protection of the rights and freedoms of others." Correspondingly, par. 1 of Article 9 guarantees everyone's right to freedom of thought, conscience and religion, while par. 2 of the same article provides that "freedom to manifest one's religion or beliefs shall be subject only to such limitations as are prescribed by law and are necessary in a democratic society in the interests of public safety, for the protection of public order, health or morals, or the protection of the rights and freedoms of others."[26]

In the context of the ECHR, the abolition of the distinction between principles and policies would amount to eradicating the boundary separating the protected rights from the grounds for their limitation. Here we have an additional legal doctrinal reason for siding with Dworkin in the debate about the relevance of the distinction between principles and policies.

VIII. CONCLUSIONS

We are ready to conclude. The position Alexy has taken with regard to the distinction between principles and policies can be discussed at different levels and in different dimensions. In the analytical, legal-theoretical dimension, one can challenge Alexy's axiological understanding of principles (in Dworkin's strict sense). This is the line followed by Habermas but not taken up in this article. Alexy's position can also be attacked at the level of normative, legal doctrinal argumentation, as has been shown by Ingeborg Maus and as I have tried to demonstrate in relation to the Finnish Constitution and the ECHR. However, my main arguments for the significance of Dworkin's distinction concern the problem of the limits of modern law.

The problem of the law's limits accompanies all law but is aggravated by the positivity of modern law: the simultaneous loss of credibility suffered by natural law in the wake of cultural modernization and the increasing instrumentalist, policy-oriented use of the law. As a result there arises the specific threat of totalitarianism of which Hayek has warned us: totalitarianism by legal means. The constitution of a *Rechtsstaat* assigns the definition and the safe-guarding of the law's limits to fundamental rights and constitutional review. However, this solution runs against a dilemma which can be termed the paradox of fundamental rights and which is akin to the paradox of the *Rechtsstaat*. The latter paradox concerns the law's relation to state power: how can the law fulfil its task of disciplining the exercise of state power, if it itself, as positive law, is a creation of this very power? In the examination of the fundamental rights' contribution to the solution to the intra-legal problem of limitation, the paradox receives the following form: how can fundamental rights fulfil the function of the law's self-limitation, if they too, in the age of modern law, must be understood as being grounded in positive law and if they, consequently, seem to be exposed to the possibility of amendments and even annulment, a possibility characteristic of positive law?

Habermas has dissolved the paradox of the *Rechtsstaat* by arguing that the *Rechtsstaat* is possible only as a democratic *Rechtsstaat* and by subjecting state power as administrative power to state power as communicative power, distilled in legitimate laws. The key to the dissolution of the paradox of fundamental rights lies in the law's multi-layered nature. In a "mature" modern legal system, fundamental-rights principles have firmly sedimented into the law's sub-surface layers and through the practical knowledge of legal actors, exercise their limiting function in everyday legal practices; for instance, every time when a judge interprets policy-oriented legislation in the light of principles. Cases of constitutional justice, where constitutional provisions on fundamental rights are expressly applied, represent only the visible top of the iceberg in the law's self-limitation, which, in a well-functioning modern legal system, primarily operates in an inconspicuous way in ordinary, every-day legal practices.

NOTES

[1] See chapters 7 and 8 of this book.
[2] Robert Alexy, *Theorie der Grundrechte*. Frankfurt am Main: Suhrkamp, 1986.
[3] Ibid., 18.
[4] Ibid., pp. 22ff.
[5] Ibid., 32.
[6] See Robert Alexy, "Zum Begriff des Rechtsprinzips," in *Recht, Vernunft, Diskurs*, Frankfurt am Main: Suhrkamp, 1995, pp. 177–212. The article was originally published already in 1979.
[7] Ibid.
[8] Cf. Ronald Dworkin, *Taking Rights Seriously*, London: Duckworth, 1978, pp. 24ff and Alexy, *supra*, fn. 2, pp. 77ff.
[9] Alexy, *supra*, fn. 2, pp. 75–76
[10] Dworkin, *supra*, fn. 8, p. 22.
[11] Robert Alexy, "Individuelle Rechte und kollektive Güter," in *Recht, Vernunft, Diskurs*. Frankfurt am Main: Suhrkamp, 1995, pp. 232–261.
[12] Alexy, *supra*, fn. 2, pp. 79ff.
[13] Ingeborg Maus, "Die Trennung von Recht und Moral als Begrenzung des Rechts," 20 (1989) *Rechtstheorie*, pp. 191–210, at pp. 197–199.
[14] Jürgen Habermas, *Faktizität und Geltung*, Frankfurt am Main: Suhrkamp, 1992, pp. 309ff.
[15] Niklas Luhmann, *Das Recht der Gesellschaft*, Frankfurt am Main: Suhrkamp, 1995, pp. 470–481.
[16] Georg Jellinek, *Allgemeine Staatslehre*, Berlin: O. Häring, 1914, pp. 386ff.
[17] François Ewald, *L'Etat providence*, Paris: Grasset, 1986.
[18] Friedrick A. Hayek, *Law, Legislation, and Liberty*, One-volume edition, London: Routledge & Kegan Paul, 1982.
[19] Habermas, *supra*, fn. 13, pp. 182ff.
[20] I have developed the idea of the law's multi-layered nature at greater length in my *Critical Legal Positivism*, Aldershot: Ashgate, 2002. My focus has been on an ideal-typical national legal system which meets the criteria of a "mature" modern legal system. An open question is whether one could employ a similar theoretical framework when examining international law in general and the role of fundamental-right provisions and principles play therein in particular. In the further elaboration of the multi-layered view of the law, due attention should also be paid to the interaction of domestic and international law, as well as to the other aspects of the legal pluralism characteristic of our contemporary legal situation.
[21] Habermas, *supra*, fn. 14, pp. 468ff.
[22] Alexy, *supra*, fn. 2, pp. 508ff.
[23] We should also bear in mind the monitoring mechanisms established by international human-rights treaties, although their role can, as I have already claimed, be regarded as complementary with respect to the constitutional arrangements of a democratic *Rechtsstaat*.
[24] The bill put forward by the government, which led to the adoption of the new fundamental rights provisions in 1995, explicitly mentioned the possibility of such a horizontal effect.
[25] The Basic Law includes an explicit provision (19(2)) on the *Wesensgehalt*: "In no case may a basic right be infringed upon in its essential content."
[26] The last chapter of the Charter on Fundamental Rights of the European Union contains general provisions on the scope of the protected rights. Thus, according to Article 52(1), "subject to the principle of proportionality, limitations may be made only if they are necessary and genuinely meet objectives of general interest recognized by the Union or the need to protect the rights and freedoms of others."

MASSIMO LA TORRE

3. NINE CRITIQUES TO ALEXY'S THEORY OF FUNDAMENTAL RIGHTS

I. INTRODUCTION

I do not intend to propose a theory of fundamental rights alternative to the one masterly outlined by Robert Alexy. Nor would I like to advocate one or the other alternative conceptions of fundamental rights based on other conceptions of discourse theory. My intention here is a more modest one. I will put forward a series of criticisms to Alexy's theory, combining my own interpretation of his theory with a rather liberal borrowing from two main sources: (1) Jürgen Habermas' overt or covert criticism of Alexy's Theory of Fundamental Rights; and (2) H. L. A. Hart's Postscript to *The Concept of Law,* where the British scholar replies to Ronald Dworkin's formidable attack against his positivism. The latter source of inspiration might seem rather intriguing, but I believe that in fact some of Hart's arguments can be reconstructed as full-blown criticism to Alexy. Before starting, I must add that not all the objections seem to me to have the same strength – I will however abstain from objecting to the objections, even if I do not fully share them. The ultimate goal is to show some possible weak points of Alexy's theory, and in that way, to contribute to its further elucidation.

II. ALEXY'S PURELY SEMANTIC CONCEPTION OF NORM

Serious doubts can be raised on the semantic notion of norm adopted *expressis verbis* by Alexy and shaped along the three deontic operators of order, prohibition and permission. "A norm is [...] the meaning of a normative statement" – we read in *A Theory*.[1]

A first problem with such a conception of norm is that it boils down to a pure semantic conception of a norm. And such a *purely semantic* conception of a norm cannot account for rules such as the rule of recognition. This is so because a central, if not the central feature of such a norm, is that of being embedded in a practice, something which falls beyond a *purely semantic* conception of a norm.

A. J. Menéndez and E. O. Eriksen (eds.), Arguing Fundamental Rights, 53–68.

This is bound to have devastating consequences. It is very important to keep in mind that without a rule such as the rule of recognition, it is simply not possible to conceptualise law as a legal order or system, or to introduce and use the idea of a hierarchy of norms. How to make sense of the concept of "fundamental right norm" (*Grundrechtsnorm*), a concept so central in Alexy's reconstruction of fundamental rights, if we have been deprived of the ideas of legal system and legal hierarchy? Quite obviously, a merely presupposed Fundamental Norm *à la Kelsen* (his famous basic norm, or *Grundnorm*),[2] will not do the trick, since such a norm is purely "presupposed," that is, it is a purely epistemological devise. It is only by giving to the ground rule the meaning of a rule "abstracted" from a practice, in the sense for instance of Leonard Nelson's "Abstraktion,"[3] and therefore in a sense somewhat close to the one given by Hart to his "rule of recognition" whose assessment "can only be an external statement of fact,"[4] that that ground rule can be conceived as a valid and effective norm; this is so given that it is from the existing practice, and not a mere semantic content, that it draws its "point." So that the latter can be a matter of "trascendental" or inductive knowledge.

Moreover, a mere semantic notion of the norm does not explain either the constitutive effects of special fundamental norms or their pragmatic character. In fact, a purely semantic notion of legal norm creates a considerable risk of a strong metaphysical jump into normative Platonism, or normative realism, that is, the assumption that deontic modalities are entities in the world.[5] This point is further proved when one considers the recent "post-Hartian" discussion on the question of legal determinacy. It has been argued that a semantic notion of the norm, understood as reflecting the reality of the world, offers a way out of the problem. However, the purely semantic conception of the norm implies as a matter of fact two highly controversial implications (1) the definition of meaning as correspondence to, or picture of, states of affairs or essences in the world, and further (2) the advocacy of moral realism, that is the assumption of normative, moral things or "entities" in the world. It thus seems that a semantic theory of norms, in order to ensure an acceptable degree of determinacy, should embrace an essentialist approach towards language.

It could be further added that a semantic notion of a norm implies a semantic theory of rights. As a matter of fact, this implication is drawn by Alexy himself.[6] Now, this semantic theory of rights is strongly criticized by Jürgen Habermas.[7] This is so on the basis that it cannot take account of two fundamental aspects of rights (1) first, of their pragmatic character of "claims to be right;" (2) second, of the circumstances of reciprocity and mutual recognition in which rights are born and embedded. The triadic relationship around which Alexy, following Hohfeld,[8] reconstructs rights positions can be plausibly be said to be the representation of a situation of subordination of one party to the other, in which no claim to correctness is raised or, for that purpose, could be raised. Hohfeld's rights do not imply any claim to be right (even if they are claims in a paradigmatic sense). This is actually the point of Dworkin's "rights thesis." As it is known, Dworkin claims that holding or claiming a right, and accordingly denying a right, cannot be fully understood if having a right is not also explained in terms of *being right*. Denying a right implies not only a certain damage to the interests of the right-holder, but also, and above all, downplaying his moral status, by means of implying that she is *wrong*.

III. ALEXY'S NOTION OF FUNDAMENTAL RIGHT NORM

The very notion of a fundamental rights norm (*Grundrechtsnorm*) can be challenged. More specifically, one can put into question that fundamental rights derive conceptually from norms or prescriptions.[9] This is very closely related to the extent of the influence of the doctrine held by the German Federal Constitutional Court over Alexy's conceptualisation of fundamental rights norms. But could it be that Alexy's theory is excessively conditioned by the German court? It is true that Alexy presents his theory as a legal-dogmatic exercise, which takes as its point of reference German law. Having said that, it is also clear that his ambitions point much higher, and that at any rate, his theory of law drives him towards a *universal configuration of fundamental legal concepts*.[10] Therefore, it is legitimate to question whether the long shadow of the doctrine of the German Constitutional Court, and the will to fit it, does not lead to a dangerous general reductionism of rights to commands.

The problem can be better illustrated with the help of a comparison with the legal theory of John Austin. The British positivist denied rights an independent legal conceptual status, which led him to the conclusion that constitutional law *as such* is an *extra-legal* enterprise.[11] Alexy clearly prefers to speak of fundamental rights norms, but still defines fundamental rights as "commands" of optimization. So, what is really a fundamental rights norm?

Alexy claims that a fundamental right norm is one which is correctly founded (*grundrechtlich*), that is, founded through valid fundamental rights. It is explicitly affirmed that "fundamental rights norms (*grundrechtsnormen*) are all those norms for which a correct justification through constitutional rights is possible (*eine korrekte grundrechtliche Begründung möglich ist*)."[12] However, it also seems that according to Alexy fundamental rights norms are a more fundamental concept than fundamental rights. Whenever there is a fundamental right, there must be a corresponding fundamental right norm. The opposite does not hold: there may well be fundamental rights norms without corresponding fundamental rights. But if this is so, the question arises what exactly a justification of a fundamental right norms is, and which role the latter plays in the production and recognition of fundamental rights. Is the justification of a fundamental rights norm a justification through fundamental rights or through fundamental rights norms? (This ambiguity is reflected in the English translation, where *grundrechtliche Begründung* is rendered as "constitutional justification").[13] In either case, Alexy's definition of a fundamental rights norm as an entity given through a *justification of fundamental rights norms* seems to be circular, especially once the fundamental right is said to be the outcome of the correspondent fundamental right norm.

IV. THE DISTINCTION BETWEEN PRINCIPLES AND RULES, AND THE DEONTOLOGICAL CHARACTER OF RIGHTS

A very common line of attack against *A Theory* is the denial of the fundamental distinction between principles and rules. In a different context, the inexistence of such different normative structure was defended by Herbert L. A. Hart:

> There is no reason why a legal system should not recognize that a valid rule determines a result in cases to which is applicable, except where another rule, judged to be more important, is also applicable to the same case. So a rule defeated in competition with a more important rule in a given case may, like a principle, survive to determine the outcome in other cases where it is judged to be more important than another competing rule.[14]

Even if Hart's point was specifically addressed against Dworkin's legal theory, it could also be very fittingly forwarded to Alexy, perhaps even more fittingly, as Alexy does not share Dworkin's central distinction between principles and policies.[15] In fact, once we conceive principles as goals (optimization commands), as Alexy does, the fact that rules, as well as rights, can be interpreted as establishing and prescribing goals (something clearly proven by the wide resort to teleological interpretation of statutes), the difference between principles and rules becomes indeed thin enough.

One could further question why couldn't we adopt Marcus Singer's view of the difference between rules and principles?:

> Moral rules – he says – do not hold in all circumstances; they are not invariant; in a useful legal phrase, they are "deafeasible". A moral principle, however, states that a certain kind of action (or, in some cases, a certain kind of rule) is always wrong (or obligatory), and does not leave open the possibility of justifying an action of that kind. Moral principles hold in all circumstances and allow of no exceptions; they are invariant with respect to every moral situation. They are thus "indefeasible".[16]

Following Marcus Singer, we might thus say that, while rules are defeasible, principles are not. In this view principles therefore are submitted to a greater deontological "discipline" than rules.

V. FUNDAMENTAL RIGHTS NORMS AS PRINCIPLES

One can further criticise the claim that fundamental rights norms (*Grundrechtsnormen*) are basically principles. To start with, one could wonder why they could not be fundamentally rules. After all, in Alexy's theory of norms, rules offer a higher degree of protection than principles, to the extent that they are not open to weighing and balancing. If this is so, why shouldn't we put at the foundation of the system rules (and thus offering stronger protection to individual freedoms) instead of principles (actually unable to guarantee freedoms in an indefeasible way)?

The reader will quickly realise that this question is closely related to one of the central tenets of *A Theory*, namely the characterisation of principles as "optimization commands." Here again – I believe – we are confronted with a reductionist (one could also say prescriptivist) strategy. At the end of the day, principles are collapsed into the category of commands and precepts.

A further objection is that principles so conceived are no longer clearly distinguished from policies, which entails that they can lose their *deontological character*. This is in a sense recognized by Alexy himself, when he equates principles to "values," and adds that the distinction principles/rules, in the sense of *prima facie* and definitive commands, applies also to values:

> The structural distinction between rules and principles can also be found on the axiological plane. Evaluative criteria correspond to principles, evaluative rules to rules.[17]

But Alexy denies that this entails the loss of the deontological character of principles. He claims that principles are deontological practical concepts,[18] and optimization commands are just ... commands, that is deontological entities.

This rebuttal based on reversing the criticism is not very convincing to me, for the following reasons. First, if principles were expressing an ought (*sollen*), were due (*gesollten)*, if thus their content were apt to be expressed through a deontic operator, deontic logic would then apply to them. But in such a case, their application will follow an "all-or-nothing" logic, and not the gradualistic logic proper of weighing (*abwägung*). Second, Alexy's characterisation has problems in dealing with standard cases of norms. Consider the following two examples. The minimum content of natural law, its bedrock (so-to-say), was traditionally summarised in two precepts: *malum vitandum, bonum faciendum*. This at least is Aquinas' view.[19] Now the question arises which kind of precepts these two are. Are *malum vitandum* and *bonum faciendum* optimisation commands? If Alexy says they are, should we then forget that they are the expression of a teleological morality, according to which values and virtues are more relevant than rules and obligations? A similar conclusion stems from the consideration of the principle which lies at the bottom of *utilitarian* moral doctrine. As it is well-known, this is the pursuit of "the greatest happiness of the greatest number." This principle can be reformulated as the "command" that the greatest happiness of the greatest number be realised or pursued. Should we then say that the utilitarian principle is the expression of a deontological doctrine or that it has a deontological content?

On this issue Habermas is strongly critical of Alexy's theory. In particular, the Frankfurter philosopher stresses two points. First, he is very keen to point out that justice is not just a value among other values:

Values always compete with other values. They state which specific goods specific persons or collectivities strive for or prefer under specific circumstances. Only from the perspective of the given individual or group can values be temporarily ranked in transitive order. Thus values claim relative validity, whereas justice poses an absolute validity claim: moral precepts claims to be valid for each and every person.[20]

Values are agent-relative and can be provisionally measured and traded-off from the agent's perspective and only from this. Such is not the case of justice, which is a value claiming "absolute," universal validity, that is, validity for all and each. Habermas' point is thus that values are particularistic, while justice is universalistic. It is true that legal norms are addressed to the concrete members of a concrete political community. However, legal norms raise a claim to correctness (as a result of their pragmatic nature) and thus transcend the concrete political community in which they are formulated and somehow refer to an ideal discourse. The key point is that *such an ideal discourse is not value-based, is not grounded on individual preferences, but is rather embedded in deontological requirements*. Second, principles, as well as rules, are not teleological devices, that is, they cannot be portrayed as optimization commands:

Neither rules nor principles have a teleological structure. Contrary to what legal methodologies tend to suggest when they refer to "weighing values" (*güterabwägung*), principles must not be understood as optimising prescriptions [commands], because that would eradicate their deontological character.[21]

VI. THE RATIONALITY OF WEIGHING AND BALANCING

The following controversial point which I would like to make is that fundamental rights according to Alexy are applied, exercised, or implemented through weighing and balancing (*abwägung*). This is again related to the discussed conceptualization of rights in terms of principles, sharply distinguished from rules. The idea of rights applicable through weighing depends on the thesis that fundamental rights are ascribed through principles, and that principles are applicable only through weighing – an idea which is shared, as is well known, by Ronald Dworkin. Now, balancing or weighing – this is the objection – is at the end of the day a procedure consigned to judicial discretion, since it cannot be given a fully formal and rational structure. Alexy believes to solve such problem through the so-called *Law of Balancing*, whose non-technical formulation reads as follows:

> The circumstances under which one principle takes precedence over another constitute the conditions of a rule which has the same legal consequences as the principle taking precedence[22]

Alexy's *Law of Balancing*, which turns principles into definitive rules, is, however no guarantee of a rational outcome, since the relevance of principles (their weight) and the configuration of the conditions of priority of a principle over another are shaped by judiciary discretion. The *Law of Balancing* gives only an appearance of rationality to a procedure which is in the end irrational and at its core decisionistic.

In this respect a further interesting objection is advanced by Habermas. The question with balancing is also that parties in a legal dispute claim each to be right and fully right and thus take the ideal stance of the one only right answer. Now, Alexy excludes – contrary to what is held by Dworkin – the ideal necessity of such one right answer, though he recognizes that in easy cases it could be reached. However, there is another implication of the claim to justice raised by parties and of their presupposition of the one right answer (which is, in Dworkin's theory, the substantive core of his "rights thesis"): such implication concerning the way a case is decided before a court. Balancing, which strikes a kind of compromise, seems to deny that parties "claim to rightness":

> An adjudication oriented by principles has to decide which claim and which action in a given conflict is right – and not how to balance interests or relate values.[23]

A very important line of criticism concerns the idea that fundamental rights can be balanced against collective goods (meant as non-distributive entities). The question here is that by so doing we are confronted with a strong re-introduction of consequentialist and utilitarian considerations in the assessment of rights. In particular, in a perspective of this kind no rights could resist an utilitarian reasoning. Rights will no longer be "trumps" (to use Dworkin's expression) against policies, and there will be no "absolute" rights whatever. Torture would thus be eventually correctly justified (*grundrechtlich*).[24] Such a conclusion might suffice – I believe – to make Alexy's theory unpalatable to any staunch liberal.

A further critical point very much connected with the latest one is the assumption of the notion of the "essential core guarantee" (*wesensgehaltsgarantie*) (Basic German Law, Article 19, Section II) as equivalent to the proportionality principle. That is, the essential core of rights is to be assessed through the principle of proportionality and in the end to be considered as embedded in such principle:

> The guarantee of an essential core contained in Article 19(2) of the Basic Law does not contain any further control on the limitability of fundamental rights beyond that already contained in the principle of proportionality.[25]

The consequence has been already announced, and is that there are no absolute rights:

> The conviction that there must be rights which even in the most extreme circumstances are not outweighed – only such rights are genuine absolute rights – may be held by an individual who is free to sacrifice himself for certain principles, but it cannot be maintained as a matter of constitutional law.[26]

Now, here the question is whether a fundamental right's fundamental task is not just to be there, that is, to protect individual autonomy and dignity, especially "under the most extreme conditions" – to use Alexy's words. Is not the function of a right to physical integrity and to dignity, like the right not to be tortured, to act as an "absolute," intangible right just for the most extreme conditions of a terrorist menace or of an impending civil war? As a matter of fact, fundamental rights apply not in normal conditions, when people recognize or ignore each other, but especially whenever there is a special occurrence that endangers the peaceful co-existence of individuals. If we deny an absolute core to individual rights, what is then left of them? Is it not a kind of *reductio ad absurdum*, and somehow cynical, to say that the "essential core" of constitutional rights is their propensity to be weighed and thus to be exposed to permanent trade-offs?

Elsewhere Alexy, replying to the accusation of irrationality launched against his equivalence between an essential core guarantee (*wesensgehaltgarantie*) and proportionality principle, has connected the notion of proportionality to the intensity of their attack brought against the right. He introduces a "disproportionality rule," which reads as follows:

> An interference with a fundamental right is disproportional if it is not justified by the fact that the omission of this interference would give rise to an interference with another principle (or with the same principle with respect to other persons or in other respects), provided that this latter interference is at least as intensive as the first one.[27]

Here, nevertheless, Alexy does not face the fundamental problem raising from his treating rights and principles as a common unity of measure, especially given that principles are not distinct from policies. Policies and fundamental rights can thus be legitimately introduced in a same structure of reasoning leading to a decision concerning fundamental rights: rights can be weighed and measured against policies, and the latter can trump the former if the omission of the policy in question would bring about an interference with another policy which is more intensive than the interference against the principle upholding the fundamental right in question:

> Fundamental rights gain over-proportionally in strength as the intensity of interferences increase. There exists something like a centre of resistance.[28]

However, this resistance is not "absolute" against policies. It is in the end a matter of intensity, a value indeed which moreover allows for an intense judicial discretion. And such resistance is not absolute and really effective, because according to Alexy fundamental rights are themselves in the end conceived as policies.

If fundamental rights are seen as policies, they will however lose their point, which is controlling and limiting State action. On the contrary, fundamental rights shaped as optimization commands – prescriptions of positive, not negative actions – would contribute to a further expansion of State powers in the social domain. One might reply to this objection by pointing out that fundamental rights are not only of the liberal kind (defensive rights, *abwehrrechte*), but that there are several very relevant fundamental rights which consist of political and social rights, demanding a positive action of the State. However, even after accepting such objection, a disquieting problem remains, that is, that *negative* fundamental rights too will then be conceived as claims for a positive State intervention, which by necessity has a tendency to expand. Thus, optimizing might know no boundaries. The limits of optimization – if there are some – are never stable and can ever be enlarged.

Robert Alexy has recently further elaborated on the notion of discretion, following a two-fold aim. On the one hand, he has articulated principles in two classes (1) formal and (2) substantive and has rendered precise the content and the shape of legislative discretion through a further distinction between (1) structural and (2) epistemic discretion. On the other side, he has introduced a "Weight Formula" based on a triadic scale, rendering it easier for constitutional adjudication to avoid a possible decisionistic slippery slope.[29] However, with all these refinements, the essential critical points – that of the ascription of a common, particular, quantifiable value to all variables considered and especially that of weighing as trade-off and prudential compromise – are really not tackled.

VII. A THREE-STAGE THEORY OF RIGHTS? COMPETENCES AND DEONTIC REDUCTIONISM

I would like to devote special attention to Alexy's three-stage theory of individual rights and his notion of a right as a possible ought (*mögliches sollen*). According to such a theory, in conceptualizing a right we should carefully distinguish three different dimensions (1) justification, (2) legal position and relation, and (3) enforcement.[30] In this way we would be able – Alexy claims – to solve the perennial controversies on the nature and range of rights. These controversies – Alexy believes – are the outcome, in fact, of a confusion of these three distinct dimensions. For instance, Windscheid's will theory would be better understood as a doctrine of the legal position dimension of rights, Ihreing's interest theory would rather offer a justification basis to them, while Kelsen's claim theory would focus on the enforcement dimension. Now, such a solution, though interesting, is not fully convincing. In particular, unconvincing is – I believe – Alexy's distinction between (1) the dimension of justification and (2) the dimension of legal position and relation, at least as far the traditional doctrinal controversy on rights is concerned. The dispute between "will theories" and "interest theories" is not really a meaningless dispute originating from a methodological confusion. In fact, it can be seen both as (1) dispute about justification (indeed, will is sometimes referred as a justification for having rights) and (2) as a dispute on legal positions: interest theories usually stress more the passive element of entitlements' ascription than the active one of claim, and are more willing to see as rights holders even individuals with a reduced autonomy or with no autonomy at all. Paradigmatic in this regard is the controversy about children's rights, which interest theories tend to affirm without additional qualifications, the analysis of which is rather embarrassing for will theories.

The second highly controversial point is the ideal of "possible or potential ought," which according to Alexy should serve to explain individual rights as powers and competences. Alexy distinguishes rights in three categories (1) rights to something (*rechte auf etwas*), (2) liberties (*freiheiten*) and (3) competences (*kompetenzen*). Accordingly, a negative right (*abwehrrecht*) against the State, the traditional type of liberal right is, according to Alexy, a bundle of three positions: a right to something, a liberty, a power or competence. Now, according to Alexy individual rights, whatever their form, are grounded on the traditional deontic modalities, that is, commands, prohibitions, and permissions. To such a reduction,[31] the right as competence or power is more resistant than the other two, since it is hardly the outcome of a command, of a prohibition, or even of a permission. Alexy's ingenious way out is based on the idea of a "potential ought" (*mögliches sollen*).[32] A power in his view would be the "potentiality" at a meta-level of commanding, prohibiting, or permitting. To this configuration nonetheless one may object that there is a fourth possibility, as far as legal powers are concerned, that is, the possibility that there would exist, at a meta-level, not only commands, prohibitions, and permissions, but also legal powers. Why should powers be banned from the meta-level? A (legal) power indeed may consist in ascribing a legal power, that is a power on or of power, a (legal) meta-power, in the same way as we have meta-rules, that is, rules concerning rules. That means, however, that its content would not be a traditional deontic modality. The contingent fact that the ascribed (second order) power may in its turn have as content a command, a prohibition, or a permission, is not sufficient to explain the contents of the first order power in terms of one or more deontic modalities. In any case, Alexy elsewhere admits that "the relation between a right and its subject matter is not a relation of identity."[33]

Alexy's explanation of individual rights in terms of traditional deontic modalities recall various legal positivistic attempts at conceptualising rights as obligations or duties and at conceiving rules of competence in terms of rules of conduct. Such are Alf Ross' attempts of reducing rights to "presentation techniques" of legal norms and of conceiving norms of competence as "fragments of norms". However, had Alf Ross been successful in the justification of his views, he would have been, at the end of the day, forced to deny that a (strong) permission, an explicit permission, could be an independent deontic modality (as it was on the contrary defended by Von Wright). Indeed, Ross ended up proposing that even (strong) permissions are to be conceived as simple negations of a command. Command here is the only pure deontic operator, the alpha and the omega of the whole of law and practical domain. Ross was therefore only consequent in defending his reductionist strategy, since according to him there held the assumption of "the unity of ought," which meant that there is one, and only one, supreme deontic modality, that is, command. Now, the postulate of the unity of ought is warmly defended by Robert Alexy in terms which are identical to Ross'. In the case of the Danish legal philosopher, it was only a matter of course that such an authoritarian view (the centrality or the fundamentality of command), I dare call it a real obsession, could not tolerate an independent notion of rights – which, as Vilhelm Lundstedt (another legal realist) proposed, should rather be referred in brackets.

Leaving aside thee two Scandinavian theorists, Alexy's notion of "potential ought" remains problematic. "Potential ought" might be conceived in analogy to the "possibility" modality of modal logic. However, this would have as a consequence to deny the normative character of legal powers – which for sure is not what Alexy intends to do. "Possible *ought*" in modal terms is equivalent to the statement "it is possible that *ought*," or, said differently, "it is possible that *ought* takes place." However, such a phrase would be trivial, since for an *ought* to hold or take place or to be meaningful, the said *ought* has not to be "necessary." But if "it is not necessary that *non-ought*," then "it is possible that *ought*." In this sense whatever ought is a "possible *ought*."

If the "possibility" in question is not the modal possibility, we have then two other ways out. (1) Either potential ought is coterminous with what is deontically possible, that is, a permission, or (2) it is a power, a competence – but then clearly is not a permission. However, this second way out is exactly what Alexy seems to intend to avoid. Thus, we are only left with the characterisation of the potential ought as a permission. However, if it is a permission, it is not a competence or power – according to the same Alexy, who carefully distinguishes between the two positions. Moreover, it is explicitly denied in *A Theory* that rules of competence should be regarded as equivalent to rules of conduct. Given that a permission is the modality of a rule of conduct, and if we reduce powers to permissions, we would accordingly agree that there is no rule of conduct distinct from a rule of competence and that competences are fully equivalent to permissions. An outcome, it seems, that is not extremely felicitous for Alexy's theory.

Finally, Alexy's (and Ross') search for the unity of the ought can be further challenged by recalling Hart's criticism against the "fragments of norms" thesis. According to the latter, rules which do not impose duties *prima facie*, for example, rules of competence or rules ascribing powers, would just set conditions for the holding of rules imposing duties, and could thus be considered as internal to the latter rules' formal structure. Hart claims that such a thesis would amount to saying that "all the rules of a game are 'really' directions to the umpire and the scorer."[34] But this would "distort the ways in which these are spoken of, thought of, and actually used in social life."[35] In a similar way the constitutional rules of a country would be only assumptions needed for the judge to inflict sanctions. In this way, however, the "puzzled man,"[36] who is the subject around whom the normative experience revolves, being rules devices to orient the disoriented, would see his being "puzzled" brought to extremes.

VIII. DISCOURSES OF JUSTIFICATION AND APPLICATION: COMING TOO CLOSE?

A further weak point in Alexy's powerful theory is that the application of law (and rights) is governed by the same criteria which guide the justification of rules (and rights). However, one could believe that the discourse of application, which should give account of the factual features of a case and of its specificity, is different from the discourse of justification, in which the validity of the final ruling is assessed. What we need in reasoning about legal facts – it has been argued – is not balancing, but coherence, or "integrity." Integrity however does not assume rights as optimization commands, and coherence is sought between strong deontological criteria which exclude policies. This seems to be Ronald Dworkin's strategy, later followed by Klaus Günther and Jürgen Habermas.

Disputable is also the view that legal positivism is inclusive, or rather, that positivism being necessarily inclusive (as Alexy seems to hold), it should be at the end of the day rejected (which is Alexy's contention). Indeed, we might assume that (moral) principles are included in the rule of recognition, and in this way are transformed in positivistic prescriptions. This is the strategy that Hart uses to rebuff Dworkin's criticism, and that he elaborated in detail in his *Postscript* to *The Concept of Law*. Such a strategy might be damaging to Alexy's theory, insofar as he ascribes to idealism (the connection thesis in the dispute on the relationship between law and morality).[37] By their inclusion in the rule of recognition, principles are legally recognizable and applicable in terms of pedigree criteria. Reference to principles accordingly does not imply that legal argumentation should lapse into moral reasoning – as is claimed by Alexy.

Nonetheless should legal reasoning be doomed to drift into general practical reasoning, there is no conceptual need to connect the theory of the nature of law with the theory of legal reasoning. We can conceive the first enterprise as fully neutral and descriptive, while advocating a moral and political characterisation of legal reasoning. This is Joseph Raz's position (i.e., "exclusive positivism"), echoed by the late Hart as well.

IX. ALEXY'S DISCURSIVE FOUNDATION OF HUMAN RIGHTS

My eighth point concerns Alexy's discursive foundation of human rights.[38] A foundational objection to his train of argumentation is that discourse theory cannot transform discursive requirements into action or conduct requirements, something which renders extremely problematic Alexy's theoretical construction. Indeed, Alexy's three steps strategy – moving from (1) a claim to correctness to (2) a claim to justifiability to eventually land into (3) a claim to justice – is bound to fail, since discourses are not the whole of human experience (one could even regret that human beings are not fully discursive beings, but still observe that this is the case). Somehow connected with this objection is Eugenio Bulygin's criticism to the pragmatic assumption of a claim to correctness embedded in legal discourse, based on contesting the meaningfulness of the idea of "normative necessity."[39]

We could add that in particular rights (as claims) cannot offer the bedrock for morality whose main task is just the control over, and the limitation of, our claims and rights. "Self-righteousness" (*rechthaberei*) is not a moral attitude, but rather the opposite. The same objection could be, and has been, directed against all "rights-based" theories of morality, and especially against those rights theories which centre around the notion of "autonomy" and "agency." In this sense, some of the perplexity directed against Alan Gewirth's monological and prudential foundation of basic rights might perhaps also be targeted to Alexy's dialogical *and* teleological perspective.

X. THE TENSION BETWEEN CRITICAL THEORY AND PRESCRIPTIVISM

There is a final issue to consider, which can serve as a conclusion and a coda for this chapter. It seems to me that any reader considering Alexy's theory of fundamental rights faces a strange incongruence between a general philosophy based on discourse and language (Alexy's Habermasian roots) and a strong insistence on a prescriptivist, behaviourist jurisprudence (resulting from the influence of Alf Ross' reductionist strategies). To put it differently, there is on the one side a development of a pragmatic, post- or anti-positivistic philosophy (whose main tenet is the idea that concepts are embedded in social practice and discourses, and that discourses are ideally free and not-hierarchical experiences) and on the other side high fidelity to a positivistic account both of social reality and of law (where the central view is that concepts are just tools external to reality, and that in law the fundamental notion is command and the central experience is hierarchy and subjection). At the one corner, the Habermasian one, there is a defense of the priority and fundamentality of communicative rationality over other forms of reason; at the other corner, the Rossian one, practical rationality is only instrumentalism (*zweckrationalität*). Alexy – it seems to me – perpetually goes to and fro between the two.

NOTES

1 TCR, p. 22.

2 Hans Kelsen, *Introduction to the Problems of Legal Theory*, Oxford: Oxford University Press, 1997; *Pure Theory of Law*, Berkeley and Los Angeles: University of California Press, 1967.

3 See Leonard Nelson, "Kritik der praktischen Vernunft," in *Gesammelte Schriften, 4 Vorlesungen über die Grundlagen der Etik*, edited by Paul Bernays et. al., Hamburg: Felix Meiner Verlag, 1972, pp. 29ff.

4 Herbert. L. A. Hart, *The Concept of Law*, Oxford: Oxford University Press, 1961, at p. 107.

5 Such is the outcome, for instance, of Georges Kalinowski's legal theory (see *La Logique des normes*, Paris: Presses Universitaires de France, 1972) and somehow of Weinberger's use of Popper's "World Three" to explain the "ideal" side of norms (see Neil D. MacCormick and Ota Weinberger, *An Institutional Theory of Law*, Dordrecht: Reidel, 1986, chapter 1).

6 Alexy, *Theorie der Grundrechte*, Frankfurt: Suhrkamp, 1986, pp. 45–46.

7 Jürgen Habermas, *Faktizität und Geltung. Beiträge zur Diskurstheorie des Rechts und des demokratischen Rechtsstaats*, Frankfurt: Suhrkamp, 1992, pp. 164–165.

8 Wesley Newcomb Hohfeld, *Fundamental Legal Concepts as applied in judicial reasoning*, New Haven: Yale University Press, 1919; originally the book was published in two parts in the *Yale Law Journal*, 23 (1913), pp. 16–59 and 26 (1917), pp. 710–770.

9 Actually, this is one of the most controversial points of Alexy's theory, at least when confronted with the liberal notion of rights, rather openly or overtly played against the notion of a rule. In fact, the history of legal positivism can be summarised as a permanent attempt at taming the idea of right by means of transferring them into the more convenient context of norms. However, such attempts are not always convincing and, at any rate, the rationale of such a move is obviously not free of strong normative and political implications.

10 See chapters 8 and 9 of this book.

11 John Austin, *The Province of Jurisprudence Determined*, Cambridge: Cambridge University Press, 1995.

12 TCR, p. 37.

13 Ibid.

14 Hart, *supra*, fn. 4, pp. 260–261.

15 Ronald Dworkin, *Taking Rights Seriously*, London: Duckworth, 1977, pp. 22–28; Cf. chapter 3 of this book.

16 Marcus S. Singer, "Moral Rules and Principles," in *Essays in Moral Philosophy*, ed. by A. I. Melden, Seattle: University of Washington Press, 1958, p. 169.

17 TCR, p. 91.

18 He follows Georg Henrik Von Wright's terminology, as proposed in his *The Logic of Preference*, Edinburgh: Edinburgh University Press, 1963.

19 "Hoc est ergo primum praeceptum legis, quod bonum est faciendum et prosequendum, et malum vitandum," in Thomas Aquinas, *Summa Theologica*, Chicago: Encyclopedia Britannica, 1978, Ia, IIae, q. 94, a. 2, co.

20 Jürgen Habermas, *supra*, fn. 7, p. 153 (I am quoting from the English translation, *Between Facts and Norms*, Cambridge (MA): The MIT Press, 1996a, p. 153).

21 Ibid., p. 255 (English translation, p. 208).

22 TCR, p. 54.

23 Habermas, *supra*, fn. 7, p. 317.

24 Cf. fn. 21 of the introduction to the book on claims to the justification of torture.

25 TCR, p. 196.

26 Ibid.

27 Robert Alexy, "Fundamental rights, Balancing, and Rationality," 16 (2003a) *Ratio Juris*, pp. 131–140, at p. 138.

28 Ibid., p. 140.

29 TCR, pp. 388ff.

30 See also chapter 2 of this book.

31 Cf. TCR, pp. 152ff.

32 Ibid., p. 155.

33 Robert Alexy, "Individual Rights and Collective Goods," in Carlos Santiago Nino (ed.), *Rights*, Dartmouth: Aldershot, 1992b, pp. 163–181, at p. 173.

34 Hart, *supra*, fn. 6, p. 80.

35 Ibid.

36 Ibid., p. 40.

37 Cf. Robert Alexy, *The Argument from Injustice. A reply to legal positivism*, Oxford: Oxford University Press, 2002b.

38 See for instance Robert Alexy, "Discourse Theory and Human Rights," 9 (1996b) *Ratio Juris*, pp. 209–235.

39 See Eugenio Bulygin, "Alexy's Thesis of the Necessary Connection Between Law and Morality," 13 (2000) *Ratio Juris*, pp. 133–137.

ERIK ODDVAR ERIKSEN

4. DEMOCRATIC OR JURIST-MADE LAW?

I. INTRODUCTION*

The interconnections between law and politics are many and intricate. For one there is a mutual relationship as only politics can give the norms that courts act upon. It is the legislative process that furnishes the legal system with normative inputs. But politicians cannot work unless they observe the legal procedures that judges monitor. No valid law without politics and no legitimate politics without the law. Law is the lingua franca of democracy and democracy is the sole remaining legitimation principle in modern societies.

However, also in another sense is there an intricate relationship as majority vote, which is the operative principle of representative democracy, cannot ensure correct decisions, viz., a rational and just outcome. The majority principle does not ensure political equality. The phenomenon of permanent minorities is well-known: certain groups are not likely ever to become a majority or to be a part of majority alliances. Outcomes of majority voting represent the voice of the winners, not the common will. But can procedures at all ensure correct results by themselves?

Discourse theory holds that it is the procedures that warrant the presumption that it is possible to reach correct decisions: *A norm N is correct when it is the result of procedure P.*[1] In a democracy the correctness of decisions depends solely on the procedures.[2] In pure procedural justice it is fair procedures that ensure the right result; there is no independent criterion for such. For example, a chance procedure like gambling is *a pure procedural model* that ensures just outcomes without any reference to extra-procedural elements.[3] But if it is the procedure itself that warrants correct results, what, then, warrants the procedure? There is a problem with a pure procedural conception of correctness, and hence with pure procedural conceptions of democratic legitimacy. Independent standards are required in order to evaluate the process or the outcome, according to *constitutionalists*. The latter make use of moral arguments, of substantive conceptions of what is right or good, in order to solve the problem of rational adjudication without this "substance"

A. J. Menéndez and E. O. Eriksen (eds.), Arguing Fundamental Rights, 69–100.

being neither legitimated nor tested democratically. It opens for jurist made law. The Supreme Court becomes the final arbiter of constitutional law.

I address the relationship between law and politics when it comes to rational adjudication of constitutional questions from a discourse theoretical point of view. The question is whether the substantial factors can be tested democratically so that we can speak of democratic made law. The specific query is whether the observance of the rules of rational communication guarantees correctness, and in that case what kind of standard for correctness, pure or imperfect, is involved. The argument is that the standard is imperfect but is itself an expression of a normative procedure for justification. This is due to a larger concept of democracy. It is not merely a voting arrangement constitutionally constrained, viz., electoral democracy, but a complex deliberative arrangement for the justification of political action.

I start out by briefly addressing the schism between constitutionalists and proceduralists in political theory and the democratic problem involved (II) before outlining the discourse model of legal argumentation (III). This is not a pure procedural theory as certain substantial elements are involved (IV). I find that the *core morality* of discourse theory can be proceduralised through the rules of argumentation, but speech rules do not fully do away with normative, substantial elements and the indeterminacy problem lingers (V). Here I address Robert Alexy's theory of rational adjudication. He sees legal discourse as a special variant of general practical discourse – *die Sonderfallthese* – that by itself can ensure rationality and correctness. But can a judicial discourse intermediate between substance and procedure in a valid manner (VI)? Law and morality are interconnected, but is the legal medium itself capable of handling normative questions adequately; or are additional procedures called for (VII)? *Die Sonderfallthese* seems to overtax the legal medium (VIII). Klaus Günther's proposal of a distinction between *a justification and an application discourse* fares better in normative terms (IX), but it cannot ensure correctness (X). The bottom line is that a core morality is presupposed in the procedure ensuring a fair process of reason-giving – alluding to a concept of constitutional proceduralism, which hinges on *discursive proceduralism* (XI). It yields, however, not more than an imperfect standard of justice (XII).

II. CONSTITUTION OR PROCEDURE?

Constitutionalists make use of substantial conceptions of justice and give priority to fair outcomes over democratic procedures. They give rise to *correctness theories*. The proceduralists put their faith in the procedures, viz., they give priority to the rights that guarantee political participation and fair processes. Among deliberationists Jürgen Habermas is supporting such a view and Robert A. Dahl is a prominent representative of this view within the "electoral camp."[4] The latter holds that the majority principle (as well as group bargaining) is an important part of democracy because it guarantees equal treatment of all the members' interests. Majority rule reflects the principle of equal citizenship and treats everyone numerically equal. It is, however, insensitive to reasons and argumentation. Majority rule obeys to numbers not to reasons. Not only can the majority simply be wrong, the procedure itself cannot ensure a rational outcome. As demonstrated in Arrows' Impossibility Theorem, it is not possible to infer from individual preferences collective choices. Voting means the choice between different alternatives is made on the same footing as the flipping of a coin. However, under certain circumstances, as when all parties are equal, or when there are only two alternatives and no authoritative "truths," votes can be used without raising problems.[5] It is when this is not the case, as when the winner takes it all and the goods are unequally distributed because of it, the relevance of *process-independent standards* or "correctness theories" becomes clear. If we want a fair distribution, we do not decide a case as if it was a lottery. Implicitly this shows that there are independent measures as to what constitutes a correct result. The problem with the majority procedure is that it cannot let any interests or demands be favoured – not even for good reasons.[6] Voting as the primary political action, based on "non-deliberative" preferences, can never represent real political equality for suppressed or excluded groups. Constitutionalists oppose the procedural model, which they find wanting as it cannot itself lay down the conditions for a fair procedure:

> The real, deep difficulty the constitutional argument exposes in democracy is that it is a procedurally incomplete scheme of government. It cannot prescribe the procedures for testing whether the conditions for the procedures it does prescribe are met.[7]

Constitutionalists such as John Rawls and Ronald Dworkin, give priority to a set of rights, which, by protecting the individuals' vital interests, have the task of ensuring fair outcomes. Basic rights, which cannot be changed by any occasional political majority as well as checks-and-balance mechanisms such as division of power and judicial review, constitute process-independent criteria. These may ultimately be said to rest on meta-theoretical, pre-political moral principles about human being's right to life and freedom, which are themselves not subjected to democratic legislation.[8] They do not emanate from political processes but are prior to them.[9] Dworkin makes use of the distinction between *principles*, referring to reasons for actions and *policies* relating to collective interests.[10] He arrives at the fundamental egalitarian principle of treating everyone as equals.[11] On the basis of this principle the Supreme Court can reason over the correct application of a norm.[12]

Rawls presupposes pre-political elements when he gives priority to individual freedom over democratic self-determination in his interpretation of justice as fairness. With the idea of equal freedom for all citizens as a point of departure he arrives – on contractual theoretical terms – at a substantial conception of justice. The theory of justice as fairness rests on the thought experiment of an original position where the actors are placed behind *a veil of ignorance*. They have no knowledge of their social situation or personal resources – they have no knowledge of their future position in society. In this position the actors will be able to agree on, among other things, the following two lexically ordered principles of justice: they will only accept solutions which guarantee equal and maximum freedom for all and a distribution of resources that only favours differences which improve the situation of the least privileged.[13] Hence *the difference principle*: only those economic and social differences that benefit the least advantageous will be accepted on a free basis.[14] Here the choice situation itself is organized in such a way that even self-interested actors will choose morally acceptable solutions. Morality as such is built into the constraints on the reflection situation.[15]

The principles of justice are the result of an impartial agreement in an initial situation devised to ensure that no one's interest is favoured at the expense of another's. The concept of justice as fairness yields an independent or *freestanding conception of right* and justice. It is independent of disputed (religious) faiths and beliefs.[16] Further, the "political conception of justice (…) specifies certain basic rights, liberties and opportunities, (…) assigns a special priority to these rights, and affirms measures" to make them effective.[17] Here public reason is limited to political questions, and more specifically such that are of a constitutional nature and concern the fairness of the basic structure of society. *Public reason* is:

(1) about the common good as it is embedded in society's concept of political justice;
(2) governed by a reciprocity norm – one appeals to reasons that are convincing enough to satisfy reasonable people – reasons that are mutually acceptable.

This reason is applicable to questions that can be decided with reference to fairness. Rawls understands public reason as an expression of the reason employed by citizens with the same political rights in democratic states. It characterizes a situation in which equal citizens in concert exercise political power over one another in the making of statutes and in amending the constitution.

To liberals such as Rawls and Dworkin it is the discussions and reflections as carried out among public decision-makers – prototypically the judges – that constitute the ideal model of deliberation. Judges can deliberate against the background of civic virtue and with an insight into what the reciprocity norm demands. Or in Dworkin's case lawyers can "imitate Hercules" as the ideal judge.[18] The Supreme Court of a well-ordered society is regarded the highest body of public reason; it is *an exemplar of public reason* according to Rawls.[19] Deliberations in the Supreme Court and the judicial discourse form the basis of the "constitutionalists" deliberation model. Here the constitution ultimately takes precedence over the citizens' self-legislation.[20] The conflict between proceduralists and constitutionalists then pertains to the problem of whether there can be a democratic enactment of a constitution. We may, thus, distinguish between "democrats" who prioritize the political process and "consititutionalists" who claim the primacy of law.

Constitutionalists have a theory for interpretation of principles and application of norms rather than a theory for creating norms and generating principles. In effect, this is an instrumental justification of democracy: it is necessary in order to realize liberal principles. "[…] according to contractualist liberalism, political institutions are justified only if they are effective instruments for enacting laws and politics that promote the justice of society's basic structure."[21] Such a justification endangers democracy: A moral argument can be used to replace democracy – when you know what is RIGHT, you do not need to consult the people.[22] Does discourse theory provide a better solution?

III. INFINITE REGRESS

One of the problems with such correctness theories is that there is little agreement on the normative standards that are used in complex and pluralistic societies. How can we know that for example, Rawls substantial concept of justice is correct? The original position is after all a mere thought experiment and as Rawls himself concedes, "Many will prefer another criterion."[23] If, for example, one should vote over whether a decision corresponds with an independent standard of justice, some would probably agree, while some will disagree.[24] It is an unstable solution. This is not to say that we need to follow Waldron who does not find more of a common basis for deciding questions pertaining to justice than he does for questions concerning the good life. "We have also to deal with justice-pluralism and disagreement about rights."[25] This may be an empirical fact, but does not exclude the possibility of an inter-subjective basis for justice-questions. Without siding with moral realism we may maintain that norms that regulate the realisation of interests can be decided in a rational manner. As consequences for affected parties can be observed, moral norms can be assessed with regard to impartiality. Such questions are quite different from deciding issues pertaining to how one should live one's life, which by their very nature are relative to a culture and a valued way of life. In this regard one may follow Rawls who prioritizes "the right" over "the good."

According to discourse theory morality is built into the procedures which grant the citizens a right to participation and guarantee their freedom, but which also force them into a process of argumentation where they must give as well as respond to reasons. Democratic procedures themselves substantiate the expectation that decisions are reasonable and fair. The legitimacy of the laws emerges from the processes and procedures that have created them. Habermas claims that it is the trust in fair procedures that keep modern societies together politically, not consensus based on substantive world views, values, or virtues. The universal principles of justice that Habermas refers to are entrenched in modern constitutions as basic rights but the only source of legitimation is the autonomous will of the people. Hence the discourse principle, which claims that only those action norms are valid to which all affected persons can agree as participants in rational discourses.[26]

In discourse theory it is the procedures that justify the assumption that it is possible to reach legitimate outcomes. This does not relieve the citizens of taking a moral stand such as in Rawls' original position, but ensures that everyone is treated with *equal concern and respect* in order for the force of the better arguments to prevail. It is the process, which, if it is a good one, guarantees the legitimacy of the laws. On the other hand, it is impossible to argue for everyone's right to participate in a debate without presupposing some substantial, normative and non-procedural argument, of for example, people's freedom, equality and dignity as postulated by natural law. Procedural and substantive conceptions of justice interchange in a justification process in so far as the claims of equal access and participation, inclusiveness and openness rest on substantive principles of tolerance, personal integrity, guaranteed private life, etc. In logical terms there is *an infinite regress* or circular argumentation because rights that are to ensure the process must be justified procedurally, something which again rests on substantial elements, which must again be justified procedurally, etc.[27]

Consequently, the discourse theory does not totally do away with substantial elements. Procedural independent standards are needed for securing a fair process. In this sense the discourse principle is in itself normatively charged, it contains a certain normative content – it "… explicates the meaning of impartiality in practical judgements."[28] However, discourse theory may also be seen to build on moral premises – on premises of a moral person who possesses certain rights and competences. There are inbuilt conceptions of free and equal citizens that are capable of reasoning about justice and the common good.[29] Such a person participates in a discourse where validity claims are raised; the person takes a critical stand to his own as well as others' statements and actions, and substantiates his standpoints with arguments. He or she has *the ability to judge*.[30] The person is prepared to apply the same norm to him as is applied to others. In other words, *a deliberative person* is reflective and responsible, prepared for and competent of self-correction.[31] A minimum of normative content is involved in so far as claims of sound mindedness, of rationality and ability to reason form the basis of the concept of a deliberative person, while everything else is left to the discursive process.[32] This comes close to Rawls' concept of reasonableness, that is, "... the willingness to propose fair terms of cooperation and to abide by them provided others do." […] and "the willingness to recognise the burdens of judgement and to accept their consequences for the use of public reason."[33] In addition to the virtue of reasonableness, citizens have to be equipped with *a duty of civility* sufficient to be competent to take a stand on the common good.

Moreover, the outcome of moral discourses is not solely depending on the qualities of the procedure as the required procedures are considered appropriate only in so far that they lead to a correct or just outcome. The consensus warranting the universalisation principle – the categorical imperative – is a bridging principle, it "... ensures that only those norms are accepted as valid that express *a general will.*"[34] Habermas' idea of a just outcome that is referring to the likelihood that "generalizable interests will be accepted," is "certainly substantive."[35] The concept of generalizable or common interests is a procedure independent criterion.

Not only in Rawls's theory of justice as fairness, but in discourse theory as well, one has to do with a concept of correctness that includes substantial elements. It is not procedural all the way down as an independent criterion and *a core morality* are presupposed.[36] Consequently, discourse theory has not been able to free itself entirely from "natural law." It seems difficult to omit such elements in establishing a principle of normative justification. In fact, then there is not much difference between discourse theory and the constitutionalists when it comes to presupposing an element of substance.

IV. THE IMPERFECTION OF ARGUMENTATION PROCEDURES

Robert Alexy tries to overcome this problem by showing that discursive rules, as well as basic human rights, do not necessarily depend on discursive justification. They can be justified empirically with regard to what is "the most basic human experience" as well as with regard to what purposive rational actors without an interest in rightness, must subscribe to.[37] The first argument, that of the nature of human existence, is weak and not without exception, as consent can be enforced or be the effect of manipulation and indoctrination.

The second argument holds that the sheer cognitive content of the speech rules will do the work as even a purposive rational person with no interest in correctness, will find it advantageous to observe the discourse rules. This can also be rebutted, first, because such rules are binding only for participants in a discourse. This has to do with the so-called collective action problem; strategists always have the possibility of opting out of communication when envisaging a better deal.[38] Secondly, because freedom and equality are constitutive of the deliberative process, they have priority only in so far as the actors possess *an interest in rightness*. An interest in justice is hence to be presupposed. Moreover, only in so far as deliberative persons are equipped with the capacity to judge, do the rules apply.

The question is nevertheless whether the observance of the rules for rational communication can guarantee correctness. In other words, even though the argumentation procedure – the discourse – itself inevitably includes substantial normative elements, can it set the terms of a fair and rational deliberation process that warrants a right outcome? After all speech rules form the core element of discourse theory. Regarding norms for how the discussion should proceed several rules and prescriptions apply.

Alexy[39] derives a number of basic rules from the formal-practical presuppositions of rational communication. First of all there is a set of *process rules*, which have to do with securing participation, equal access, openness, freedom and non-coercion. These rules are based on the rights ensuring every communicative competent actor real opportunity to participate and that the members can utter what they want. The rules stem directly from the discourse principle. But such rules do not ensure a rational discussion, viz., the testing of the standpoints. Therefore, *validation rules* that ensure objectivity and coherence in deliberation are required. These rules pertain to norms such as participants voicing their real opinions without contradiction, that they consider the arguments of the opponent, and that discussions last long enough to make sure that the issues are thoroughly discussed, that is, that all stands are made clear and that all relevant information has been presented.[40] In addition, principles for the allocation of the duty to justify are required in order to ensure the fairness of the deliberative process. This includes the obligation to state the reasons for why one is not willing to provide a justification, if that is the case. We are here talking about *rules for reason giving*. Why should for example, participants be treated unequally, why is one obliged to produce further arguments only when met with counter arguments, etc? On the other hand one should stop doubting a specific point of view once it has been defended adequately. The burden of proof is on the parties who doubt the arguments of another participant.[41]

These rules operationalize and proceduralize the moral core of the discourse to a large extent but cannot guarantee rational outcomes – one single correct solution. They do not guarantee agreement because of partial compliance, unfixed argumentation steps, and because of historic contingent and changeable normative conceptions.[42] In other words, they cannot solve the problem of rational decision-making, because of:

(1) *the burdens of judgement*: even reasonable actors may remain at odds with each other after a rational discussion;[43]

(2) *linguistic uncertainty*: grammatical rules underdetermine linguistic meaning because of multiple contributions of context and usage.[44]

However, Alexy maintains that the legal medium itself raises a claim to (moral) correctness in adjudication. Even though judicial discourses aim at rational outcomes, the question is whether they accomplish this all by themselves or whether other "extra-legal" procedures are called upon to redeem the claim to correctness. This pertains to the controversy between Alexy and Klaus Günther. The former holds on to *die Sonderfallthese,* the latter to the distinction between application and justification discourses.

V. CORRECTNESS AND INDETERMINACY

Against legal realists, discourse theorists maintain that law raises *a claim to correctness* as it is inescapably linked to the basic stipulations of justice: *suum cuique tribuere*, to each his due, equal concern and respect, due consideration of all interests and values, etc. that are reflective of the *impartiality norm* of general practical reason, viz., the reason that binds the free will of autonomous human beings. This moral norm is constitutive of the idea of a justly organised legal process. Judges make up their minds about practical questions, and through justifying arguments they arrive at presumptively *correct answers*, that is, that equal cases be treated equally. This is why the kind of reasoning carried out in courts can be referred to as a practical discourse, and not as logical deduction or strategic interaction. Even in a lawsuit, where lawyers struggle to obtain the best possible result on behalf of their clients and themselves, reference is made to objective legal norms and principles when they justify their claims. When appeal is made to impartial judges or to the members of the jury, it must be made with reference to principles on which rational actors can agree, even if the aim is not to convince the opponent.

A legal discourse is constituted and regulated by the existing laws. But positive legal norms are too unclear to give unambiguous, correct answers to normative problems. Rules are under-specified with regard to action.[45] They are reflective and subject to interpretation and contextualisation. This is so because there can be no rule for the correct application of rules – such a claim opens for an infinite regress. As rules or norms cannot determine their own application in particular cases there is a *cognitive indeterminacy* of general practical discourse.[46] But also legal discourses are faced with indeterminacy as positive law as well has an *open texture*. Also the legal language is vague, full of rationality gaps and norm collisions.[47]

Just as norms cannot apply themselves, a legal system as such cannot produce coherence. To achieve this, persons and procedures are necessary for feeding in new contents.[48]

Lawyers make use of a *know-how* that is partly determined by the prevailing conceptions of law and partly by how the law has been practiced earlier (precedent, custom, common values, etc.). However, legal norms must, according to Alexy, first and foremost be in accordance with the criteria of rightness or justice. They must in fact claim to be correct, even though the criteria are not given by positive law itself. This is what the discourse theory accomplishes; it specifies the criteria for correctness:[49] The rules for legal and practical argumentation penetrate each other without destroying each other's respective logics. Judicial procedures guarantee symmetrical conditions for communication within the legal community.[50] They do not govern practical argumentation directly, but establish the institutional framework which makes possible a rational discourse on which norms are appropriate in a given case. How is this possible?

According to discourse theory, both judicial and argumentative procedures aim at rational outcomes, but none of them can guarantee success because the demanding procedural presuppositions are rarely met. In legal discourses time is tight as a decision has to be reached within a given deadline. The problem with argumentation in a practical discourse is that only the participants can judge if a consensus is qualified; there is no procedure-independent criterion for the evaluation of a rational argumentation process. The legal procedure compensates for this weakness, because it subjects argumentation to spatio-temporal, social and substantive constraints. Legal procedures regulate what topics and questions may be raised, the use of time, who the participants are, the distribution of roles, etc. The judge as a neutral third party controls that the norms are followed. These procedures limit the access of premises, they ensure an unambiguous and binding result, and they connect argumentation to decision-making. Hence, the judicial procedures compensate for the fallibility of communicative processes and improve their incomplete or quasi-pure procedural fairness.[51]

This takes place in two ways: First, argumentation is disciplined in relation to judicially binding decisions through the institutionalisation of *an expert discourse* that can interpret and adapt codified law in a professional manner, according to internal criteria and specified procedures. Judicial institutions are designed to systematise and adapt prevailing law to the matter which is to be regulated. Secondly, correct outcomes can be ensured because the discourse is tied to a legal public sphere characterised as an open, inclusive and transparent discussion forum. This can be referred to as the external justification of the principles that are operative in the expert discourse, as it provides those premises which are not derived from positive law itself.[52] In addition to a wide supply of source material – preparatory works, customs, precedent – moral and political considerations are also taken into consideration, as is demonstrated in the discussion of so-called *hard cases*, that is, fundamental, precedent-forming cases with a legal political significance.[53] These are *extra-legal factors* that are used to decide which norms should have priority, on the basis of substantial conceptions of justice and freedom.[54]

The judges cannot avoid evaluating the validity of approved norms because only a uniform and consistent legal system can ensure a rational decision – a single correct solution. The conclusion must be inferred from rational normative premises. This is a prerequisite for solving conflicts of norms and practical-ethical dilemmas in the court-room. Legal norms must be interpreted and operationalised, and even a valid legal norm, for example a constitutional norm, must be given a legal interpretation in relation to validity criteria before its correctness and relevance can be established.[55]

In democracies legal procedures are meant to guarantee decisions that are legally correct and rationally acceptable, viz., decisions that can be defended both in relation to legal statutes and in relation to public criticism. But can the legal system through the discretion of the judges itself – without normative inputs from the political system – settle moral questions which by their very nature are political as they refer to what *ought to* be accomplished? Moral and legal questions point to different audiences, raise different validity claims and require different procedures for the resolving of conflicts.

VI. LAW AND MORALITY

Following Kant's law and morality, which both concern practical questions and claim to regulate interaction in the interest of all parties involved – the resolving of interpersonal conflicts, refer to different contexts of cooperation and have different validity bases. Whereas the law applies to a concrete community of people which can be subjected to the same duties, viz., a political community, morality refers to humanity as such. Law is also different from morality in that it only regulates external behaviour. The law says nothing about the citizens' motives for abiding by the laws; it only tells us what actions are illegal and indictable. Morality presupposes freedom to make one's own choices. Moral duties cannot be enforced. A final distinction between legal and moral questions is that the law is also a means to realise collective goals, while moral norms are ends in themselves. Legal norms apply to territorially demarcated communities and regulate behaviour that has consequences for the prevailing interests, values and concerns of the citizens. Hence, they are too concrete to be justified only on a moral basis.

With regard to the claim to correctness there is a clear difference between moral and legal norms, as the latter claim validity for the members of a particular legal society, while moral norms claim to be universalistic as they claim to be valid for everyone – on the basis of free and rational deliberation.[56] But if legal norms are binding only within a community of citizens how can they be trans-culturally valid, absolute, deontological principles? This determination of legal norms as relative to their spatio-temporal embeddedness does not sit very well with the concept of legal norms as deontological – as absolutely binding.[57] Alexy proposes to see principles as non-conclusive *optimization commands*.[58] Principles such as freedom, equality, rule of law, democracy are not merely deontological norms on par with anti-utilitarian trumps in collective decision making processes; rather they are to be seen as norms to be weighted and balanced in the adjudication of particular conflicts, they are to be optimized to the greatest extent possible. Principles only take the character of a trump "… when some competing principle has a greater weight in the case to be decided."[59] In the wording of Alexy: "A principle is trumped when some competing principle has greater weight in the case to be decided (…) Principles represent reasons which can be displaced by other reasons."[60] To be able to reach an optimal decision principles must be weighted and balanced. Alexy operationalizes the weighing process through an economic model of justification (for details see the Alexy's and Bernal's chapters in this volume). Principles neither protect the separation of power unconditionally – *the red-tape argument* – nor human rights – *the fire wall argument.*[61] I return to this problem.

According to Alexy, the law cannot all by itself establish a sufficient account of the normative premises at work in legal adjudication. On the one hand legal argumentation is faced with the requirement of identifying right decisions, on the other hand due to the contested and open texture of positive law – a law is never absolutely lucid – correctness cannot be provided by legal standards alone. "Therefore only recourse to standards other than legal standards is available, such as general reflection on utility, traditional and common ideas of what is good and evil, as well as principles of justice."[62] Legal norms certainly are premised not only on moral reasons but on utilitarian considerations, prudent reasons, collective values, etc., as well. But how is it possible to ensure correctness in adjudication? Alexy claims that this requirement can be fulfilled by conceiving of legal argumentation as *a special case* of a general practical discourse.

> Under the conditions of a non-positivist concept of law nothing is left to be connected because substantial correctness, and therefore morality, are already part of law.[63]

The special case thesis is objected to by legal positivists, legal realists (such as Niklas Luhmann) as well as discourse theorists such as Jürgen Habermas and Klaus Günther: It is not for the legal discourse to justify normative claims. Günther has therefore introduced the distinction between a justification and an application discourse maintaining that it is in the particular ruling, in the individual case, that the weight of rules, norms and values can be determined. The norms that have passed the test of justification have to be implemented correctly.

VII. JUSTIFICATION AND APPLICATION

Practical rationality is about normative questions or reasons for actions and refers to what is obligatory, prohibited or permitted. Such decisions are so to say a compartment of moral obligations and conscience. The relation between autonomous morality, that refers to irreplaceable human beings or humanity as such, and positive law, which regulates actions that have diverse consequences, is a complementary one; moral norms must be implemented and the law must be justified. Moral norms can only be realised if they are formulated in legal categories which allow sanctions, and the law can only obtain legitimacy to the extent that there is equality before the law. It is the legal medium that transforms such obligations and concerns of conscience that are legally valid into practical results. It entails institutional mechanisms for connecting validity and facticity such as secondary rules for legal adjudication.

While justification discourses require that all interests are considered and judged impartially, application discourses require a procedure where all relevant features of the situation are given equal treatment.[64] Application discourses are due to the limitedness of our actual knowledge and of the interests and values of the members. In a legal debate where concrete matters are to be decided, the question of the universal validity of the norms is put into parenthesis. This validity is simply presupposed, and one proceeds to ask which norms are relevant and should apply to a particular case.[65]

It is the consequences which are at issue in application discourses. The point of interest is what the effects would be if justified moral norms are implemented. In an application situation, we are faced with a choice between justified norms, which must be decided in relation to a number of factors: empirical elements, the type and quality of the information available, actual power relations, the important values at stake as well as the balancing of non-generalisable interests. Legal norms have a much more complex validity basis than have moral norms. The law realises political values and ethical and moral norms by positivising them. Through this procedure, they become sanctionable and collectively binding. Morality, on its part, tests and justifies positive legal norms. Whether legal decisions are correct, ultimately depends on whether the decision process has made possible *impartial judgement*, which requires that certain higher-ranking conditions for argumentation have been met. While discourses of justification pertain to justifying general legal norms *in abstracto* and in light of the consequences its observance may have for affected parties, discourses of application have an hermeneutic structure and relate to the justification of concrete judgements given already justified norms.

These two discourses are dealing with two kinds of questions, but the question of what is correct in a situation and which moral norm is correct cannot easily be distinguished.[66] In practice they are intertwined, and to give up the claim of moral justification with regard to situational features is to renounce rational decision-making.[67] Hermeneutics takes everything into consideration but cannot tell what is valid as it contains no standards for rational adjudication. This strategy, according to Alexy, means giving up the claim that the application of norms should be correct. "It is empty, because it does not say which aspects are to be considered in what way."[68] Hence, it cannot solve the problem of rational adjudication. Consequently, Günther cannot uphold the claim to correctness. This can only be accomplished by seeing that every application necessarily involves a justificatory discourse, complying with the rules of rational argumentation.[69]

VIII. OVERTAXING THE LEGAL MEDIUM

For Alexy a practical discourse does not merely comprise moral questions of justice and universalisation (as in Habermas' and Günther's set up), but rather encompasses the whole spectre of normative, non institutional reasons that have to be employed to settle what ought to be done, to reach a single correct decision in case of interpersonal conflicts.[70] A legal discourse differs from a practical discourse in that it deals with what is correct within the legal framework and within a time frame, and not with what is ultimately right.[71] But the judge cannot avoid making use of political or moral arguments in order to justify *the balance he strikes* when it comes to the basic principles and their subprinciples. "It follows, then, that the claim to legal correctness necessarily attached to the decision includes a claim to moral correctness."[72]

Alexy's analysis is based on the reconstruction of a four-stage procedural model of legal argumentation, which combines law and rational practical arguing in such a way that rational decision-making is possible.[73] His point of departure are the rules of rational practical discourse, which are easy to justify; but this easiness comes at a price, since discourse rules are "compatible with very different outcomes." Hence practical discourse needs to be complemented by law, first by the legislative procedure, which " … is not capable of establishing in advance just one solution," then by a legal discourse which has to " … respect statue, precedent, and legal doctrine … but … uncertainty of outcome is not totally eliminated." There is thus need for a fourth procedure – the court process – in which one and only one decision is made and which can claim to be rational because of its designs.

The problem that emerges here pertains to the limits of the law and those of the judges' competence. How can we know that judges are right when they do not merely apply politically laid down laws and reasons but make use of their own discretionary know-how and value-base? In Alexy's theory there are the dangers of assimilating law and morality and of overburdening the legal medium itself. These dangers are interlinked:

(1) The first problem is simply this: How can the imported substance, the norms and values that are needed for reaching a single decision, be tested? How can we know they are right and that the decision is correct? According to discourse theory only norms that have been accepted by the parties in a free and rational debate can be considered legitimate. As well as it is only in a discourse among affected that we can know what justice really consist in, we cannot know whether the adoption of rights clauses in particular situations are right unless the ones affected have been heard. This is underpinned by the fact that the right is permeated by the good, as also Alexy himself points to. One's conception of justice is affected and can be changed according to altered self-understandings and revised self-descriptions. Even human rights require democratic legitimation and public deliberation to be correctly implemented. They are unfulfilled until they have been codified and interpreted (and subsequently transformed into basic rights). This means there are no fixed moral precepts, principles or concepts of justice that judges in a non-controversial way can appeal to in order to adjudicate conflicts.

According to legal positivists[74] as well as legal realists[75] this cannot be settled by the law: the medium of law, based on the binary coding legal/non-legal cannot justify normative questions themselves. What is correct/right have to be settled outside the legal medium. The law itself simply can neither deny nor confirm the validity of a moral argument. This directs us to the overtaxing problem.

(2) This pertains to the question of the addressees. There is a claim to correctness as the judges both out of conceptual and moral reasons have to contend that their decisions are right. But can the lawyers really establish the premises for redeeming this claim all by themselves? Are they so to say the right addressees? Alexy distinguishes between institutional and non-institutional circles of addressees. The former refers to the ones affected by respective legal acts, the latter to relevant participants who can use all arguments allowed in a

legal discourse – in the legal public sphere, as mentioned. The non-institutional circles include everyone who takes the point of view of a participant in the respective legal system. It is an inclusive public forum which can bring forward the interests and viewpoints of legal consociates that are all relevant for passing a correct judgement. The premises that cannot be derived from the ordering of legal norms and previous jurisprudence have to be justified by the external "jury."[76] But who are the participants in such a process and what arguments are permitted? It follows from the constraints of a legal discourse that only judicial arguments are allowed and that it is not the participants but the judge who has the last word.[77] Admittedly the equality criterion can be approximated by making more open and inclusive forms of participation possible, but legal argumentation is from its inception constrained: the participants are legal consociates and a judge is the adjudicator:

> No matter how many schemes we conceive in order to increase the number of interests and arguments to which judges are exposed, the fact that it is they and not the parties who have the last word precludes any direct reference to participation as a source of legitimacy.[78]

In a practical discourse there is no impartial judge, no limited number of participants or constraints on time, themes and topics for debate, etc. In a justification discourse there can only be participants. Only the participants themselves can pass judgment over their *equal interest and their common good*. Here there are no procedure independent criteria of correctness. From a democratic point of view these two questions, that is what is legal and what is normative or politically valid, branches out in two kinds of procedures – *the legal one* where the addresses are confined to the circle of legal consociates, and *the political one* referring to circle of citizens, which are not merely bound by the legal medium but also authorized as *le pouvoir constituant* to constitute power and give the law new normative content: Common action norms can only be legitimately tested in the wider public sphere where competent citizens and all affected parties are present.

> Once the judge is allowed to move in the unrestrained space of reasons that such a "general practical discourse" offers, a "red line" that marks the division of powers between courts and legislation becomes blurred. In view of the application of a particular statute, the legal discourse of the judge should be confined to the set of reasons legislators either in fact put forward or at least could have mobilized for the parliamentary justification of the norm.[79]

IX. DELIBERATIVE DEMOCRACY AND LEGAL UNCERTAINTY

The question is whether legal argumentation can satisfy the conditions for legitimate law-making, as the special case thesis holds, or whether other procedures must be called upon as Günther and Habermas suggest. From a democratic point of view the latter solution fares better. Alexy may be right in maintaining that application discourses cannot solve the problem of rational adjudication of interpersonal conflicts, but the procedures for tackling normative content, substance, are better specified in the formers' suggestion.

Procedural rights guarantee each legal person the claim of a fair procedure that in turn guarantees not certainty of outcome but a discursive clarification of the pertinent facts and legal questions.[80]

The general problem with the special case thesis in this perspective is that judges should apply norms, not make them. Conceiving of the legal discourse as a special variant of the practical discourse blurs the distinction between legislation and application because it allows the judge to make use of normative reasons in general, not only the ones given by the legislators. Now Alexy may defend his thesis by pointing to the fact that in modern societies heavily strained by complexity, the political system becomes overburdened and does not produce the required set of norms. When the legislator does not fulfil its functions, the courts have to intervene and upgrade the legal system so that it becomes possible to handle the complexities facing it. It leaves the generation of norms to be handled autonomously by the discretion of the judges – hence the prevalence of delegation and framework legislation. The politicians are not doing their job in furnishing the legal system with the required normative premises and leaves to the discretion of the judges to find the "correct" normative basis for adjudication.

As far as this is the actual situation of the legal system in a comprehensive welfare state, the *Sonderfallthese* is plausible in descriptive terms. But it cannot be sustained normatively. It does not sit with the basic principle of democratic legitimacy that the people should be the final arbitrator of constitutional law (subjected only to a limited set of constraints). Alexy's solution gives too much leeway to the discretion of the lawyers as they become authorized to choose the decisive reasons themselves. But how can the problems of legal uncertainty be avoided when judges have to make use of extra-legal premises in order to decide in conflicts over the law? How can affected parties know that the decision is correct and how can they check that the premises of a ruling are the right ones?

These queries makes us aware that another concept of democracy is required than the one based on majority vote. As mentioned the majoritarian model of democratic politics is inadequate. The voting procedure cannot ensure correctness because of its un-attentiveness to reasons. Rather we should conceive of democracy as a procedural constellation where citizens are involved in inclusive legislative processes, and where inputs as well as outputs are subjected to public critical debate. We should thus see it as *deliberative democracy*. The essence of the deliberative conception of democracy is that citizens have a right to justification of those action norms that affect them. It is based on "the rule of reasons" and on the moral principle of reciprocal and general justification.[81] Deliberative democracy is consistent with the republican idea of popular constitutionalism conceiving of the people and not the judge as the interpreter of last resort. Democracy is depicted as a set of procedures that set the conditions for getting things right in politics. Thus it takes a rational debate among affected parties to settle what is just and the legitimacy of popular rules depends on satisfying stringent prerequisites such as equal access, autonomy, full information, openness. These prerequisites may be hard to fulfil in any real existing form of democracy, and deliberative democracy should be conceived more of as a regulative idea than blueprint of an organizational form.

From this point of view, not only formal aggregative procedures revolving on voting but the whole spectre of demanding communicative arrangements – extra-electoral forms of participation – in the political sphere of action comes into consideration. In the discourse-theoretical reading, modern democracy is based on the circular movement between state-based decision-making and civic participation made possible by elections and public debate that links the citizens and the legislative. In the public sphere of civil society proposals are subjected to unrestricted debate prior to law enactment. Prior to adjudication there are comprehensive processes of norm-testing deliberation: In the general public sphere in civil society – in media and newspapers – in networks, social movements, popular assemblies etc., problems are discovered, thematized and dramatized, and social concerns are verbalised and claims are justified. Here a moral discussion over what norms should prevail and how different and similar cases be treated, take place. The general public sphere, the generic principles of which are participation, inclusion, equality, freedom, open agenda, is the locus of popular sovereignty and practical reason. Here people can address the political questions of the day, can assemble and try to influence the political system and in rare moments – in constitutional moments – also change its basis rules.[82]

However, deliberative democracy is brought to the fore in yet another sense as the required extensive norm-production of the modern welfare state cannot legimately be facilitated through the formal political and legal only. As the situation of jurist-made-law has become problematic and the parliament is overburdened a plethora of quasi-legal and quasi-political bodies outside of the political system are initiated, in order to settle the problem of legitimate normative inputs to legal and political system. These bodies are involved in the generation of the norms. On the input side of the political system we find different kinds of public hearings, popular meetings, citizens juries, experiments with deliberative reflection groups, ethical committees, consensus-conferences, etc., which all are oriented towards the elucidation and resolving of controversial value- and norm-questions. On the output side of the political system, as well, we find a plethora of bodies where citizens are involved in the concretization and operationalisation of the political laws and regulations, which also may be deemed necessary from a democratic point of view, as the discretion of the street-level bureaucracy has increased as a result of the amplification of welfare state service production.[83]

The new participatory forms of governance of a deliberative kind are important. First, because here legitimacy is not merely a matter of the citizens' preferences as they are expressed by the voting slip, but what reasons the participants have for agreeing or disagreeing with a standpoint. In these bodies the affected parties or their representatives are involved in a deliberative process over which norms and rules should apply. Second, because such bodies may alleviate the problem of an overburdened political system. Some of these deliberative sites may be seen as forms of delegation of the norm-production of the society as they involve the citizens in reflective moral deliberation. Their democratic value pertains to the proviso that only through a fair process of argumentation between affected can one tell whether a norm is unbiased or not. A legitimate political decision is not an expression of preconceived ideas of what is just or the common good, but the outcome of everybody's deliberation in a free, open and rational process. Consequently, there is, in principle, an alternative, or rather, a supplement to an institutionalised legal public sphere when it comes to the settling of normative questions.

X. PROCEDURALISM AND JUDGEMENT CAPACITY

But also on a deeper level there is a problem with Alexy's architectonic. This has to do with the aforementioned notion of *principles as optimization commands* and the implied weighing criterion, which rules out the possibility of being able to criticise the principles themselves in light of higher ranking norms and validity claims. Principles conceived of as optimization commands are subject to weighting and balancing and hence are framed on merely axiological values and weak evaluations. They are reflective of wants and preferences and not moral norms in the Kantian sense.[84] What happens then when rules, which are definitive norms related to permissions/prohibitions, collide, and when it is necessary to recur to higher ordered principled debates on what norms should have priority? The problem is how to solve collisions of norms rationally when the procedures for discursive meta-legal assessment are lacking.

While Alexy, on the one hand, subscribes to the discourse principle he holds, on the other hand, certain moral norms as valid prior to a discourse. The procedural concept of correctness says that a norm N is correct when it is the result of the procedure P. However, P is not reserved for discursive justification:

"P kann durch ein Individuum durchgefürt werden …".[85] Norms can so to say be justified in a monological way. As we have seen, Alexy justifies basic human rights in a way that does not depend on discursive justification. In this respect Alexy sides with the constitutionalists. His concept of procedure is not connected to the criterion of a rational consensus as is the justification program of Habermas,[86] but to the carrying out of the discourse procedure. He disconnects consensus and correctness. The norm N is not correct because of a rational acceptance in actual or ideal discourses, but because of the way the procedure is carried out enables *judgement capacity*, viz., the way the members manage to distinguish good from bad reasons. "Was ein guter Grund ist, kan sich erst im Prozess der diskursiven Überprüfung zeigen."[87] The achievement of the procedure depends on the judgement capacity of the members. It is the purpose of the procedure to develop such. The *raison d'être* of the procedure is to enhance the capacity to judge by the particular discourse members, to distinguish between good and bad reasons with regard to what should be done. But, then, what is the criterion of correct decisions? There is no second procedure for testing the fallible outcomes of actual discourses. In other words, there is no appeal to a more basic justification procedure. What is at stake in this conceptual strategy is the space for discretion left over to judges, and hence the expansion of "constitutional legal reasoning" to the detriment of the political process itself and of the citizens self-government.

The substance involved, the restrictions within legal discourses needs to be checked, and this check cannot take place at the same level – it can only be tested by a higher order, justificatory discourse.[88] Because the rules of the discourse are basic to justification, their correctness must be justified on a deeper level.[89] Thus there is a problem of *relativism* in Alexy's theory. He has not provided an "objective" correctness theory. His concept of correctness is relative: It depends on the (arbitrary) judgement capacity of the judges. Alexy is a proceduralist who is not a "democrat" in the present use of the term.[90] The substantial rest in Alexy's program is larger than in Habermas', in which the rational consensus establishes a criterion for correctness, that is, when affected parties comply under free and equal conditions. Here constitutional proceduralism hinges on *discursive proceduralism*. The task is therefore to establish a procedural standard for legitimacy where the democratic deliberation process itself makes the result right. But does the discourse theory of popular sovereignty really accomplish this?

XI. EPISTEMIC OR MORAL JUSTIFICATION?

According to Habermas any substantial standpoint raises claims of justification and makes demands on knowledge which can only be met argumentatively.

On the one hand, only substantial standpoints can justify outcomes. We do not know whether a case has been correctly dealt with until we know the parties' arguments – their views, reasons, valuations, etc. On the other hand, no grounds are beyond justification in a political context, something that is due to the fact that there is no reality-check of normative statements. Norms are only "valid" to the extent that actors agree on them in a rational discourse.

All contents, no matter how fundamental the action norm involved may be, must be made to depend on real discourses (or advocacy discourses conducted as substitutes for them).[91]

Discourse theory brings together substance and procedure when it is maintained that in a free argumentation process the validity of the reasons can be tested, viz., they can be assessed in relation to autonomy and universality. It is therefore the process that justifies the outcomes.[92] Neither the formal qualities of the procedure nor substantial grounds justify the outcomes. Rather, it depends on whether the process has included objections and counter-arguments in such a way that outcomes can stand up to public criticism. "[L]egitimacy through procedure does not result from the structure of procedure itself, which guarantees the right of participation, but rather from the quality of discursive processes which they make possible."[93] It is a qualitative good process of argumentation that is able to test the justifiableness and reasonability of claims and interests involved that bears the burden of legitimation in discourse theory. Thus it is neither the participation of all, nor expressions of will and the respect for preferences that give the democratic process its legitimating power, but rather the deliberative process. This power lies in the access to a process where standpoints can be tested in such a way that one can expect reasonable and publicly acceptable, that is, rational results.

Discourse theory thus subscribes to an epistemic account of deliberative democracy: Democratic deliberation is a cognitive process for the assessment of reasons in order to reach correct decisions. It builds on the assumption of an internal connection between deliberation, subjected to certain procedural conditions, and truth or more generally rationality – concerning political results. Discourse theory offers a procedural account of justice and defines moral rightness as what rational agents could agree to under ideal conditions: "An agreement about norms or actions that has been attained discursively under ideal conditions carries more than merely authorizing force: it warrants the rightness of moral judgements."[94] Habermas sees "rightness" as an epistemic notion based on redeeming knowledge claims. Moral judgements and legal decisions have an epistemic status as they can be right or wrong. Actors can reach the single correct answer to practical questions. Regarding moral questions, they can be settled through *an universal-reciprocal discourse* allowing the participants to test whether the norm satisfies the interests and values of those affected. Similarly, in legal discourse a single correct answer would mean the appropriate answer – appropriate according to the impartial application of norms given that all relevant aspects of a particular situation of norm appliance are taken into account.

The problem with this solution is that the standard for evaluating the quality of the outcomes is given independently of an actually performed deliberation process. The standard is constituted by *an ideal procedure*, which specifies the contra-factual conditions for a public discourse where all limitations on time and resources have been suspended, and where the only authority is that of the better argument. Real communication processes can only approximate such ideals. To Habermas the rational consensus is the standard by which the correct outcome can be defined. It represents the criterion of legitimacy. By observing the ideal conditions of justification – the demanding presuppositions for impartial argumentation – one would arrive at the correct decision – one that everyone could approve of. The problem is that this does not explain why the reasons for an actual decision are good reasons. How can public deliberation be both moral and epistemic, that is, how can features of the process justify the outcome at the same time as it has good effects? Under non-ideal conditions the problem with justifying the epistemic value of deliberation arises. This is due to the fact that actual deliberations will not generally meet ideal requirements: they will be marked by, for example, ignorance, asymmetric information, power and strategic action. Estlund[95] and Gaus[96] therefore ask the question of whether the reasons that can be stated publicly also are good (convincing or correct) reasons.

Ideal proceduralists attempt to avoid these problems of justification. Their claim is that the ideal deliberative procedure is constitutive for correctness as long as certain conditions are met. But if correctness is seen as what the actors will support under ideal conditions, it will be difficult to prove the epistemic qualities, that is, that actual deliberation leads to better and fairer decisions.[97] This is only possible when one can appeal to a process-independent standard of truth or correctness. This is what the constitutionalists put forth when they operate with a substantial measure of justice as it is formulated, for example, in the theory of justice as fairness as we have seen.

In order to defend the epistemic qualities of deliberation, process-independent standards are needed. An epistemic justification of outcomes will in that case become independent of ideal deliberative conditions, but dependent on what the deliberation leads to with regard to rational decisions – independently defined. We are therefore faced with the following paradox: if deliberative democracy defends its claims on moral qualities via an ideal process, it cannot legitimate its claims on epistemic value. On the other hand, if deliberative democracy claims to have epistemic qualities, it can only be defended by standards that not only are process-independent, but also independent of actual deliberation.[98]

Gutmann and Thompson[99] argue that deliberative justification is neither entirely procedural nor substantial (constitutional) – none of them have priority, but both are necessary. They argue that substantial principles should be included but these are to be seen as morally and politically provisional.[100] Then little is achieved. David Estlund also argues for a mixed principle that does not make the legitimacy of the result dependent on its correctness, but on the epistemic value of the process that created it:

> Democratic legitimacy requires that the procedure is procedurally fair and can be held, in terms acceptable to all reasonable citizens, to be epistemically the best among those that are better than random.[101]

This is a weak principle that involves a "thin substance."[102] The only requirement is that the citizens agree that there are more or less favourable ways of evaluating arguments. The normative problem with this solution is that it lacks a theory of criteria specification and of conflict resolution based on a theory of public justification.[103] The analytical problem is that this solution does not pick up on the moral authority of the process, that is, that the process itself has the ability to bring forth results worthy of respect. It is only the moral qualities of the procedure that can explain that political decisions have a binding power also on those who disagree.[104] It is hard to see how discourse theorists can maintain that it is the epistemic value of deliberation that makes results correct, when the procedure itself is constituted by moral (non-deliberative) norms. But what kind of standard are we talking about?

XII. DISCURSIVE PROCEDURALISM

The tension between substance and procedure that occupies such a prominent place in contemporary political theory reflects the very constitutional structure of modern democracies in which the citizens have the opportunity to give themselves the laws that they have to obey, but where participation is regulated by non-disposable procedures and inalienable rights. Fundamental norms like equality, autonomy, human dignity, legal certainty, democracy, which make up the basic procedures of the modern constitutional state, are higher-ranking principles. They belong to the deontological realm. The procedures themselves are normatively charged and are subjected to *judicial review* of one sort or the other, monitored by judicial bodies. The tension then is involved in the medium of law itself as it claims to hand down correct solutions but cannot accomplish this without importing (normatively untested) substantial reasons of what is right or wrong, good or poor. This tension reemerges in discourse theory as only procedures can determine which argument is a good one, but speech rules constituting the process reflect substantial elements. So are the constitutionalists right after all?

The standard for democratic justification that is at work here is not an objective one. It involves actors, their arguments and fallible opinions and it refers to the idea of a justly organised process. Hence a concept of justice is presupposed. This standard is an intrinsic critical standard for assessing existing imperfect democratic procedures: it can be used in assessing every actual institutionalisation of political deliberation and decision-making.

> What it can argue for are improved forms of justification if there are grounds to assume that good reasons have been neglected, but there is no independent way to "find" an objective truth beyond reciprocal and general argumentation.[105]

Regarding this it becomes clear that the alleged problem of *infinite regress* is only a problem for foundationalists – it may be seen as a " … product of an old providential model of authority that leads us to look for authorization prior to action rather than the other way round."[106] In discourse theory, which builds on a pragmatic conception of validity, there is a departure from induction and deduction as rightness warranting principles. Argumentation replaces propositional inferences as the central area of logic in practical contexts. The theory is based on the connection between a speech act and its pragmatic presuppositions. There are basic rules of argumentation that cannot be opposed, because they are presupposed as valid already when the discussion starts. The constitutive rules of the game can be criticized, ridiculed, changed, modified, but cannot be disposed of if the game is to be played at all. It is this idea of procedure that makes criticism and correction of established processes possible. Thus an independent standard – but not a pure procedural justice standard – is given for the evaluation of actual procedures and political decisions. This standard is not objective in a simple scientific sense as it includes normative elements (such as a notion of justice and democracy) and cannot yield absolutely correct results as the ideal conditions of discourse can only be approximated. *It is only a question of better answers compared to those that can be reached by means of democratic processes, in the sense that an argumentative process will bring about more justified standpoints.*

The standard is thus imperfect. It is itself an expression of a normative procedure for justification, which is entrenched in the legal and moral nexus of modern constitutional democracies. Discourse theory regards fundamental rights as procedural arrangements for substantiating the presumption of popular made law. In this specific meaning, procedures overrule correctness theories, but the procedure itself is constituted by substantial claims to *freedom and equality*. The latter cannot be explained procedurally, because the very procedural claim of *equal right to participation* itself presupposes the basic substantial claim of everybody's equality and the right to equal freedom. Such basic moral or human rights have priority over other claims – this is why they are constitutionalised in the first place – and they also must have priority in order for democracy to be acceptable for all.[107] Consequently, in discourse theory there is a substantial residual element that leaves room for judicial review and for judges as guardians of the constitution.

Generally, discourse theory holds that correctness is more a question of what can be *justified* in a process, than what is right or fair according to some external (theoretical) standard. It is the citizens', not the judges or the political philosophers' moral judgement that is decisive. But the process must be secured by reference to substantial elements, because it is required that the procedure is fair. According to discourse theorists, in contrast to contractarian constitutionalism, the task of philosophy is to clarify *the moral point of view* and the criteria for democratic legitimacy through an analysis of the procedural requirements for a rational debate. It does not include deducing certain norms or criteria for distribution of resources. *Neutrality* in this context has to do with ensuring mutual respect and equal conditions for communication, so that everyone can express their opinion and that arguments can be tested.

XIII. CONCLUSION

The debate on substance and procedure is not merely a theoretically one because it has to do with whether there can be a democratic enactment of a constitution. What can popular sovereignty mean under the rule of law in modern society? In short, should the legislators or the judges have the upper hand? Should the Supreme Court's or the politicians be the final arbiter of constitutional law? This article has established that proceduralists cannot do without substance in conceiving of popular rule. For the people to be free to make their own constitution some moral properties are presupposed. Hence, the rights-based perspective of the constitititutionalists has a case against proceduralists. But what is meant by procedure? If it comes down to solely majority vote, a procedural approach cannot be sustained. If, on the contrary, it designates the procedures for ensuring a fair deliberative process – a fair procedure of reason giving – the case is a bit different. Deliberationists like the discourse theorists plead for a larger concept of democracy than the one depicting it as merely a voting arrangement and hold that substantive and procedural conceptions of justice interchange in justificatory processes.

In this regard one may conceive of politics as a special variant of practical reason. It is specialised on collective goal attainment revolving on common good considerations constrained by the principle of justice. Moral and legal principles are seen as constraints that ensure equal access, autonomy and equality. The constitutive power – *le pouvoir constituant* – always lies with the people; all law and public authority stem from citizens. Moreover, it is the deliberative process itself that bears the burden of legitimation in so far it manages to define and mobilize support for collective goals and secure a fair treatment of all actors' interests and needs. In this model, judging the legitimacy of the arguments is in the last instance left to the participants involved in the discussion. A legitimate decision is not an expression of preconceived ideas of what is just or the common good but the outcome of everybody's deliberation in a free, open and rational process. Such a procedure is constituted by substantial moral norms that cannot themselves be proceduralised. What then from a democratic point of view seems to be the contribution of discourse theory is the way it does not fix substantial conceptions of what should be done in final categories, left over to the politicians, judges and bureaucrats to implement, but constantly subjects them to argumentative testing and higher-ordered procedural constraints based on idealized deliberative preconditions.

NOTES

* I am grateful for comments from Anders Molander, Agustín J. Menéndez and Synne Sæther Mæhle to an earlier variant of this chapter.

1 Robert Alexy, *Recht, Vernunft, Diskurs,* Frankfurt: Suhrkamp, 1995, p. 110.

2 Jürgen Habermas, "Reply to Symposium Participants," 17 (1996b) *Cardozo Law Review*, pp. 1477–1558, at p. 1495.

3 John Rawls, *A Theory of Justice,* Oxford: Oxford University Press, 1971, p. 86.

4 See for example, Robert A. Dahl, *Democracy and its Critics,* New Haven: Yale University Press, 1989.

5 See Brian Barry, *Democracy and Power,* Oxford: Oxford University Press, 1991.

6 David Estlund, "Beyond Fairness and Deliberation: The Epistemic Dimension of Democratic Authority," in James Bohman and William Rehg (eds.) *Deliberative Democracy,* Cambridge, Mass.: The MIT Press, 1997, pp. 176ff.

7 Ronald Dworkin, *Freedom's Law,* Cambridge, Mass.: Harvard University Press, 1996.

8 On whether this is a "natural law" conception, see Rawls, *supra*, fn. 3, pp. 505ff, and John Rawls, "Reply to Habermas," 92 (1995) *The Journal of Philosophy*, pp. 132–180, p. 159; and Ronald Dworkin, "What is Equality? Part 2: Equality of Resources" 10 (1981) *Philosophy and Public Affairs*, pp. 283–345; Stefan Gosepath, "The Place of Equality in Habermas' and Dworkin's Theories of Justice" 3 (1995) *European Journal of Philosophy*, pp. 21–35; and Rainer Forst, "Die Rechtfertigung der Gerechtigkeit. Rawls' Politischer Liberalismus und Habermas' Diskursteorie in der Diskussion," In Hauke Brunkhorst and Peter Niesen (eds.) *Das Recht der Republik*. Frankfurt: Suhrkamp, 1999a, p. 113 and p. 143; Jürgen Habermas, *The Inclusion of the Other: Studies in Political Theory*, Cambridge, Mass.: The MIT Press,

1998, especially chapters "Reconciliation through the Public Use of Reason" and " 'Reasonable' vs. 'True', or the 'Morality of Worldviews.' "

[9] Consider the views of Dworkin: "Justice is a matter of the correct or best theory of moral and political rights, and anyone's conception of justice is his theory, imposed by his own personal convictions, of what these rights actually are," in Ronald Dworkin, *Law's Empire,* Cambridge, Mass.: Harvard University Press, 1986, p. 97. Cf. Frank I. Michelman: " …*justice* (…) is unalterably what we may call a 'perfectly' process-independent standard: in judging whether fundamental laws are just (…), no reference can ever be called for to the process of their legislation," in "How can the People ever make the Laws? A Critique of Deliberative Democracy," in Bohman and Rehg, *supra*, fn. 6, pp. 145–171, at p. 147.

[10] Ronald Dworkin, *Taking Rights Seriously*, London: Duckworth, 1977, pp. 82ff.

[11] Dworkin, *supra*, fn. 9.

[12] Dworkin, *supra,* fn. 10, pp. 397ff. And also at p. 227: "According to laws integrity, propositions of law are true if they figure on or follow from the principles of justice, fairness, and procedural due process that provide the best constructive interpretation of the community's legal practice."

[13] Rawls, *supra*, fn. 3, p. 302.

[14] "Because the parties start from an equal division of all social primary goods, those who benefit least have, so to speak a veto. Thus we arrive at the difference principle," in John Rawls, *A Theory of Justice.* Revised Edition, Cambridge, Mass.: Harvard University Press, 1999a, p. 131.

[15] Rainer Forst argues that Rawls rather conceives of the private use of public reason in public affairs than of the public use of reason, see *Kontexte der Gerechtigkeit,* Frankfurt: Suhrkamp, 1994, p. 156. See also Jürgen Habermas, *supra*, fn. 8, pp. 51ff and 75ff; and Seyla Benhabib, *The Claims of Culture. Equality and Diversity in a Global Era*, Princeton: Princeton University Press, 2002, chapter 5.

[16] John Rawls, *The Law of Peoples*, Cambridge, Mass.: Harvard University Press, 1999b, p. 3.

[17] John Rawls, "The Idea of Public Reason Revisited," 64 (1997) *The University of Chicago Law Review*, pp. 765–807, at p. 774.

[18] Dworkin, *supra,* fn. 10, pp. 263ff.

[19] Rawls, *supra*, fn. 17.

[20] For criticism along these lines see Roberto Alejandro, "What is Political about Rawls's Political Liberalism?," 58 (1996) *The Journal of Politics,* pp. 1–24, at p. 22; Jürgen Habermas, *supra*, fn. 8, pp. 49ff; Forst, *supra*, fn. 9*;* and Rainer Forst, "The Basic Right to Justification: Toward a Constructivist Conception of Human Rights," 6 (1999b) *Constellations*, pp. 35–60; Rainer Forst, "The Rule of Reasons. Three Models of Deliberative Democracy," 14 (2001) *Ratio Juris,* pp. 345–378; Seyla Benhabib, *supra*, fn. 15. See also John Rawls, *Political Liberalism,* New York: Colombia University Press, 1993, p. 239; and John Rawls, *supra*, fn. 8 (1995), for reply.

[21] Paul J. Weithman, "Contractualist Liberalism and Deliberative Democracy," 24 (1995) *Philosophy & Public Affairs*, pp. 314–343, at p. 316. Cf. "The best institutional structure is the one designed to produce the best answers to the essentially moral questions of what the democratic conditions are, and to secure stable compliance with those conditions," in Dworkin, *supra*, fn. 10, p. 34.

[22] Cf. Ingeborg Maus, "Die Trennung von Recht und Moral als Begrenzung des Rechts," 20 (1989) *Rechtstheorie*, pp. 191–210, at p. 193.

[23] John Rawls, *supra,* fn. 20, p. 227.

[24] Cf. David Estlund, *supra,* fn. 6, p. 175.

[25] Jeremy Waldron, *Law and Disagreement*, Oxford: Oxford University Press, 2001, p. 158.

[26] Jürgen Habermas, *Between Facts and Norms,* Cambridge, Mass.: The MIT Press, 1996a, p. 107. Cf. Alexy, *supra,* fn. 1, p. 131; and Robert Alexy, "Discourse Theory and Human Rights," 9 (1996b) *Ratio Juris*, pp. 209–235, p. 212.

[27] Frank I. Michelman, *supra,* fn. 10, pp. 162ff.

[28] Jürgen Habermas, *supra*, fn. 26.

[29] For criticism of this point see Karl Otto Apel, *Auseinander-setzungen in Erprobung des transzendental-pragmatischen Ansatzes,* Frankfurt: Suhrkamp, 1998. See also chapters in Hauke Brunkhorst, Wolfgang Köhler and Matthias Lutz-Bachmann (eds.) *Recht auf Menschrechte,* Frankfurt: Suhrkamp, 1999; Alexy, *supra*, fn. 26; Otfried Höffe, *Vernunft und Recht. Bausteine zu einem interkulturellen Rechtsdiskurs*. Frankfurt: Suhrkamp,1996.

[30] Alexy, *supra*, fn. 26.

[31] Klaus Günther, "Welchen Personenbegriff braucht die Diskurstheorie des Rechts?," in Brunkhorst and Niesen, *supra,* fn. 9, (1999) pp. 83–104, p. 87.

[32] Rainer Forst, *supra,* fn. 8, p. 151.

[33] John Rawls, *supra*, fn. 20.

[34] Jürgen Habermas, "Discourse Ethics: Notes on a Program of Philosophical Justification," in *Moral Consciousness and Communicative Action,* Cambridge, Mass.: The MIT Press, 1990, p. 63.

[35] John Rawls, *supra,* fn. 9, p. 173.

[36] It does not amount to pure procedural justice in Rawls's terminology.

[37] Alexy, *supra,* fn. 26, p. 220.

[38] For the point that there is a decisionistic rest in discourse theory as the commitment to enter the discussion cannot be derived from the principle of non-contradiction. Rationality presuppositions are different from the presuppositions of morality, see Albert Wellmer, *Ethik und Dialog,* Frankfurt: Suhrkamp, 1986, pp. 106ff.

[39] Robert Alexy, *A Theory of Legal Argumentation. The Theory of Rational Discourse as Theory of Legal Justification,* Oxford: Oxford University Press, 1989.

[40] Ibid., p. 188.

[41] Ibid., pp. 192 and 196ff. See also Robert Alexy, "Die Idee einer prozeduralen Theorie der juristischen Argumentation," in Aalius Aarnio et. al. (eds.) *Methodologie und Erkenntnistheorie der juristischen Argumentation,* Berlin: Duncker & Humbolt, 1981, pp. 94ff, pp. 244ff. I.M.A.M. Pröpper, "Argumentation and Power in Evaluation-Research and in its Utilization in the Policy Making Process," in Rene von Schomberg (ed.) *Science, Politics and Morality. Scientific Uncertainty and Decision Making,* Dordrecht: Kluwer Academic Publishers, 1993, pp. 138ff; Erik Oddvar Eriksen and Jarle Weigård, *Understanding Habermas. Communicative Action and Deliberative Democracy*, London: Continuum, 2003, pp. 199ff.

[42] Alexy, *supra*, fn. 39, p. 206.

[43] Rawls, *supra*, fn. 20, pp. 54ff.

[44] Ludwig Wittgenstein, *Philosophical Investigations,* Oxford: Basil Blackwell, 1978.

[45] "Rules are certainly not determinate enough to be predictive; they are not followed in the same way by all agents, and many often are not followed at all," James Bohman, *New Philosophy of Social Science: Problems of Interderminacy,* Cambridge, Mass.: The MIT Press, 1991, p. 64.

[46] Klaus Günther, *The Sense of Appropriateness: Application Discourses in Morality and Law*, Albany: State University of New York Press, 1993b.

[47] Herbert L. A Hart, *The Concept of Law*. Oxford: Clarendon Press, 1961, p. 128; Robert Alexy, "Law and Correctness," 51 (1998a) *Current Legal Problems,* pp. 205–221, at p. 215.

[48] Robert Alexy, "The Special Case Thesis," 12 (1999b) *Ratio Juris*, pp. 374–384, at p. 383.

[49] Alexy, *supra*, fn. 39, pp. 11 and 18.

[50] Jürgen Habermas, *supra*, fn. 26, p. 234.

[51] Alexy, *supra*, fn. 39, p. 179.

[52] Ibid., p. 228. I return to the problem of who are the participants in the legal public sphere.

[53] Cf. Jürgen Habermas, *supra*, fn. 26, p. 232. Although the law has rules that regulate collisions between norms, for example *lex superior, lex posterior,* and *lex specialis*, these are too unspecified to solve disputes in a consequent and systematic manner.

[54] Jürgen Habermas, "Om förhållandet mellan politik, rätt och moral," In Erik Oddvar Eriksen and Anders Molander (eds.) *Habermas: Diskurs, rätt och demokrati,* Gothenburg: Daidalos, 1995, p. 55; and Dworkin, *supra*, fn. 8, pp. 81ff.

[55] Robert Alexy, *A Theory of Constitutional Rights*, Oxford: Oxford University Press, 2002a, p. 23; Cf. Dworkin, *supra,* fn. 10 and Hart, *supra*, fn. 47.

[56] Habermas, *supra*, fn. 9, p. 256. "The moral universe, which is *unlimited* in social space and historical time, includes *all natural persons* and their complex of life histories; morality itself extends to the protection of the integrity of fully individuated persons (*Einzelner*). By contrast, the legal community, which is always localized in time and space, protects the integrity of its members precisely in so far as that they acquire the artificial status as *rights bearers*."

[57] Robert Alexy, "Jürgen Habermas' Theory of Legal Discourse," 17 (1996a) *Cardozo Law Review*, pp. 1027–1034, at p. 1030.

[58] Alexy, *supra*, fn. 55, pp. 47–48: "(…) characterised by the fact that they can be satisfied to varying degrees, and that the appropriate degree of satisfaction depends not only on what is factually possible, but also on what is legally possible."

[59] Ibid., pp. 58 and 102.

[60] Ibid., pp. 58 and 57.

[61] On the problems of principles as trumps see Alexy, *supra*, fn. 55, p. 102; and *infra,* fn. 72, pp. 77ff; Günther, *infra*, fn. 46, pp. 214ff, 219 and 227.

[62] Alexy, *supra,* fn. 57, p. 216.

[63] Ibid., p. 219.

[64] Klaus Günther, "A Normative Conception of Coherence for a Discursive Theory of Legal Justification," 2 (1989) *Ratio Juris*, pp. 155–166, at p. 155.

[65] Klaus Günther, "Criticial Remarks on Robert Alexy's Special-Case Thesis" 6 (1993a) *Ratio Juris*, pp. 143–156, at p. 151: "Everybody who uses a valid moral norm as a reason for a justification of singular normative propositions has to observe at least two principles: (1) A justification of a singular normative proposition requires a complete description of the concrete case with respect to all those moral reasons which are relevant. (2) A justification of a singular normative proposition requires a coherent interpretation of those morally valid reasons which are directly or indirectly relevant to the concrete case."

[66] Robert Alexy, "Justification and Application of Norms," 6 (1993) *Ratio Juris*, pp. 157–170, at p. 167: "From the fact that those two questions have to be distinguished it does not follow that there exist two essential different kinds of discourse."

[67] Ibid., p. 163: "The fundamental moral demand of equal treatment runs empty because in the sparsely furnished normative universe of this construction there is nothing that could grant equal treatment."

[68] Alexy, *supra*, fn. 57, p. 1032.

[69] This is possible as "the law is not only open to moral criticism from the outside. The critical dimension is replaced into the law itself," see Klaus Günther, "Welchen Personenbegriff braucht die Diskurstheorie des Rechts?" in Brunkhorst and Niesen, *supra*, fn. 9, pp. 83–104, p. 382. It is worth quoting at length from p. 384: "General practical arguments have to float through all institutions if the roots of these institutions in practical reason shall not be cut off."

[70] Alexy, *supra*, fn. 48, pp. 375ff.

[71] Ibid., p. 375: "It is not concerned with what is absolutely correct but what is correct within the framework and on the basis of a validly prevailing legal order (… it …) is bound to the statutes and to precedents and has to observe the system of law elaborated by legal dogmatics."

[72] Robert Alexy, *The Argument from Injustice. A Reply to Legal Positivism*, Oxford: Clarendon Press, 2002b, p. 77.

[73] Alexy, *supra*, fn. 55, pp. 370–371.

[74] The following statements originate from one of the founding fathers of legal positivism. Cf. Paul Laband, *Das Staatsrecht des Deutschen Reiches*, vol. 2, Tübingen: Mohr, 1911, p. 178, cited from Massimo La Torre, "Theories of Legal Argumentation and Concepts of Law. An Approximation," 15 (2002) *Ratio Juris*, pp. 377–402, at p. 379. "Legal decision consists of a given case's subsumption under valid law; like any other logical conclusion it is independent from will. There is no freedom on the resolution whether the consequence should take place or not; it is produced-as it were-by itself, by intrinsic necessity."

[75] "Das, was richtig is, wird nun durch eigenen Programme fixiert" … and … , Die frage nach der Richtighkeit der Programmatik als solcher hat keinen erkennenbaren Sinn – es sei denn, … , im context einer Rejektion des Rechtscodes", Niklas Luhmann, *Das Recht der Gesellschaft*, Frankfurt: Suhrkamp, 1995, p. 192.

[76] Alexy, *supra*, fn. 39, p. 228: "It is the task of the external justification to justify those premises which cannot be derived from positive law:" Cf. also Hart, *supra*, fn. 47, p. 89.

[77] Alexy, *supra*, fn. 48, p. 377: "[O]ne cannot deny that it is the court which is to decide and argue in the last instance."

[78] Agustín José Menéndez, *Justifying Taxes*. Dordrecht: Kluwer, 2001, p. 240.

[79] Jürgen Habermas, "A short Reply," 12 (1999) *Ratio Juris*, pp. 445–453. Cf. also Habermas *supra*, fn. 26, p. 234: Legal discourses refer "*from the outset* to democratically enacted law."

[80] Habermas, *supra*, fn. 26, p. 220.

[81] Forst, *supra*, fn. 20 (2001).

[82] Cf. Bruce Ackerman, *We the People: Transformations*, Cambridge, Mass.: Harvard University Press, 1998.

[83] Ranging from Conflict councils and law mediators, family courts to user-participation in a broad range of public service institutions, Cf. Erik Oddvar Eriksen, *Demokratiets sorte hull*, Oslo: Abstrakt Forlag, 2001.

[84] According to Günther, Alexy presupposes "a teleological reinterpretation of principles" and he reduces "the justification problem to justifying decisions of preference." Cf. Günther, *supra*, fn. 46, p. 227.

[85] Alexy, *supra*, fn. 1, pp. 96, 104 and 110.

[86] Habermas, *supra*, fn. 34.

[87] Alexy, *supra*, fn. 1, p. 121.

[88] George Pavlakos, "The Special Case Thesis. An Assessment of R. Alexy's Discursive Theory of Law," 11 (1998) *Ratio Juris*, pp. 126–154. See also, of the same author, "Persons and Norms: On the normative groundwork of Discourse-Ethics," 85 (1999) *Archiv für Rechts- und Sozialphilosophie*, pp.1–22, at p. 9: "If one allows a picture of the discourse, where these is no room for any substantive norms at its starting point, and where

consequently all discourse-rules are simply speech rules (…) then one should renounce the idea of a substantive claim for rightness; in this case the rightness-claim would remain a sheer formal concept, which would be nevertheless too weak to justify the whole enterprise of practical discourse."

[89] Peter Gril, *Die Möglichkeit praktischer Erkenntnis aus der Sicht der Diskursteorie*, Berlin: Duncker and Humbolt, 1998, pp. 158 and 162.

[90] In *The Argument from Injustice*, fn. 72, it becomes clear that Alexy prioritizes justice over democracy, as he holds the former to be a more fundamental value.

[91] Habermas, *supra*, fn. 34, p. 94. On this point see also Jürgen Habermas, *Wahrheit und Rechtferdigung*, Frankfurt: Suhrkamp, 1999, pp. 302ff.

[92] Habermas, *supra*, fn. 2, p. 1508.

[93] Ingeborg. Maus, "Liberties and Popular Sovereignty: On Jürgen Habermas's Reconstruction of the System of Rights," 17 (1996) *Cardozo Law Review*, pp. 825–882, at pp. 880–881.

[94] And further, "Since the 'validity' of a norm consists in that it would be accepted, that is, recognized as valid, under ideal conditions of justification, 'rightness' is an epistemic concept." Habermas, "Rightness versus Truth: On the Sense of Normative Validity in Moral Judgments and Norms," in *Truth and Justification*, Cambridge, MA: MIT Press, 2003, p. 258.

[95] David Estlund, "Who's Afraid of Deliberative Democracy? On the Strategic/Deliberative Dichotomy in Recent Constitutional Jurisprudence" 71 (1993) *Texas Law Review*, pp. 1437–1477.

[96] Gerald F. Gaus, "Reason, Justification and Consensus: Why Democracy Can't Have it All," in Bohman and Rehg, *supra*, fn. 6, (1997) pp. 205–242.

[97] Bohman and Rehg, *supra*, fn. 6, pp. ix–xxx, at p. xix.

[98] Cf. James Bohman, "Survey Article: The Coming of Age of Deliberative Democracy," 6 (1998) *The Journal of Political Philosophy*, pp. 400–425, at p. 403.

[99] Amy Gutmann and Dennis Thompson, *Democracy and Disagreement*, Cambridge, Mass: Harvard University Press, 1996, p. 27.

[100] Amy Gutmann and Dennis Thompson, "Deliberative Democracy Beyond Process," 10 (2002) *The Journal of Political Philosophy*, pp. 153–174.

[101] Estlund, *supra*, fn. 6, p. 174.

[102] Estlund, *supra*, fn. 95.

[103] Bohman, *supra*, fn. 98, p. 407.

[104] Tom R. Tyler, *Why People Obey the Law*, New Haven: Yale University Press, 1990.

[105] Forst, *supra*, fn. 20 (2001).

[106] Bonnie Honig, "Dead Rights, Live Futures. A reply to Habermas's 'Constitutional Democracy' " 29 (2001) *Political Theory*, pp. 792–805, at p. 796.

[107] Stefan Gosepath, "Democracy out of Reason. Comment on Rainer Forst's 'The rule of Reasons'," 14 (2001) *Ratio Juris*, pp. 379–389, at p. 389.

CARLOS BERNAL PULIDO

5. ON ALEXY'S WEIGHT FORMULA

I. INTRODUCTION

There are two basic kinds of norms in every modern legal system: rules and principles. They are applied by means of two different rational procedures: subsumption and balancing.[1] While rules apply by means of subsumption, balancing is the way to apply principles. For this reason, balancing has become an essential methodological criterion for adjudication, especially for the adjudication of fundamental rights, which have the structure of principles. However, balancing is at the heart of many theoretical discussions. One of the most important questions is whether balancing has a rational structure, and whether balancing is a rational procedure or a mere rhetoric device, useful to justify any kind of judicial decisions. In *A Theory of Constitutional Rights*[2] and in other papers, Alexy supports the thesis that balancing has a rational structure and offers a well developed conception of the structure of balancing. In the last version, three elements form the structure of balancing: the law of balancing, the weight formula, and the burden of argumentation. The aim of this chapter is to analyze the role and the structure of the second element: the weight formula (III), but first it is necessary to clarify the concept and the general structure of balancing (II).[3]

II. THE CONCEPT AND THE STRUCTURE OF BALANCING

A. The Concept of Balancing

Principles are optimization commands. Principles are norms which do not establish exactly what should be done, but require "that something be realized to the greatest extent possible given the legal and factual possibilities."[4] The scope of the legally possible is determined by opposing principles and rules, and factual statements about the case determine the scope of the factually possible.

To establish this "greatest extent possible" to which a principle should be carried out, it is necessary to confront it with opposing principles or with principles supporting opposing rules. In this case, all of them are competing principles; they support *prima facie* two incompatible norms (for instance,

A. J. Menéndez and E. O. Eriksen (eds.), Arguing Fundamental Rights, 101–110.

*N*1 forbids ø and *N*2 commands ø), which can be proposed as solutions for the case.

Balancing is the way to resolve this incompatibility between *prima facie* norms. Balancing does not guarantee a systematic articulation of all the legal principles which, taking into account their hierarchy, resolves beforehand all the possible conflicts between them, and all the possible incompatibilities between all the *prima facie* norms they underlie. On the contrary, as a syllogism, balancing is only a structure, composed of three elements by means of which "a conditional relation of precedence between the principles in the light of the circumstances of the case"[5] is to be established in order to reach the legal decision.

B. *The Structure of Balancing*

Robert Alexy explains the structure of balancing with great clarity and precision. If we agree with Alexy, to establish the conditional relation of precedence between competing principles, it is necessary to consider three elements, which form the structure of balancing: the law of balancing, the weight formula and the burden of argumentation.

a. The Law of Balancing According to the law of balancing,

> The greater the degree of non-satisfaction of, or detriment to, one principle, the greater must be the importance of satisfying the other.[6]

Consistent with this rule, the structure of balancing can be broken down into three different stages, which Alexy clearly identifies: "The first stage involves establishing the degree of non-satisfaction of, or detriment to, the first principle. This is followed by a second stage in which the importance of satisfying the competing principle is established. Finally, the third stage establishes whether the importance of satisfying the competing principle justifies the detriment to, or non-satisfaction of, the first."[7]

It is important to note that the first and the second stages of balancing are rather analogous. Both operations consist of establishing the importance of the principles at stake, so we will refer to both as such.[8] Indeed, in both cases Alexy claims that commensurability can be established by reference to a triadic scale: "light," "moderate" and "serious."

The importance of the principles at stake is not the only relevant variable. A second one is the "abstract weight" of the principles.[9] Different abstract weight might derive from the different legal hierarchy of the legal body in which the principle is affirmed or from which it stems, but it might be established by reference to positive social values. Thus, for instance, it could be claimed that the principle of protection of life has a greater abstract weight than that of liberty, if only because to be able to exercise one's liberty, it is pretty obvious that one must be alive. Similarly, many national constitutional courts assign a high abstract weight to freedom of speech, on account of its close connection with democracy, or to privacy, given its close association with human dignity.

A third variable R should be added, which refers to the reliability of the empirical assumptions concerning what the measure in question means for the non-realization of the first principle and the realization of the second under the circumstances of the case. R is based on the recognition that the empirical assumptions relating to the importance of the competing principles can have a different degree of reliability, something which should affect the relative weight of each principle in the balancing exercise.

Now the question is: how should the importance of principles, their abstract weight, and the reliability of the empirical assumptions concerning the importance of the principles be assessed in order to come to a concrete balancing outcome? According to Alexy, the answer is provided by the weight formula.

b. The Weight Formula The weight formula has the following structure:[10]

$$WPi{,}jC = \frac{IPiC \cdot WPiA \cdot RPiC}{SPjC \cdot WPjA \cdot RPjC}$$

This formula states that the concrete weight in a given case of principle *Pi* in relation to principle *Pj* results from the quotient between, on the one hand, the product of the importance of principle *Pi*, its abstract weight and the reliability of the empirical assumptions regarding its importance and, on the other hand, the product of the importance of principle *Pj*, its abstract weight, and the reliability of the empirical assumptions regarding its importance. Alexy says that it is possible to give a numerical value to the variables of the importance and abstract weight of the principles with the help of the triadic scale: light 2^0 that is, 1; moderate 2^1 that is, 2; and serious 2^2, that is, 4. In contrast, the reliability of the factual premises must be given a quantitative expression in the following way: reliable, 2^0, that is, 1; maintainable or plausible 2^{-1}, that is, $\frac{1}{2}$; and not evidently false, 2^{-2}, that is, $\frac{1}{4}$.[11]

Applying these numerical values, it is possible to determine the "concrete weight"[12] of principle *Pi* in relation to principle *Pj* in the case at hand. If the concrete weight of principle *Pi* in relation to principle *Pj* is greater than the concrete weight of principle *Pj* in relation to principle *Pi*, the case should be decided according to principle *Pi*. On the contrary, if the concrete weight of principle *Pj* in relation to principle *Pi* is greater than the concrete weight of principle *Pi* in relation to principle *Pj*, the case should be decided according to principle *Pj*. If *Pi* supports the norm *N*1 that forbids ø and if *Pj* supports the norm *N*2 that commands ø, ø should be forbidden in the first case and ø should be commanded in the second case.

c. The burden of argumentation The third element of the structure of balancing is the burden of argumentation.[13] This burden operates when the application of the weight formula results in a stalemate, that is, when the weight of the principles is identical (or to express it formally, $WPi,jC = WPj,iC$). Alexy seems to defend two different ways of breaking the stalemate, one in the final chapter of *A Theory of Constitutional Rights*, and another in the *Postscript* to the just referred book, written fifteen years after the publication of the first edition. This double solution is problematic to the extent that it could lead to rather different results, as we will see.

In *A Theory of Constitutional Rights*, Alexy claims that stalemate cases should be decided in favour of legal liberty and legal equality, or what is the same, his position could be summarized by reference to the principle of *in dubio pro libertate*.[14] Any principle in conflict with the principles of legal liberty or legal equality would not be applied in the case at hand, unless "stronger reasons"[15] are put forward in its favor. In the *Postscript* to *A Theory of Constitutional Rights*, Alexy defends a different solution. In stalemate cases, he says, a restriction mandated by an act of Parliament should be considered as proportionate and therefore declared in accordance with the Constitution. In other words, ties would have to be sorted out by fostering the democratic principle, and not necessarily legal liberty and equality.[16]

III. THE ROLE AND THE STRUCTURE OF THE WEIGHT FORMULA

A. *The Role of the Weight Formula*

We should now consider the role played by the weight formula in the general structure of balancing. First, it should be remembered that the weight formula is a rational procedure to determine the concrete weight of principle *Pi* in relation to principle *Pj* in the light of the circumstances of a case. Alexy, thus, presents the weight formula as a complement to the law of balancing, based in the classical formulation of the third limb of the proportionality principle, or proportionality in the narrow sense.[17]

However, it seems to me that the weight formula, as described by Alexy, calls for a new law of balancing. The aim of the weight formula is to establish "a conditional relation of precedence between the principles in the light of the circumstances of the case." The key observation is that the relation of precedence is not determined by means of merely comparing the importance of the principles in the case at hand ("the degree of non-satisfaction of, or detriment to, one principle" and "the importance of satisfying the other"), but by a wider operation which includes reference to their abstract weight and to the reliability of the empirical assumptions relating to the importance of the principles.

That is, the weight formula is a reformulation of the basic insight behind the original law of balancing which is more sophisticated in analytical terms, as it renders explicit the need of considering another two variables, namely abstract weight and reliability of the empirical assumptions.

The new formulation of the law of balancing should be as follows:

The greater the concrete weight of principle *Pi* in relation with principle *Pj* in the light of the circumstances of the case, the greater must be the concrete weight of principle *Pj* in relation with principle *Pi* in the light of the circumstances of the case.

This reformulated law of balancing could also be expressed as:

$$WPi,jC \leq WPj,iC$$

Or more explicitly,

$$\frac{IPiC \cdot WPiA \cdot RPIC}{SPjC \cdot WPjA \cdot RPjC} \leq \frac{SPjC \cdot WPjA \cdot RPjC}{IPiC \cdot WPiA \cdot RPiC}$$

This could be rendered clearer with the help of a concrete example. Imagine that the life of a child is dependent on a blood transfusion, which her parents refuse in the name of their religious beliefs. This implies a conflict between the right to life and the right to religious freedom. Is it constitutionally sound to mandate the transfusion contrary to the will of the parents? The Court could consider that the degree of non-satisfaction or detriment of principle *Pi* (freedom of religion) is serious (4), as is the importance of satisfying principle *Pj* (protection of the life of the child) (4). The Court could further consider that the abstract weight of freedom of religion *Pi* is moderate (2) and that the right to life is high (4); finally, that the empirical assumptions concerning the importance of both principles are reliable (1). In this case, the application of the law of balancing leads to the following conclusion:

$$\frac{4 \cdot 2 \cdot 1}{4 \cdot 4 \cdot 1} \leq \frac{4 \cdot 4 \cdot 1}{4 \cdot 2 \cdot 1}$$

That is to say:

$$\frac{8}{16} \leq \frac{16}{8}$$

$$\frac{1}{2} < 2.$$

In this example, the blood transfusion should be undertaken against the will of parents because the right to life of the children meets the requirements of the law of balancing. The infringement of the right to religious freedom should be considered as proportionate and, therefore, as permitted by the Constitution.

B. *The Structure of the Weight Formula*

The structure of the weight formula sets out many interesting problems. But paramount among which is whether there are objective criteria to determine the value of the relevant variables which form the weight formula. Whether this or not the case is what I will explore in this section, by means of considering each of the variables in detail.

a. *The degree of importance of the competing principles* It is certain that sometimes rational judgments about degrees of intensity and importance of competing principles are possible. Or what is the same, there are easy cases concerning the degree of importance of principles. For example, if a satirical magazine calls a handicapped officer a "cripple," this clearly constitutes a serious offence against his honour (4), while at the same time contributes very slightly to the protection of freedom of speech (1). However, there are also hard cases in which the premises, both factual and normative, which should be considered in determining the importance of a principle are uncertain. This is typically the case when religious freedom is at stake. It can be doubted whether the degree of interference of a given measure with religious freedom can be determined in abstract terms, without taking into account subjective views on religious experience. Thus, the perceived degree of interference with religious freedom of a forced blood transfusion is clearly dependent on how the individual lives her religious faith. It might be fully negligible for most believers, and very serious for a Jehova witness. An assessment of the importance of the principle can only be made after taking a concrete stand which cannot be determined by the weight formula in itself. Thus, reference to the weight formula implies a grant of discretion to the judge and to his critical moral views, as well as political ideology. However, even in such cases, the weight formula has a role to play, as it renders clear the margin of discretion left to the judge, and the room made to critical morality and political ideology in the balancing exercise.

Likewise, the judge can exercise discretion when it is not clear if the case is an easy or a hard one with respect to the first variable in the weight formula, namely the importance of principles. This can be done with the help of a concrete case, the *Tobacco* Judgment of the German Constitutional Court, which Alexy tends to refer as an example of a clear case. The *Tobacco* case concerned the statutory duty imposed upon tobacco producers to make consumers aware of the health risks associated to smoking in the label of cigarettes, and more precisely, whether this was constitutionally sound or not. In principle, the judgment shows that there are easy cases in which "rational judgments are possible about intensity of interference and degrees of importance," so that "an outcome can be rationally established in way of balancing."[18] The labeling duty is a "relatively minor interference with freedom of profession,"[19] especially when compared to potential alternative measures, such as the prohibition of the sale of tobacco, or the imposition of restrictions on its sale. Moreover, it is clear that the measure fosters the protection of health. Therefore, Alexy concludes that "The Federal Constitutional Court was not exaggerating when it stated in its decision on health warnings, that 'according to the current state of medical knowledge, it is certain', that smoking causes cancer and cardio-vascular disease."[20] The minor interference with the freedom of profession would be balanced against satisfying the protection of health. However, different assessments of the relevant variables are not impossible. From a factual point of view, it could be said that it is not certain that the duty to advertise the heart risks stemming from tobacco in tobacco labels actually contributes to fostering consumers' health. It could be the case that such a measure is inefficient, perhaps because consumers are already aware of what the labels tell them; or because tobacco addiction persists even if consumers are informed of its consequences, because it is to be traced back to weakness of will, and not to lack of information; or perhaps because providing information in the labels would render smoking more desirable.

What at any rate is clear is that the range of variation of the importance of the relevant principles depends on factual and normative premises.

A first normative premise concerns the "meaning"[21] (*M*) of the relevant positions of the principles, from the standpoint of the concept of person that any legal and political system must presuppose.[22] In a liberal society *à la Rawls,* liberty rights closely connected to the moral capacities of the person should be given more weight. They have greater meaning, and therefore, if they are interfered by an act of public power, this results in a serious violation of the principle that underlies them. In a Rawlsian society, the more connected with the moral capacities of the person a position of a principle is, the more importance should be attributed to a principle.[23]

A second kind of normative premise is the importance of the legal position (*LP*) at stake, from the point of view of the content of the relevant principles. For instance, an act of censorship of the government against the opposition's party is a more serious detriment to the freedom during an electoral campaign of speech than a strict regulation of a journal that publishes every day details about the sexual life of the actors of Hollywood. It could be also said that a restriction of access to the basic education for many children is a more serious detriment to the right of education than a strict regulation of post-graduate studies (LLM or PhD).

On what regards the empirical premises, they concern the variation of the importance that the case at hand projects onto the relevant principles. Empirical variation depends on the efficiency (*E*), speed (*Sp*), probability (*P*), reach (*Re*) and duration (*D*) of the controversial act in non-satisfying and satisfying the principles at stake.[24] The more efficient, fast, probable, powerful and long is the act under review in non-satisfying or satisfying the relevant principles, the greater will be the importance of these principles.

Regarding these normative and empirical premises, it could be said that the variables *IPiC* and *SPjC* in the weight formula could be formulated in a more explicit and extended way as follows:

$$IPiC = (MPiC \cdot LPPiC) \cdot (EPiC \cdot SPPiC \cdot PPiC \cdot RePiC \cdot DPiC)$$

$$SPjC = (MPjC \cdot LPPjC) \cdot (EPjC \cdot SPPjC \cdot PPjC \cdot RePjC \cdot DPjC)$$

b. The abstract weight of the competing principles Further room to judicial discretion derives from the measurement of the abstract weight of the principles. Abstract weight is a very singular variable, which always refers back to moral and ideological considerations. Its measurement requires the judge to take a position about the Constitution, the role of the State in the given society, and the very concept of justice. It is clear that the variable of abstract weight loses its importance when the competing principles are of the same nature. On the contrary, abstract weight becomes very relevant in solving the case when the nature of the competing principles is different. Even then, some cases might be relatively easy. It could be assumed, for example, that the protection of life, or fundamental rights closely related to the principles of human dignity and democracy should be given a higher abstract weight than others.[25] However, judges have a considerable discretion when determining the abstract weight of principles. Quite obviously, there is no complete pre-established graduation of abstract weights. The protection of life might be said to deserve the highest value (4), but one could discuss whether such a value should not also be granted to the rights closely connected to human dignity and democratic decision-making. Furthermore, should the value be the same for all rights connected to human dignity and democratic decision-making, or should it vary depending on the closeness of the connection? What about other principles like legal equality or the right to factual, and not merely legal, equality? It might be said at this point that the measurement of the abstract weight of principles according to the triadic scale clearly depends on the ideology of the judge. An individualistic judge will give the highest abstract weight to liberty, while a communitarian judge might give the greatest weight to the common good. The judge should solve the case according to the best moral argument, but sometimes it is not easy to know which the best moral argument is. Thus, the right answer is that there is no right answer.

c. The reliability of the premises Some limits to rationality are also observable on what concerns the determination of the reliability of the empirical assumptions relating to the importance of principles. The importance can be said to depend on its efficiency, speed, probability, reach and duration. The limits of rationality are related to several factors. First, it is difficulty to determine the reliability of the empirical assumptions from all these perspectives. The empirical knowledge of the judge is limited. Sometimes he does not know the right value of each one of these variables. Second, the combination of these variables is a highly complex affair. What should be the reliability of an empirical assumption whose little efficiency is plausible $(\frac{1}{2})$, its high speed is not evidently false $(\frac{1}{4})$, its high probability is reliable (1), its great reach is plausible $(\frac{1}{2})$ and its long duration is reliable (1)? And, correlatively, will this reliability be greater, if the same variables have the same values but in a different order?

This is what explains that, at the end of the day, Alexy limits himself to consider the reliability of the empirical assumptions as such. However, there could be also an epistemological problem concerning the reliability of the normative premises that determine the variation and abstract weight of a principle. This leads opens up the "normative epistemic discretion"[26] of the Parliament and other public decision-making powers. This requires clarifying whether the relevant normative premises are reliable, plausible or not evidently false. If we distinguish the reliability of the empirical premises (*REIPiC* and *RESPjC*) from the reliability of the normative premises concerning the importance of principles in the case at hand (*RNIPiC* and *RNSPjC*) and their abstract weight (*RNWPiA* and *RNWPjA*), we have an extended definition of reliability as follows:

$$RPiC = REIPiC \cdot (RNIPiC \cdot RNWPiA)$$
$$RPjC = RESPjC \cdot (RNSPjC \cdot RNWPjA)$$

IV. CONCLUSION

I have tried to show that the weight formula should not be regarded as algorithmic procedure which produces the right one answer in all cases. On the contrary, there are diverse rationality limits that leave a margin of discretion to judges. In that regard, his ideology matters and plays an important role. This does not impair the analytical value of the weight formula. Despite its limits, the weight formula provides a clear argumentative structure that helps clarifying the different relevant variables when balancing conflicting principles. Therefore, it renders explicit all the elements the judge should take into account, and all decisions that need be justified.

NOTES

1 See Robert Alexy, "On the structure of legal principles," 13 (2000) *Ratio Juris*, pp. 294–304.
2 Robert Alexy, *A Theory of Constitutional Rights*, Oxford: Oxford University Press, 2002a.

[3] On the concept of balancing, see: Carlos Bernal Pulido, *El principio de proporcionalidad y los derechos fundamentales*, Madrid: Centro de Estudios Políticos y Constitucionales, 2003, pp. 757ff.

[4] See Alexy, *supra*, fn. 2, p. 47.

[5] Ibid., pp. 52ff.

[6] Ibid., p. 102.

[7] Ibid., p. 401.

[8] Following the notation of Alexy, we will symbolize the degree of variation or non-satisfaction of the first principle in the case as *IPiC* and the importance in the satisfaction of the second principle in the case, as *SPjC*. See Ibid., p. 406.

[9] Following the notation of Alexy, we will symbolize the abstract weight of the first principle as *WPiA* and the abstract weight of the second principle as *WPjA*.

[10] Ibid., p. 408. See also Robert Alexy, "Die Gewichtsformel," in Joachim Jickeli, Peter Kreutz and Dieter Reuter (eds.), *Gedächtnisschrift für Jürgen Sonnenschein*, Berlin: De Gruyter, 2003b, pp. 771–792.

[11] See Ibid., pp. 789ff.

[12] Robert Alexy, "On Balancing and Subsumption. A Structural Comparison," 16 (2003c) *Ratio Juris*, 433–449, at pp. 433ff.

[13] On the burdens of argumentation, see Bernal Pulido, *supra*, fn. 3, pp. 789ff.

[14] Alexy, *supra*, fn. 2, pp. 384ff.

[15] Ibid., p. 385.

[16] Ibid., pp. 410 ff.

[17] Cf. BVerfGE 30, 296 (316).

[18] Ibid., p. 402.

[19] Ibid.

[20] Ibid.

[21] John Rawls, *Political Liberalism*, New York: Columbia University Press, 1993.

[22] See Bernal Pulido, *supra*, fn. 3, p. 760.

[23] An analogous observation could be made when considering the concept of person from a different standpoint, more precisely, as a citizen, the dignity of which requires the protection of social rights.

[24] See Bernal Pulido, *supra*, fn. 3, p. 763.

[25] Ibid., pp. 760, 770 and 772.

[26] See Alexy, *supra*, fn. 2, p. 420.

PART III

SUBSTANTIVE ISSUES

MATTIAS KUMM

6. WHO'S AFRAID OF THE TOTAL CONSTITUTION?

I. INTRODUCTION: FROM THE TOTAL STATE TO THE TOTAL CONSTITUTION?

In 1931 Carl Schmitt published an article titled "The Turn to the Total State."[1] The total state that Schmitt describes is not yet a totalitarian state. Germany is still a liberal democracy and the Weimar Constitution is still the supreme law of the land. But the total state Schmitt describes is a state in which the traditional lines between a sphere in which the private law society governs itself and the public domain (properly the sphere of state intervention) have been undermined. According to Schmitt the pluralistic forces of civil society have captured the state and made it an instrument to serve their purposes. *Everything is up for grabs politically*. It is a state of political mobilization and deep ideological conflict, reflected in the plurality of deeply divided political parties in parliament. Three features of the total state illustrate the total prevalence of politics over law.

First, the idea of an autonomous domain of private law as an integral part of an apolitical state-free sphere had collapsed. The belief in a civil society that organizes itself by means of private law, the content of which is defined by apolitical legal experts, no longer resonated. Private law, too, had become the object of self-conscious broad-based political struggle. Private law was wrested from the legal priesthood and became a mundane object of regulatory intervention. The frame of mind of scholarly mandarins who conceived of private law in natural law, historicist or conceptual terms, or alternatively conceived "the" code as the authoritative embodiment of legal rationality was replaced by legal conceptions according to which private law was also the proper subject of political choice. In such a context, the regulatory state, featuring a "motorized legislator" and an increasingly powerful executive branch which responded in a flexible manner to eventual crisis, was in full swing. Governments had already enacted competition laws prohibiting cartels and trusts, laws limiting freedom of contract to legislatively determine minimum wages and maximum hours, and more generally legislatively shape the employer-employee relationship. More radical proposals concerning the

A. J. Menéndez and E. O. Eriksen (eds.), Arguing Fundamental Rights, 113–138.

transformation of the economy were on the table. All this occurred in the context of a severe economic crisis and heated ideological disagreement about the basic terms of social cooperation.

Second, like it was the case in most parliamentary democracies in the first half of the twentieth century, the Weimar constitution did not contain any judicially enforceable fundamental rights. The constitution, for all practical purposes, established only the procedure that determined what was to count as judicially enforceable law. The long list of substantive fundamental rights that adorned the Weimar constitution were not judicially enforceable. Courts were regarded as unsuitable institutions to make the political judgments necessary to give meaning to the abstract principles it contained (in the drafting process of the Weimar constitution the U.S. experience with the Supreme Court was cited as a reason *not* have fundamental rights be judicially enforced, given that court's hostile attitude towards economic and social reforms in the late nineteenth and early twentieth century).

Third, the constitution and the parliamentary process itself were not protected by either an aura of reverence and legitimacy or the prohibition of amending those provisions guaranteeing its basic democratic structure. Instead the Weimar constitution, Schmitt observed, was widely thought of as a value neutral technical procedural device. Its legitimacy was believed to lie in the very fact that it established a legal order and provided for legal procedures, not in the fact that it established a specific kind of order – a parliamentary democracy. By the early 1930s an increasing number of groups did not regard the parliamentary system as the institutional embodiment of a shared ideal of procedural fairness, but merely as a *modus vivendi*: Something to accept for so long as they lack the political clout to replace it with something more favorable, some form of nationalistically inspired monarchical or authoritarian government perhaps, or a fascist or communist dictatorship. Since 1930, the parties in support of the Weimar constitution ("Systemparteien" – "parties of the system") no longer held a parliamentary majority.[2]

The relationship between law and politics in contemporary Germany is in important ways the mirror image of Weimar. Under the guardianship of the Federal Constitutional Court (hereinafter FCC) the German Basic Law has (hereafter, BL), over the course of the second half of the twentieth century, developed to become what Carl Schmitt might well have referred to as a total constitution. If a total state is a state in which everything is up for grabs politically, a total constitutional state inverts the relationship between law and politics in important respects. The constitution serves as a guide and imposes substantive constraints on the resolution of any and every political question. The legislative parliamentary state is transformed in a constitutional juristocracy.[3]

First a total constitution immunizes itself against the possibilities of radical political change by entrenching its basic structural features – fundamental rights, democracy and the rule of law among them – precluding their abolition by way of constitutional amendment.[4] The constitution furthermore clarifies that it is not a neutral procedural order, but one that is able to identify its enemies and authorize their effective political neutralization: Political parties, for example, can be prohibited if instrumental in the fight against the liberal democratic constitutional order (Article 21 II BL); moreover, the individual right to participate in the political process can be withdrawn under similar circumstances (Article 18 BL).

Second, a total constitution provides the constitutional resources to constitutionalize all political and legal conflicts – it constrains and guides their resolution in the name of fundamental rights. By means of its fundamental rights provisions a total constitution provides the general normative standards – even if stated in terms of abstract principle – for the resolution of all legal and political conflicts that occur within its jurisdiction. It also gives a Constitutional Court the jurisdiction to pronounce itself on what constitutional justice requires, if called upon by persons whose interests are at stake. A total constitution functions as a kind of juridical genome (Ernst Forsthoff untranslatably called it "ein juristisches Weltenei"): It establishes a general normative program for choices to be made by public authorities *vis à vis* individuals. It commits public authorities to either intervene or abstain from intervention, and guides public authorities with regard to the appropriate means of intervention. Democratic politics, executive decision-making and ordinary judicial decision-making become constitutional implementation, subject to the supervision of the Constitutional Court. The total constitution transforms a parliamentary legislative state into a juristocracy.

In a total constitution, fundamental rights not only establish a comprehensive system of defenses of the individual against potential excesses of the state. Instead, a key function of fundamental rights is to provide the basis for claims against public authorities to intervene on behalf of rights-claimants in response to threats from third parties. These third parties can be terrorists threatening to kill a hostage,[5] nuclear power plant operators imposing dangers on neighboring residents,[6] creditor banks enforcing a contract against a debtor,[7] employers firing an employee or landlords threatening to evict a tenant. The public authorities to whom these claims are addressed can be the legislature (for not having enacted the appropriate protective legislation), the executive (for not taking the appropriate protective measures) or the judiciary (for not interpreting the law in the appropriately protective way). If the politicization of the relationship between private individuals is a feature of the total state, the constitutionalization of that relationship is a defining feature of the total constitution.

Drawing on the work of Robert Alexy[8], the following will provide a brief account of the basic *structural* interpretative choices that have made fundamental rights the basic instrument for the constitutionalization of politics in Germany (II). These choices will then be assessed with a particular focus on the implications of the constitutionalization of private law – the background laws of contracts and torts at the heart of both the great continental codes and the common law. Here the claim is that the doctrine of indirect effect achieves practically the same result as a constitutional provision that explicitly makes individual persons addressees of fundamental rights provisions. It leads to the constitutionalization of private law (III). The following section will provide a critical assessment. It will conclude that those who lament the constitutionalization of private law may be making the same mistake as Schmitt who lamented the politicization of private law. Both are guided by mistaken ideas about the nature of private law as it relates to politics and fundamental rights respectively. The chapter argues that there are no specific features of private law that suggest there is something particularly problematic about the constitutionalization of private law or the recognition of the individual as addressee of fundamental rights norms. There is no justification for exempting private law decisions by legislators and courts from the kind of constitutional review that all other acts of public authorities are subjected to in Germany (IV). The final section very briefly provides a historical perspective on contemporary rights practice and suggests that the loaded formula of a "total constitution" as applied to the constitution of the Federal Republic of Germany is as inappropriate as the formula of a "total state" was inappropriate to refer to the struggling Weimar Republic. If a formula is desirable to describe the commitment of a constitution to an expansive conception of fundamental rights that includes the constitutionalization of private law it would be more appropriately referred to as "complete constitutional justice."

II. THE STRUCTURE OF RIGHTS AND THE DOMAIN OF CONSTITUTIONAL JUSTICE

A. *The Scope of Negative Rights: Liberty, Equality and Proportionality*

The German constitution, as interpreted by the FCC, guarantees rights to specific liberties, such as freedom of expression and freedom of religion, along with rights against certain forms of discrimination, such as that on grounds of sex or race. It also grants a general right to liberty and a general right to equality. This has radical implications for the understanding of fundamental rights and the role of constitutional courts in reviewing acts of public authorities. Every act of legislation that restricts an individual from doing what she pleases as well as any legislative classification requires constitutional justification of the sort described above. The domain of constitutional justice and, institutionally, the domain of judicial control of public authorities, are thus radically expanded. In the following I will briefly describe the choices the FCC has made focusing on the general right to liberty.[9]

Article 2 Sect. 1 of Basic Law states:

> Every person has the right to the free development of their personality, to the extent that they do not infringe on the rights of others or offend against the constitutional order or public morals.

Compare this to the text of the fifth and fourteenth Amendment of the U.S. Constitution which in the relevant passage states:

> No person … shall be deprived of liberty … without due process of law.

When confronted with texts of this kind two questions present themselves. The first focuses on the scope of the right. How narrowly or how broadly should it be conceived? What is meant by the free development of personality? What is meant by liberty? The second focuses on the broad or narrow understanding of the constitutional limitations of such a right. The texts mention "the rights of others, offenses against the constitutional order or public morals" and "due process of law" respectively. What does this mean for the purposes of articulating a judicially administrable test for acts by public authorities that is subject to constitutional litigation?

In constitutional practice there are two competing approaches to choices of this kind.

The first is to define both the scope of the right and the limitations narrowly. This is generally the approach taken by the U.S. Supreme Court. The U.S. Supreme Court insists that only particularly qualified liberty interests, liberty interests that are deemed to be sufficiently fundamental, enjoy meaningful protection under the Due Process Clause. When an interest is deemed to be sufficiently fundamental, the limitations that apply are narrow too. They are narrow in the sense that the requirements that must be fulfilled to infringe a protected interest are demanding. Only "compelling interests" are sufficient to justify infringements of the right. The "compelling interest" test loads the dice in favour of the protected right and raises the bar for justifying infringements when compared to the requirements of proportionality. A measure may be proportional, but not meet the "compelling interest" test.

The FCC has taken a different approach. Both the scope and the limitations of fundamental rights have been given an expansive interpretation. First, the court was quick to dismiss narrow conceptions of the "free development of personality" that limited the scope of the right to "expressions of true human nature as understood in western culture" as was suggested by influential commentaries.[10] Instead, the FCC opted for an interpretation that the right guaranteeing the free development of the personality should be read as guaranteeing general freedom of action understood as the right to do or not to do as one pleases.[11] This means that the scope of a general right to liberty encompasses such mundane things as the *prima facie* right to ride horses in public woods[12] or feeding pigeons in public squares.[13] If public authorities prohibit such actions they would infringe the general right to liberty.

As a corollary to the wide scope of the right, the court has embraced a broad interpretation of the limits of the right. Any infringement of the right is justified if it follows appropriate legal procedures and is not disproportionate. The triad of requirements stipulated by Article 2 Sect.1 (rights of others, constitutional order, and public morals) in the jurisprudence of the court translate into the requirements of legality and proportionality. This is a move that has been characteristic of the interpretative approach that courts have taken to rights limits. The proportionality test is at the center of most of the human rights jurisprudence not just in Germany. The proportionality test, generally consists of four subtests. A measure infringing a constitutionally protected interest has to be (1) enacted for a legitimate purpose (2) has to actually further that legitimate purpose (3) it must be necessary (a measure is necessary if no equally effective but less intrusive measure is available) and it must be (4) proportional in a narrow sense (the benefits of infringing the protected interests must be greater than the loss incurred with regard to the infringed interest). It is important to point out that even though the substantive limit of proportionality is broad, it does have bite. It is not adequately compared to the analysis – or lack of it – that generally characterizes the application of the "rational basis" test in cases involving liberty interests that are not deemed fundamental by the U.S. Supreme Court.[14]

There are three characteristic features of rights reasoning as practiced by the FCC. First, practically any action taken by the state is open to challenge on constitutional grounds. Any such action will distinguish between persons in some respect, therefore raising equality concerns. And most actions are likely to infringe on someone's liberty interest. Second, even though fundamental rights are virtually always at stake whenever the state acts, they cannot be regarded as trumps in any meaningful sense. More specifically, the fact that a right holder has a *prima facie* right does not imply that he holds a position that gives him any kind of priority over countervailing considerations of policy. An infringement of the scope of a right merely serves as a trigger to initiate an assessment of whether the infringement is justified. But the fact that rights are not trumps in this sense does not mean that they provide no effective protection. Even without such priority, constitutional practice in Germany clearly illustrates how rights are formidable weapons. The third characteristic feature of rights reasoning is the flip side of the second. Since comparatively little is decided by acknowledging that a measure infringes a right, the focus of rights adjudication is generally on the *reasons* that justify the infringement. Furthermore, the four-prong structure of proportionality analysis provides little more than a structure which functions as a checklist for the individually necessary and collectively sufficient conditions that determine whether the reasons that can be marshaled to justify an infringement of a right are good reasons under the circumstances. Assessing the justification for rights infringements is, at least in many cases where the constitution provides no specific further guidance, largely an exercise of general practical reasoning without many of the constraining features that otherwise characterizes legal reasoning. Rights reasoning under this model, then, shares important structural features with rational policy assessment.[15]

B. *From Negative Rights to Positive Rights: The Idea of Protective Duties*

The discussion so far has focused on fundamental rights in their classic liberal understanding as defensive rights against the state. An important question is whether and to what extent fundamental rights also establish rights to positive state action. In terms of text and legislative history the Basic Law is primarily oriented towards defensive rights. Except for the right of mothers to the protection and support of society,[16] the text of the constitution does not contain references to any entitlements. There is a reference to the duty of all state power to protect human dignity[17] as well as a clause postulating that the Federal Republic of Germany is a social state[18], but that is the extent of it. Yet there is a rich jurisprudence on various entitlements ranging from duties of the state to protect the individual from third parties, entitlements concerning the provision of certain procedures and organizations as well as social rights. How is that possible?

The key lies in an early judgment of the court concerning a private law dispute between individuals. In *Lüth*[19] the central issue was whether fundamental rights merely apply as defensive rights against the state or whether they also have horizontal effect and apply to the relationship between individuals.[20] In that judgment the court held for the first time what would become a standard mantra: that "fundamental rights are not just defensive rights of the individual against the state, but embody an objective order of values, which applies to all areas of the law … and which provides guidelines and impulses for the legislature, administration and judiciary."[21] Fundamental rights norms "radiate" into all areas of the legal system. Freedom of expression, for example, is not just a right of an individual against the state, but a value or principle that gives impulses and provides guidelines to all areas of the law to which it is relevant. As such it has implications for questions such as whether an individual can recover civil damages against another for having been subjected to derogatory remarks[22] and other private law norms. The idea that constitutional principles radiate to affect the rights and duties of all actors within the jurisdiction is the basis not just for an expansion of the court's rights jurisprudence to private law cases. It is also the basis for establishing individual rights to positive actions by the state.

As far as the scope of fundamental rights is concerned, the consequences of the "radiation thesis" have been enormous. First, the court insisted that fundamental rights required the institutionalization of certain procedures and forms of organization. These ranged from specific court and administrative procedures to complex statutory intervention to secure freedom of broadcasting and establish a television broadcasting system that is free from state control and pluralistic. Second, the door was opened to claims in which the state was required to take specific action to protect individuals adequately from acts of third parties.[23] The claims the FCC has been asked to adjudicate upon range from demands to the state to tighten up the standards of nuclear reactor safety to adequately protect the rights holder from dangers of a nuclear power plant[24] to claims that the state is under a constitutional duty to comply with terrorist kidnappers demands and free certain prisoners in order to protect the life of the kidnapped victim threatened by the terrorist kidnappers.[25] But the best-known and most consequential case concerning protective rights involves the issue of abortion. Under the Basic Law the issue did not come to the court as a challenge to criminal sanctions by a woman invoking a right to choose. Instead the minority faction brought the case after the parliamentary majority enacted a law that decriminalized certain kinds of abortions. The partly successful claim made by the minority faction was that the state was under a constitutional duty to criminalize abortion to a greater extent in order to effectively protect the right to life of the unborn.[26] Finally, the radiation thesis also provided the grounds for the development of a jurisprudence concerning social rights.[27] These rights are all linked to help sustain the necessary preconditions for the meaningful realization of liberties. The court has in fact recognized a right to minimal subsistence. It has even come close to recognizing the right to choose a profession as a basis for the duty of the state to create a sufficient number of university spaces at universities for anyone qualified to study her subject of choice.[28]

III. CONSTITUTIONALIZING PRIVATE LAW: HOW "INDIRECT EFFECT" IS LIKE "DIRECT EFFECT"

But does any of this support the claim that the German constitution in effect constitutionalizes relationships, between private individuals? After all the

German Basic Law provides that "basic rights shall be binding for the legislative, executive and judicial powers."[29] Generally, the fundamental rights guaranteed by the Basic Law are not addressed to individuals. Individuals may not rely on them against one another in private litigation directly. Fundamental rights are in play in private litigation only *indirectly* as duties of the respective public authorities, and in particular the civil courts, to respect fundamental rights in the legislation and interpretation of private law. This is the core point of the doctrine of "indirect horizontal effect" of fundamental rights (the so-called "mittelbare Drittwirkung").

The practical difference between indirect and direct effect, however, is negligeable. It concerns merely the formal construction of the legal issue and has no implications whatsoever for questions relating to substantive outcomes or institutional competence. Not only is private law in Germany already fully constitutionalized. If, in a surprise move, the constitutional legislator were to amend the constitution and explicitly determine that fundamental rights are also applicable to relationships between individuals, *this would change practically nothing*. There would be a difference in the way complaints could be framed. Instead of bringing to court public authorities, that are currently the addressees of complaints, the plaintiff could simply sue some other private party. (It goes without saying that the act under judicial review would then be the private act, rather than the act of public authorities which in a way upheld the private act. But this change in the legal construction of the issue would have no implications whatsoever either substantively with regard to outcomes, or institutionally with regard to the jurisdiction of the Constitutional Court. The following examples serve to illustrate this point.

A hypothetical to begin with: A, a consumer in dire financial straights, contracts with a credit card company C. The card he signs up for is advertised as offering high credit limits, no questions asked, and 0% interest for the first 6 months. The standard contract then establishes that after six months interest goes up to 35% p.a. After running up the maximum amount of debt possible, A pays back the original amount borrowed over a number of years but refuses to pay the interest claimed by the credit card company on the ground that it is ridiculously high. After having verified that A is actually able to pay, C decides to sue A for the remaining interest.

The question to be focused on here is not who would prevail or the details of the existing consumer protection law, but how the issue would be framed and how fundamental rights could enter the dispute. To begin with this seems to be a straightforward private law contract case that does not involve fundamental rights at all. Substantively what is at issue is on the one hand freedom of contract, and on the other hand, the protection of the weak contractual party against usurious interest rates. The standard justifications for holding someone to a contract – promise, legitimate expectations and general considerations of economic efficiency – goes only so far and allow for some degree of protection of the weak contractual party. According to received wisdom, there is a line to be drawn somewhere. This line-drawing exercise can be legally structured in different ways. The German code contains a general clause that invalidates contracts that "violate the good customs of the community."[30] One of the purposes of this clause has traditionally been to provide some degree of protection to the weak party in certain cases.[31] In the United States, the doctrine of unconscionability has been developed as part of the common law by courts[32] and has a comparable function. In both cases the line-drawing exercise is effectively managed by ordinary courts balancing the relevant concerns and, over time, articulating more specific rules that determine the conditions under which a contract will not be judicially enforced. Today it is just as likely that this balance is struck by the legislator. Beyond the general code or the common law some consumer protection legislation exists in most jurisdictions. In Europe national consumer protection legislation, complemented by EU directives, addresses such issues as standard contracts, installment sales contracts or consumer credit contracts.[33] To the extent that this legislation consists of specific and clear easily administrable rules, the line-drawing exercises between freedom of contract and consumer protection are no longer undertaken by the respective courts, but by legislators.

A. *How then Could Fundamental Rights Come Into the Picture?*

Imagine first, counterfactually, that fundamental rights were directly horizontally effective in Germany and could be enforced by ordinary courts. The (hypothetical) newly amended Constitution would state: "Fundamental rights are addressed to all public authorities and, where applicable, individuals." Everything else, let us assume, would remain the same. In Germany both C and A would be able to plausibly invoke fundamental rights to support their claims. The German Constitution as interpreted by the FCC recognizes an all-encompassing right to liberty understood as the freedom of a person to do or to abstain from doing whatever he pleases.[34] The violation of any liberty interest potentially raises constitutional questions and requires constitutional justification.[35] C could file a constitutional tort action claiming that A, by refusing to recognize the validity of the contract, was bridging C's freedom to enter into legally binding contracts, guaranteed under the German constitution as an instantiation of a general right to liberty.[36] But C's fundamental rights would not be the only constitutional rights at play. A could also invoke a general right to liberty as a defense against C. C effectively wants to force A to part with his money against his will, only because A, under dire financial circumstances, happened to have accepted an unfavorable contract. With two competing liberty interests at stake, both of them enjoying constitutional protection *prima facie*, the conflict would be resolved by balancing the respective reasons that can be marshaled in support of each of these liberty interests against one another. Proportionality analysis is at the center of the jurisprudence of the Court not just when the issue is a conflict between an individual right and some collective good, but also when rights collide. Such a balance would require the assessment of a rich set of considerations including, but not limited to, (1) the degree of hardship A was under and the effect this had on his making a promise; (2) the reliance interests of C in circumstances where he is charging interest rates outrageously above market rates, (3) whether ex-post relief provided by the Court actually improves the position of the weak party, as well as (4) general efficiency considerations. Whatever the right way of thinking about these kinds of conflicts of interests in a contractual setting may be, that is also the right way to sort out the constitutional issue. Of course it is generally the function of ordinary private law legislation, precedent and doctrine to strike the right balance between relevant concerns. No doubt the court would engage and give some degree of deference to ordinary legislation, precedent and doctrine that exist on these kinds of matters. But constitutional law as the supreme law of the land would trump ordinary legislation, precedent or doctrine as the ultimate ground for the resolution of private law disputes. Existing private law would only be applicable, if and to the extent it could be shown to strike a reasonable balance between competing fundamental rights as assessed by the relevant court charged with the adjudication of fundamental rights issues applying proportionality analysis.

Why waste all this time on the counterfactual hypothetical that fundamental rights have horizontal effect? In the real world any German civil court would immediately dismiss the idea of A violating C's fundamental rights or vice versa. The fundamental rights enshrined in the German constitution are generally addressed to public authorities, and not to private individuals. Individuals, the civil judge would claim, citing well established doctrine, are not the addressees of fundamental rights norms, but public authorities are. Fundamental rights are the rights of individuals against the state and not the rights of individuals against one another. Fundamental rights do not have direct horizontal effect.

But this does not mean that fundamental rights would be fully out of the picture. Of course fundamental rights are rights only against public authorities, but ever since the *Lüth* case[37] it is generally accepted that civil courts, as the interpreters of private law are a public authority that is bound by fundamental rights. C may not have a constitutional right of freedom of contract that he can invoke against A directly, nor can A invoke a liberty right against

C directly. Instead of a constitutional tort, C's or A's cause of action for a claim against the other must always be grounded in private law, an action for specific performance or damages, for example, grounded in the law of contracts or torts. But in the course of private litigation C and A can invoke fundamental rights *against the court*. Indeed, C could insist that the court, within its jurisdiction, is required to do what is in its power to ensure that freedom of contract as guaranteed as an instantiation of the general Constitutional Right to liberty, is adequately protected. In that sense the basic value commitments underlying fundamental rights "radiate" throughout the legal order, so to establish requirements for the *interpretation* of private law by civil courts. The court must therefore interpret private law, including the general clauses of the code, in a way that conforms to the basic value commitments expressed in the constitution. This means that private law is to be interpreted so as to reflect an adequate balance between the respective constitutional interests at stake.[38] In this case it means interpreting the "good customs" exception of the code narrowly because of the centrality of freedom of contract as an instantiation of the general right to liberty. On its turn, A could claim that, though C is right to insist that the courts are under a constitutional duty to interpret private law so as to reflect an adequate balance of the respective constitutional interests at play, he is wrong about what that entails. In light of A's constitutional right to liberty, and the undue burden it would inflict on him, were he held to the unfair terms of this contract, the court has no choice but to interpret the "good customs" clause as invalidating the contract. Failure to interpret the law in such a way will result in the plaintiff appealing the decision and, if ultimately necessary, filing a complaint with the Constitutional Court claiming that his fundamental rights have been bridged by the judgment of this court and any other civil court inclined to affirm it.

It turns out, then, that under the guise of interpreting the general clause, the judge is required to make *exactly* the kind of determination that he would have been required to make, were he directly to adjudicate competing fundamental rights claims. As the court interprets the general clauses of the code it has to strike a balance between the relevant competing considerations. And just as would be the case if a doctrine of horizontal direct effect was recognized, the door is opened to the involvement of the Constitutional Court as the final arbiter of private law claims: When a party feels that a civil court has failed to take fundamental rights adequately into account while interpreting civil law, a complaint can be filed before the Constitutional Court.

But what if the law is clear and there is nothing to interpret? Does the practical difference between direct and indirect horizontal effect not lie in civil courts having to worry about constitutional concerns only when making *interpretative* choices? Can civil courts ignore constitutional concerns, when provisions of private law are clear? Imagine the civil judge discovers that she is not required to interpret a highly abstract clause in the code in light of highly indeterminate constitutional principles to dispose of the case. Instead, let us assume that the legislature has established a clear rule applicable to cases such as these. It turns out that the national parliament has enacted special legislation establishing a safe harbor provision determining that no credit card contract charging 35% p.a. interest or less could be challenged as in violation of good customs, or as otherwise unfair. The judge breathes a sigh of relief, glad that the difficult task of striking the balance between the competing concerns has been assumed by the legislature, leaving no textual ambiguity, no difficult task of interpretation, and it seems, no constitutional issue to be resolved.

But of course the judge has no reason to breath a sigh of relief. If the constitutional interests of one party cannot appropriately be taken into account in anything plausibly deemed as interpretation of the law, given its clarity and specificity, this does not settle all constitutional issues once and for all. The question remains whether the law – here the safe harbor clause for credit card contracts charging 35% or less – is unconstitutional because it does not adequately take into account one side's constitutional liberty interests, by holding him to unfair burdensome contracts.

Even though fundamental rights are not directly horizontally effective, constitutional liberty interests are relevant not merely for the *interpretation* of the law by courts. They need also to be taken into account by *legislatures* enacting private law. Legislative acts, including legislative acts on issues of private law, are undisputedly acts by public authorities and thus subject to fundamental rights constraints. A civil court judge would be violating a constitutional right to liberty if he enforces a law that unduly infringes on the constitutional right to liberty. It may well be that the civil judge has no competence to simply set aside legislation on the grounds that it is unconstitutional. If the statute was enacted *after* the constitution entered into force, the Constitutional Court may enjoy a monopoly of constitutional review.[39] But if the law does not meet constitutional standards, the civil court is required to make a reference to the Constitutional Court so that the latter reviews its constitutionality, and eventually declares the law to be unconstitutional. If the ordinary court refuses to bring the case to the attention of the Constitutional Court, the party whose rights may be violated as a result may file a constitutional complaint with the Constitutional Court on the ground that both the ruling (of the ordinary court) and the legislative act underlying it violate its constitutional right to liberty.

The doctrine of indirect horizontal effect, then, seems to have much the same consequences, substantively and institutionally, as the embrace of the doctrine of direct horizontal effect. In both cases civil courts are required to interpret existing private law so that it is compatible with constitutional requirements. Where that is impossible because of a clear legislative rule, the court must make a reference to the Constitutional Court to determine the constitutional issue and, if necessary, declare private law legislation to be invalid. Furthermore, in both cases a party to a private dispute could file a constitutional complaint claiming that his fundamental rights were violated and requiring the Constitutional Court to review either the constitutionality of private law legislation or of the interpretation provided by civil courts.

It is true that the FCC in fact accords a significant degree of deference to legislatures and civil courts.[40] Only when civil courts have either failed completely to address relevant constitutional concerns or seriously misassessed their significance, does the Constitutional Court determine that a civil court has violated a party's constitutional right.[41] The private law legislator too enjoys considerable discretion in balancing the relevant policy considerations.[42] But that does not mean that constitutional review of civil court's decisions and legislatures enacting private law has no bite. In Germany contracts in the area of creditor/debtor law,[43] landlord/tenant law[44] and prenuptials[45] have been reshaped by the jurisprudence of the Constitutional Court, and not just the law of defamation[46] or labor law.[47] But more importantly, *the degree of discretion accorded to various constitutional actors has nothing to do with the distinction between direct and indirect horizontal effect*. The court accords discretion for reasons relating to the division of labor between various institutions and perhaps pragmatic considerations relating to docket management. There is nothing inherent in the doctrine of indirect horizontal effect that requires discretion to be granted and there is nothing inherent in the doctrine of direct horizontal effect that prohibits it.

The FCC plausibly insists that fundamental rights do not apply directly to individuals, but only to state actors. And it is right to do so, given a constitutional text that suggests legal issues should be constructed by focusing on the relevant action by public authorities.[48] But the court recognizes that there is always action by public authorities when the state establishes norms that govern the relationship between individuals, and when a court interprets and enforces such rules. If the state action requirement is always met, the question arises whether there is any difference whatsoever between construing an indirect horizontal effect grounded in a "radiating effect" of fundamental rights norms, and acknowledging that fundamental rights bind individuals. The counterfactual example used here illustrates that nothing would change outcome-wise, or even institutionally, if the court simply acknowledged that fundamental rights bind private individuals. Indirect horizontal effect and direct horizontal effect are merely alternative, but in all relevant respects equivalent, constructions of a legal problem.[49]

A constitutional amendment explicitly establishing that fundamental rights have direct horizontal effect in Germany would neither impede the liberty of economic actors, nor would it provide additional protection for weaker economic parties. As a matter of substantive law and institutional division of labor, it would simply leave things as they are. With the comprehensive scope of constitutionally protected interests in Germany, private law in Germany is already applied constitutional law.

IV. WHO'S AFRAID OF THE TOTAL CONSTITUTION?

Conceptually then, private law, like any law in Germany, qualifies as a branch of applied constitutional law. If, like in Germany, the Constitutional Court recognizes a general constitutional right to liberty and private law is about determining the limits of the respective spheres of liberty in the interest of all, then private law is in effect *applied* constitutional law. It implements the constitution with regard to the concerns it addresses. It works out the implications of a general commitment to a constitutional right to liberty that citizens enjoy equally in their relationship with each other. As the hypothetical illustrates, civil litigation could always be conceived as litigation about competing fundamental rights, the specific contours of which private law attempts to define.

This may be a conclusion that even many constitutional lawyers may find unfamiliar and are hesitant to support, even when they embrace the doctrine of the indirect horizontal effect and support the generally expansive understanding of rights that informs the jurisprudence of the FCC. But for private jurists the challenge is greater still. Such an understanding of private law goes against some deeply engrained ideas that still resonate in the intellectual universe that German scholars inhabit. Could it be that the German Civil Code (BGB), originally thought of as the crowning glory of the legal system and the final product of centuries of civil law scholarship, is merely an implementing device of constitutional commitments? To private lawyers, hardly so. Indeed, the idea that private law is merely worked out constitutional law is deeply insulting to private law jurists, who, since the heyday of nineteenth century codification debates have suffered a comparative status loss in the academy as public law increasingly took center stage in the twentieth century. It also seems incompatible with the idea that there is a deep significance to the distinction between public and private law. In Germany you are either a public lawyer or a private lawyer. A constitutional lawyer may also teach administrative law or even municipal law. He will never teach contracts or torts. Conversely a private lawyer will never teach constitutional law. The idea that a public lawyer, using concepts and categories of a public law discipline, could intrude on the domain of civilian expertise, borders on the preposterous. The conceptual issue is therefore deeply linked to turf battles over traditional disciplinary boundaries and prestige. It is not surprising to see it heavily resisted by private law jurists.

But besides habits of thought, disciplinary turf wars and losses of prestige, are there not also good reasons for the resistance by the private law establishment to the constitutionalization of private law? Are there serious concerns that need to be addressed? Beyond inevitable complaints about the court having decided one or the other case in the wrong way, is there anything deeply problematic about current practice?

There are at least two levels on which the basic structure of current practice can be challenged. The first, more general question concerns the expansive scope of rights under the German constitution generally[50] and questions the wisdom of an understanding of rights that is so expansive that it effectively constitutionalizes every political and legal issue. On this level some have questioned whether the court should recognize a general right to liberty or only more restrictive, specifically defined liberty rights.[51] Others question the use of a balancing test and propose that the court should restrict itself to the assessment of the legitimate purposes, suitability and necessity of a measure.[52] Still we find those who have questioned the wisdom of the idea of protective duties and advocate the return to a conception of negative rights.[53] Restrictions of this kind would significantly limit the role of the Constitutional Court, both concerning its supervision of private law and its supervision of public authorities more generally. These questions can't be addressed here.

Instead, the discussion in the remaining of this chapter will focus on a second, more specific critique. It goes that whatever the best general conception of rights may be, *private law is special* and should be exempted from constitutional scrutiny. There are two main arguments against using fundamental rights as a standard to review private law, one substantive, the other one institutional.

Substantively speaking, the claim is that there is something important about the distinction between private and public law that is directly connected to the question whether fundamental rights should also have an impact upon private law through the doctrine of indirect effect. Private law regulates relationships between private parties, whereas public law establishes the normative framework of relationships between the state *and* private individuals. Fundamental rights ought to be conceived primarily as rights of the individual against the state, whereas private law applies to relationships between individuals.[54] Not recognizing that difference will result in undermining private autonomy. To illustrate the point: Freedom of speech paradigmatically protects against legal sanctioning of speech because of its content. If a Professor aggressively advocates tax reforms aimed at establishing a flat tax, he may well be advocating a position that is unjust and harmful to the weaker segments of society. But any legal sanctions against someone advocating such reforms would be clearly unconstitutional and in violation of his right to freedom of speech. He could not, for example, be forced to give up his chair at a public university. But even if public authorities may not legally discriminate against or sanction a person based on his political views, individuals, to some extent, may. Private law in a liberal society rightly allows individuals to discriminate against and sanction those whose political views they dislike in many social contexts. No freedom of expression claim ought to be successful against a person who invites only those who share his political views to a private dinner party and excludes the advocate of a flat tax. The general point is that in liberal societies individuals may often do things and act on reasons that public authorities may not act upon. The idea of private autonomy, the central organizing principle of private law, expresses this idea. When individuals are effectively constrained by fundamental rights in the same way as public authorities, this undermines the core of private autonomy. The total constitution, it seems, is a twin of the total state. Both of them fail to appropriately respect private autonomy.

This argument is unpersuasive. It is true that the liberal commitment to private autonomy implies that individuals may often do things that public authorities may not. The dinner host who excludes flat tax adherents does not violate their right to freedom of expression. But it does not follow that fundamental rights are not appropriately applied to private law and the relationships between private individuals. Within the context of proportionality analysis the relevant difference in the context of application can be taken into account. All that follows is that fundamental rights guarantees have to be applied to conflicts between private individuals in a manner that takes into account the principle of private autonomy. The task of the Constitutional Court engaged in fundamental rights adjudication is to assess whether the decision a civil law court or by the private law legislator concerning the relationship between individuals did in fact take into account the competing constitutional principles at stake and struck a reasonable balance between them.

Substantively, then, the application of fundamental rights to private law and the relationship between individuals does not prejudice any particular outcome about where the relevant lines ought to be drawn. It neither implies a libertarian nor a social-democratic bias and is certainly not totalitarian. Fundamental rights provide a way of structuring legal debates about private law. The structure provided – and the open-ended proportionality requirement in particular – is open to the whole range of considerations that legal actors deem relevant for the design and interpretation of good, just and efficient private law rules that give the right weight to the principle of private autonomy. If existing private law strikes the right balance between the relevant concerns, then existing private law rules can be justified within the fundamental rights paradigm. If certain parts of contract law are either too libertarian, or too paternalistically focused on consumer protection, then fundamental rights provide a structure within which this criticism can be legally articulated in a reasoned form. The only bias inherent in such a construction of the legal issue, is that it requires *reasoned reconstruction* of any tradition-guilded baselines and conceptual and doctrinal structures that lawyers are socialised into. If such a reconstruction succeeds, then the tradition can proudly claim to stand on more solid grounds than mere habit of thought. Else, if the tradition fails the test, then that should be celebrated as a further step in the overcoming of deeply inculcated prejudices.

But perhaps the problem of applying fundamental rights to private law is not primarily substantial, but *institutional*. If private law at its heart is about balancing competing fundamental rights, the FCC – whose jurisdiction is limited to constitutional questions – has general jurisdiction to review decisions by civil courts, to assess whether civil courts or legislators have struck the balance between the respective liberty interests correctly. The constitutional court would have the jurisdiction to effectively review all civil court decisions and all private law legislation on the ground that civil courts or private law legislators may have struck the balance between the competing liberty interests in the wrong way and thus violated the plaintiffs or the defendant's constitutional right.

This is significant because civil law and administrative courts are still organized as different branches of the judiciary in Germany. Whereas no-one disputes that decisions by public law courts can be reviewed by the constitutional court on fundamental rights grounds, the role of the constitutional court as a supervisory institution over the civil courts depends on how fundamental rights affect civil litigation in civil court. As was demonstrated above, the doctrine of indirect horizontal effect effectively subjects civil courts to the same constitutional discipline as public law courts. Under the current jurisprudence of the FCC the proud civil courts are mere equals of public law courts, with both of them subject to supervision by the Constitutional Court.

The institutional question that must be posed is whether is adequate for the Constitutional Court to review the decisions of civil courts. What reasons are there to assume that a review by a non-specialized court that is not attuned to the intricate doctrinal points of private law doctrine and private law culture is likely to lead to better decisions? What is wrong with leaving private law questions to be decided by private law courts supervised by the private law professional establishment and their critical commentary?

Here there are two answers. The first turns the question around. What grounds are there to assume that it is appropriate for the FCC to review the decisions reached by *other* specialized courts, administrative agencies or legislators, generally aided by capable research services, but not the decisions of the civil courts? Both Finance Courts which decide tax cases and administrative law courts which adjudicate upon administrative law cases have special expertise, and yet their decisions are subject to constitutional review. If this is so, what reasons are there to exclude from constitutional review decisions by civil courts or the "private law" legislator? What exactly is so special about the expertise of private law courts and lawyers to justify exemption from constitutional scrutiny?

Of course the FCC respects the idea of special expertise and comparative institutional advantage of other institutional actors, and it also upholds a division of labor between itself and other courts. But respecting an adequate division of labor does not amount to an abdication of jurisdiction to review legal issues on constitutional grounds. Such abdication would undermine the very clear and explicit commitment of the German Basic Law to fundamental rights review by a Constitutional Court. Instead the FCC tends to accord some degree of *deference* to other institutional actors, when it reviews their decisions. In private law cases, for example, it intervenes only when civil courts or private law legislatures have either failed completely to address relevant constitutional concerns or seriously misassessed their significance.[55] The Court insists that it is not a general "super-court" of final appeals (*Superrevisionsinstanz*) that will review the finer points of private law. It will only review cases that raise serious constitutional issues.

It is true, of course, that if the development of the civil law is subject to the guardianship of the Constitutional Court, different elites, socialized into different sets of assumptions and sensibilities will determine what the content of private law should be. A shift from the civil to the Constitutional Court as final arbiters of private law claims may also affect outcomes. But to the extent that there is such a shift, it need not necessarily reflect the lack of expertise of public jurists and institutions relating to the specific requirements of private law. Such a shift could also indicate that private law as a discipline – occupied with its internally generated occupations and distinctions – has failed to be responsive to legitimate concerns and societal shifts that a more generally focused Constitutional Court is responsive to.

V. CONCLUSION: THE TOTAL CONSTITUTION OR COMPLETE CONSTITUTIONAL JUSTICE?

When Carl Schmitt first described "the total state" he was not describing the totalitarian state that he would later enthusiastically endorse. One must remember that he was citizen of a Republic in which the traditional baselines that had informed the thinking and writing of mainstream private law jurists during much of the Wilhelmine era were subjected to political challenges and were redefined as a result of legislative intervention. Under such circumstances, the reference to the total state must be constructed as a critical description of a struggling liberal Republic in which the domain of private law had become a realm of political disagreement and legislative intervention. Schmitt did *not* deny that there was a line to be drawn between the public and the private sphere, between "the state" and "society." He would claim that, but only at a later and dark time in his career. Rather, his original intention was to challenge the way that the line between public and private was drawn by the Civil Code, as interpreted by the civil courts, and to propose alternative ways of conceptualizing the distinction between public and private, so that it could be possible to strike a fairer balance between the interests of employers and employees in their contractual relationships. These line-drawing exercises were no longer thought of as appropriately within the competence of a professional elite of private law experts, but instead the task of a responsive and socially aware democratic legislator. The delimitation of spheres of liberty between equally ranked persons was recharacterised as a political question, and no longer regarded as a conceptual craft expertly performed by those schooled in the doctrines and history of private law.

In an important sense modern liberal constitutional democracies remain very much the "total state" that Schmitt polemically describes. Private law remains subject to political debate and regulation, and any idea of a concrete "natural" baseline remains discredited, even if highly abstract principles, such as private autonomy, enjoy general recognition. The "motorized legislator" continues his work. As Habermas puts it, the scope and limits of private autonomy need to be determined by citizens exercising their public autonomy in a democratic process.[56] Politically contested rules relating to topics as diverse as the rules relating to the work place, consumer protection laws, and product liability rules continue to redefine the scope and limits of private autonomy. One central feature of what Schmitt describes as the "total state" is simply the demise of a very particular and historically contingent understanding of a self-governing private law society.

But if the politicization of private law within liberal constitutional democracies is one defining feature of private law in the last century (and arguably in the present one), the constitutional assessment of political choices by a constitutional court is a central feature law in post-war liberal constitutional democracies. If the production of private law rules, either by the legislator or by courts interpreting abstract, ambiguous or indeterminate legal provisions involves a political choice, and political choices are subject to fundamental rights review using proportionality analysis, why should decisions relating to private law be excluded from fundamental rights scrutiny? In a world where decisions on private law rules are conceived as political questions, and the political process is constitutionally guided and constrained by fundamental rights, private law is necessarily constitutionalized. In Schmittian parlance one might say that the total state is complemented by the total constitution.

But a Schmittian vocabulary should not bias the assessment of such an expansive conception of fundamental rights. When the government acts in a way that detrimentally affects the interests of an individual, it is not outrageous to require that those acts have to be justifiable in terms that take that individual seriously. The language of rights provides the vocabulary to assess whether that burden of justification can be met in a particular case. All you need in order to make a rights claim is an interest that is sufficient to establish a duty of public institutions to take account of it.[57] The Constitutional Court, applying Alexy's conception of rights as principles helps assess whether the commitment to take individuals seriously was honored by public institutions in a particular case.

There is nothing new in understanding rights in this expansive way. In the French revolutionary tradition rights were understood in just this way. The 1789 *Déclaration des droits de l'Homme et du citoyen* establishes that everyone has an equal right to liberty.[58] The task of the political process in a true republic is to delimitate the respective spheres of liberty between individuals in a way that takes them seriously as equals, and does so in a way that best furthers the general interest. In this respect there is no difference between private law and public law. Courts, of course, had no role to play whatsoever in the exercise of determining the specific content of what it means to be free and equal in specific circumstances. Courts, discredited as part of the *ancien régime* – the *noblesse de robe* – were to function as the mouthpiece of the law as enacted by the legislature and nothing more. Even today, France is something of an outlier in its choice of institutions in charge of protecting rights. True, the *Conseil Constitutionnel* engages in rights analysis not very different from the one described by Alexy.[59] Still, it is significant that is labeled a Council, not a Court. This corresponds to its status a veto player or negative legislature. It can preclude statutes from entering into force by holding them to be in bridge of rights, but does not hear claims brought by other than "public persons." In such a sense, it can be properly said to remain a "Council" to the legislature.

But in the post-war era, the institutional choice of the vast majority of countries has been different. Haunted by traumatic experiences of national-socialist, fascist-authoritarian, communist or simply racist rule, many European countries have made a transition to a reasonably inclusive liberal constitutional democracy and have decided not only to constitutionalize rights, but also to give a standing before the Constitutional Court to those whose non-trivial interests are affected by the actions of public authorities, allowing them to challenge the constitutionality of such actions (and norms). Such institutional design implies that constitutional courts assess whether, under the circumstances, the acts of public authorities, even of elected legislatures, can reasonably be justified.

It goes without saying that the primary task of delimitating the respective spheres of liberty is left to the legislatures. Legislatures remain the authors of the laws in liberal constitutional democracies. But courts have assumed an important editorial function[60] as veto players. Courts, as guardians and subsidiary enforcers of human and fundamental rights, serve as institutions that provide a forum in which legislatures can be held accountable at the behest of affected individuals claiming that their legitimate interests have not been taken seriously. The point of fundamental rights is to focus and structure the court's assessment of whether the actions of public institutions are reasonable under the circumstances. The language of rights has provided the authorization for courts to play a role in protecting the legitimate interests of individuals, thereby helping to hold public institutions to standards of good government in liberal constitutional democracies worldwide.

There are good reasons to mistrust Schmitt's vocabulary and the not so subtle normative biases it reflects. After all, Schmitt's concept of the "total state" was unable to distinguish the Weimar Republic from the National Socialist state.[61] The idea of a total constitution is similarly unhelpful. Of course much more would need to be said both to gain a deeper understanding of the moral significance of having courts playing the role that they do in constitutional democracies such as Germany. This is not the place to rehash debates about the legitimacy of constitutional courts reviewing democratically enacted legislation[62] or to discuss the various doctrines of deference courts use to respond to and mitigate these concerns.[63] But what Schmitt might call a total constitution may turn out to be nothing more than a constitution committed to complete constitutional justice.

NOTES

[1] Carl Schmitt, "Die Wendung zum Totalen Staat" in *Positionen und Begriffe im Kampf mit Weimar-Genf-Versailles 1929–39*, Berlin: Duncker and Humblot, 1994 (3rd edn.), at pp. 166–178.

[2] Not surprisingly the leading jurists writing during this time share two traits that distinguish them from the giants of nineteenth century legal scholarship. They tend to be public law rather than private law jurists, often focusing on constitutional and legal theory. And many of them (Schmitt, Kelsen and the American Realists among them) insisted that, to

paraphrase Clausewitz, law is the continuation of politics by other means. Schmitt develops a constitutional theory featuring the concept of the political at its core. Kelsen, on the other hand, develops a theory of legal science committed to eliminate the political (empirical and moral) from its scope to rescue the idea of scholarly detachment. Yet, as Kelsen himself rightly points out, the Pure Theory of Law, in all its modernist abstraction and formality, reveals *legal practice* as political all the way down. It is exactly the formal structure and substantive emptiness of Kelsen's theory that makes it a potent weapon for exposing the prevalence of politics in legal practice and legal scholarship: If a pure theory of law can say nothing about how a law should be interpreted, then every act of legal interpretation is revealed to be a political act, not a requirement of law. The achievements of the American Realists, finally, are not limited to legal theory: After denouncing all forms of "legal formalism" most quickly assume practical roles either as litigators or administrators in newly created administrative agencies, using law as a pragmatic instrument to bring about social change – law becomes a political tool in the hand of social engineers working through the legislative, administrative or judicial process.

3 The term constitutional juristocracy was introduced to contemporary debates by Carl Schmitt's probably most brilliant late pupil, Ernest Wolfgang Böckenförde, see for example his *Recht, Staat, Freiheit,* Frankfurt: Suhrkamp, 2000. In the Anglo-American world the term has been popularized by Ran Hirschl, *Towards Juristocracy*, Cambridge (MA): Harvard University Press, 2004.

4 See Article 79 Sect. I Basic Law referring to Article 20 Sect. 1 Basic Law.

5 BVerfGE 46, 160 (*Schleyer*).

6 BVerfGE 49, 89 and BVerfGE 53, 30.

7 BVerfGE 89, 214.

8 Robert Alexy, *A Theory of Constitutional Rights,* Oxford: Oxford University Press, 2002a (hereinafter TCR).

9 TCR chapter 7, pp. 223–259. Alexy deals with a general right to equality in chapter 8, pp. 260–287.

10 For further references see TCR, p. 224 fn. 5.

11 BVerfGE 6, 32 (*Elfes*).

12 BVerfGE 39, 1, BVerfGE 88, 203.

13 BVerfGE 54, 143 (147).

14 See Lawrence Tribe, *American Constitutional Law*, vol. 1, New York: Foundation Press, 2000 (3rd edn.), at p. 1362.

15 That does not mean that the two are identical. There are at least four differences between substantive rights analysis and general policy assessments. First, courts are not faced with generating and evaluating competing policy proposals, but merely assess whether the choices made by other institutional actors are justified. Second, they only assess the merit of these policy decisions in so far they affect the scope of a right. Third, specific constitutional rules concerning limits to fundamental rights or judicial precedent establishing rules that fix conditional relations of precedence frequently exist. Fourth, proportionality analysis leaves space for deference to be accorded to other institutional actors. The European Court of Human Rights refers to this as the "margin of appreciation."

16 Article 6 Sect. 4 Basic Law.

17 Article 1 Basic Law.

18 Article 20 Sect. 1 Basic Law.

19 BVerfGE 7, 198 (*Lüth*).

20 For Alexy's discussion of horizontal effect see TCR, pp. 351–365.

[21] BVerfGE 39, 1 (41).
[22] BVerfGE 86, 1.
[23] TCR, pp. 300–314.
[24] BVerfGE 30, 59 and BVerfGE 49, 89.
[25] BVerfGE 46, 160.
[26] BVerfGE 39, 1 and BVerfGE 88, 203.
[27] TCR, pp. 334–348.
[28] TCR, p. 292.
[29] Article 1 § 3 Basic Law.
[30] See § 138 Sect. 1 BGB: "Ein Rechtsgeschäft, dass gegen die guten Sitten verstöst ist nichtig."
[31] For a discussion of usury see the comment by Helmut Heinrichs in Otto Palandt, *Bürgerliches Gesetzbuch*, Munich: Beck, 2003 (62nd edn.), para. 242, recital 65–76.
[32] See *Campbell Soup Co. v Wentz* [1948] 172 F.2d 80, 3rd Circ. See also Section 2–302 Uniform Commercial Code, available at http://www.law.cornell.edu/ucc/search/display.html?terms = unconscionable&url = /ucc/2/Article2.htm#s2–302: "If the courts as a matter of law finds a contract or any clause of the contract to have been unconscionable at the time it was made, the court may refuse to enforce the contract, or it may enforce the remainder of the contract without the unconscionable clause, or it may so limit the application of any unconscionable clauses as to avoid any unconscionable result."
[33] See for example EC Directive 13/93 addressing consumer protection against unfair practices. See also the Swedish Law 112 of 1971, on Consumer Contract Terms (Lag 1971:112 om avtalsvillkor i konsumentförhållanden), which indeed was pioneering on what concerns unfair contractual terms. Such law was amended by laws 1512 and 1513 of 1994 to adapt it to the abovementioned Council Directive 93/13/EEC of 5 April 1993 on Unfair Terms in Consumer Contracts, Official Journal L 95 , of 21.4.1993, pp. 29–34.
[34] Article 2 I Basic Law states: "Everyone has the right to freely develop their personality." The Federal Constitutional Court (hereinafter FCC) has interpreted this right expansively to mean that everyone is free to do or to abstain from doing whatever they like. See BVerfGE 6, 32 (*Elfes*).
[35] This has propelled the Constitutional Court into the role of assessing, for example, the constitutionality of restrictions on feeding pidgeons in public squares (see BVerfGE 54, 263) or riding horses through public woods (BVerfGE 80, 137).
[36] In Ireland such constitutional tort actions are recognized. See J. Walsh in the 1973 case of *Meskell v Coras Iompair Eireann*: "If a person has suffered damage by virtue of a breach of a constitutional right … , that person has the right to seek redress against the person or persons who infringed that rights." [1973] I.R. 121, 133. Article 40.3.1. of the Irish Constitution states that "the state guarantees in its laws to respect, and, so far as practicable, by its laws to defend and vindicate the personal rights of citizens."
[37] BVerfGE 7, 198 *Lüth* (1958).
[38] See BVerfGE 30, 173 *Mephisto* (1971).
[39] This is the case in many European countries, which follow the "Kelsenian" model of constitutional review, according to which it is *the* Constitutional Court that has the monopoly for setting aside legislation on constitutional grounds. This is the case in Germany.
[40] For a general theory of deference, see Marius Raabe, *Grundrechte und Erkenntnis*, Baden-Baden: Nomos, 1998.
[41] For an account of the relationship between the Constitutional Court and the branches of the judiciary see Christian Starck, "Verfassungsgerichtsbarkeit und Fachgerichte," 51 (1996) *Juristenzeitung*, pp. 1033–1042.
[42] See Johannes Hager, "Grundrechte im Privatrecht," 49 (1994) *Juristenzeitung*, pp. 374–376.

[43] See BVerfGE 89, p. 214 (holding unconstitutional a civil court decision that failed to interpret the general clauses of the code as invalidating a contract between a bank and income- and assetless relatives of bank debtors to assume high liability risks in case the debtor default on the grounds that it failed to take into account the parties constitutional liberty interests).

[44] See BVerfGE 89, p. 1 (holding that both the interests of both the landlord and the tenant in a property are deemed property rights under the constitution that need to be taken into account in the interpretation of landlord-tenant law).

[45] BVerfGE 103, p. 89 (limiting the kind of prenuptials that can be enforced against the structurally weaker party).

[46] BVerfGe 7, p. 198 (*Lüth*). It is certainly not an accurate description of the German case law at this point that the Constitutional Court's forays into private law disputes is mainly focused on freedom of speech issues as they relate to defamation law. For such a claim see Basil M. Markesinis, "Privacy, Freedom of Expression and the Horizontal Effect of the Human Rights Bill: Lessons from Germany," 115 (1999) *Law Quarterly Review*, pp. 47–88, at p. 64.

[47] BAG 47 (1984), 363 (Employer fired employee who, as a press operator, refused on grounds of conscience to print books he believed glorified war. The BAG interprets labor law requirement that decisions laying off workers have to be "socially justified" as requiring that weight has to be given to freedom of conscience. Under the circumstances of the case the BAG held in favor of employee).

[48] See Article 1 Sect. 3 Basic Law, *supra* note 2.

[49] See TCR, at p. 351.

[50] For a more general discussion see my "Fundamental rights as Principles: On the Structure and Domain of Constitutional Justice," 2 (2004) *International Journal of Constitutional Law*, pp. 574–596.

[51] See the dissent by Judge Grimm in BVerfGE 6, 32 (*Equestrian* Case).

[52] Bernhard. Schlink, "Der Grundsatz der Verhältnismässigkeit," in Peter Badura and Horst Dreier, *Festschrift 50 Jahre Bundesverfassungsgericht*, vol. 2, Tübingen: Mohr Siebeck, 2001, at p. 445.

[53] Cf. Böckenforde, *supra*, fn. 3.

[54] The debates about what the defining features of private law really are and what makes a dispute a private law dispute is a significant practical issue in Germany, because it determines whether the Administrative Courts or the Civil Courts have jurisdiction to hear the case. Although there are a number of practical rules that are used in practice, a standard treatise describes the issue thus: "The dogmatic attempts to define the distinction between private law and public law have endured now for over a century, without any of the offered theories having gained general acceptance." See Rainer Pitzner and Michael Ronellenfitsch, *Das Assessorexam im Öffentlichen Recht*, Neuwied: Werner Verlag, 1996 (9th edn.), p. 51.

[55] This is the generally accepted doctrine used by the FCC, see for example, BVerfGE 43, 130 (137), BVerfGE 61, 1 (7).

[56] Cf. Jürgen Habermas, "Law and Morality," 8 (1988) *Tanner Lectures on Human Values*, pp. 217–279.

[57] This understanding of the purpose of rights is very similar to that proposed by Joseph Raz, *The Morality of Freedom*, Oxford: Oxford University Press, 1986, pp. 180–192.

[58] Cf. Article 1: "Les hommes naissent et demeurent libres et égaux en droits".

[59] The reasons published by the *Conseil Constitutionnel* are, however, famously cryptic. For a discussion of this phenomenon see Mitch Lasser, *Judicial Deliberations: A Comparative Analysis of Transparency and Legitimacy*, New York: Oxford University Press, 2004.

[60] Phillip Pettit, *Republicanism: A Theory of Freedom and Government*, Oxford: Oxford University Press, 1997 chapter 6.

[61] When Schmitt first wrote *The Total State* he intended to criticize the absorption and capture of the state by the pluralistic forces of civil society. When the vocabulary of the total state was affirmatively embraced by anti-liberals who advocated a totalitarian state, Schmitt distinguished between the total state out of weakness (Weimar) and the authentic total state out of strength, that he would later associate with the National Socialist Movement. See his "Weiterentwicklung des totalen Staates in Deutschland" 9:2 (1933) *Europäische Revue*, pp. 65–70 and "Totaler Feind, totaler Krieg, totaler Staate" in *supra*, fn. 1, at p. 268.

[62] The debate about the appropriateness of endowing courts with the authority to strike down acts of the legislature remains alive. See on the one hand Ronald Dworkin, "Introduction: The Moral Reading and the Majoritarian Premise" in *Freedom's Law*, Cambridge (MA): Harvard University Press, 1996, pp.1–46 and on the other hand Jeremy Waldron, "The Constitutional Conception of Democracy", in *Law and Disagreement*, Oxford: Oxford University Press, 1999, pp. 282–312.

[63] See TCR, pp. 394–425. See also David Dyzenhaus, *The Unity of Public Law* Oxford: Hart Publishers, 2004, pp. 6–19 (focusing on the Canadian case); Yukati Arai-Takahashi, *The Margin of Appreciation Doctrine and the Principle of Proportionality in the Jurisprudence of the European Court of Human Rights*, Antwerp and New York: Intersentia, 2002.

PART IV

APPLIED PERSPECTIVES

JULIAN RIVERS

7. FUNDAMENTAL RIGHTS IN THE UK HUMAN RIGHTS ACT

I. INTRODUCTION[1]

In my introduction to the English edition of *A Theory of Constitutional Rights*,[2] I try to show how the *Theory* can be used to clarify fundamental rights reasoning in one common law jurisdiction: the English legal system. That argument is controversial, because there are several points at which an orthodox, or traditional, understanding of the British Constitution departs from the picture I paint. The principal purpose of this chapter is to give a brief overview of the impact of the Human Rights Act on the British legal systems, and then to see what recent case-law is doing in a number of areas relevant to the *Theory*. The question here is whether there are signs of convergence, or indeed of divergence. At the same time I want to raise more openly than was appropriate in the book some of the difficulties that still remain. The root of these difficulties lies in the claim of the *Theory* to be a structural theory, which ought to be neutral (or at least, neutral to a high degree) on matters of substance, procedure and institutional design. The problem is that the *Theory* may be more implicated in a particular conception of substantive rights, legal procedures and institutional structures than at first sight appears. To put it crudely, it may be more German than it looks.[3] If the argument for transferability to other systems is to succeed, one has to show that this more particular conception of the Constitution is still general enough to apply more widely within liberal democracies.

II. OVERVIEW OF THE HUMAN RIGHTS ACT 1998

The United Kingdom was one of the first European states to ratify the European Convention on Human Rights, which came into force in 1953. In 1966 the UK permitted its own citizens to bring actions against the Government for violation of the Convention, but it was not until the late 1970s that this possibility for legal action entered the mainstream legal consciousness. The official position of the Government was always that Convention rights were in substance, if not in legal form, protected under the British legal systems. There was no need to incorporate the Convention as

A. J. Menéndez and E. O. Eriksen (eds.), Arguing Fundamental Rights, 141–154.

a "Bill of Rights" or "Charter of Rights." But as the UK started to lose cases in Strasbourg, the calls for transformation into domestic law increased, even among the senior judiciary.[4]

At the same time a process of informal transformation was taking place. The British constitution is dualistic in respect of treaty law, although customary international law is taken to be part of the common law. This means that strictly speaking a treaty which has not been transformed by Act of Parliament into domestic law may only be used as an aid to interpretation if the related legislation is ambiguous. But some judges from the 1980s onwards were willing to make more frequent reference to the Convention, sometimes in developing the common law, sometimes in interpreting statute. Nevertheless, the overall impact remained small. Research carried out in 1997 found that in the 316 reported cases between July 1975 and July 1996 in which the Convention was cited, in only 16 could the Convention be said to have affected the judgment, in the sense that the decision might well have been different had it not been taken into account.[5]

The Human Rights Act 1998,[6] which "gives further effect" to Convention rights in the British legal systems, was part of a set of constitutional measures proposed by the Labour party in its manifesto for the 1997 election. This programme of constitutional reform also included regional government for Scotland and Wales, freedom of information, reform of Parliament and the electoral process. In many ways the Human Rights Act has proved to be the least problematic politically. It was passed very early on, with relatively few changes to the original proposals, and came into force on 2 October 2000.[7]

From a formalistic perspective, the Human Rights Act should have had no impact at all. It simply provides a more effective remedy for violations of Convention rights. Even allowing for the dynamic nature of the Strasbourg case-law, one might have thought that almost 50 years after ratification, and 30 years after the right of individual petition, a reasonable degree of convergence would have been achieved. But of course this view ignores the inevitable creation of a complex body of domestic human rights law. Again, the statistics, crude though they may be, give some idea of what has happened. In 18 months (from 2 October 2000 to end March 2002) the Human Rights Act was cited in 431 cases in the higher courts and affected the outcome, reasoning or procedure in 318. A claim based on the Act was upheld in 94 of these cases.[8]

As far as the impact on substantive law is concerned, some effect has been felt in all areas, and in respect of all rights, The right to life, freedom of expression, the right to privacy, property rights, have all been given greater effect. But with the possible exception of privacy the impact has been sporadic and peripheral. The one clear exception to this is in the area of legal processes, criminal, private and administrative. Here the Human Rights Act has had a major impact, with most of the reported cases being based on Article 6 of the European Convention.

III. THE CONSTITUTIONAL STATUS OF CONVENTION RIGHTS

The doctrine of parliamentary supremacy is traditionally understood to mean that there is no higher law-making body than Parliament, and that the latest expression of the will of Parliament prevails.[9] Even if Parliament states its intention of binding its successors, a future Parliament could ignore those restrictions. On this account, the British Constitution is purely procedural and highly minimal. It makes it impossible to argue that any particular legislation is constitutional in the formal sense of being superior in hierarchy to ordinary law. If human rights were enacted as ordinary law in an Act of Parliament, they would override all previous legislation, but could not be used to restrict any future legislation. Rather, if there were an inconsistency, the future incompatible legislation would override the Human Rights Act under the doctrine of implied repeal.

In the light of this, the Human Rights Act is very clever, because it does not enact Convention rights as ordinary law. Instead it imposes a strong obligation on the courts to interpret all law compatibly with Convention rights, and makes it unlawful for any public body to act incompatibly with Convention rights.[10] The only public body to be treated differently is Parliament itself in its law-making capacity.[11] If it is not possible to interpret primary legislation compatibly with Convention rights, the courts are empowered to issue a formal declaration of incompatibility.[12] This does not affect the validity of the legislation, but it empowers the Government to make amending legislation under delegated legislative authority.[13] In fact, the issuing of a declaration of incompatibility has been rare – courts have made declarations in about a dozen cases, and most have been overturned on appeal.[14]

The effect of this approach is to protect the Act from the doctrine of implied repeal. Put another way, if Parliament wants to depart from Convention rights it must do so expressly,[15] and that is a weak procedural constraint which makes it legitimate to argue that Convention rights are constitutional in a formal sense. It connects the Act to the common law doctrine of fundamental rights, which states that certain rights are so important that legislation which appears to violate or limit them will be interpreted narrowly.[16] It also connects the Act to European law, which will take precedence over an incompatible Act of Parliament, unless the Act expressly departs from European law.[17]

This argument now has some judicial support. In *Thoburn v Sunderland City Council*,[18] the Divisional Court had to consider the legality of the prosecution of traders for using imperial weights and measures rather than metric ones. The use of metric measures was required by European directive, which had been implemented in 1994 using delegated legislative authority under the European Communities Act 1972 to amend primary legislation, namely the Weights and Measures Act 1985. It was argued that the Weights and Measures Act 1985 had impliedly restricted the power to pass delegated legislation in this field under the (earlier) European Communities Act 1972. But Laws LJ held the prosecution lawful, because the European Communities Act 1972 was a constitutional statute which could not be repealed impliedly. Parliament had indeed delegated the power to amend primary legislation to ensure conformity with European law, and had done so in a way which protected the power from subsequent implied limitation or repeal. The judge argued that this "protected status" for certain statutes (and for the powers granted by those statutes) was granted by the common law, and extended to include other constitutional legislation such as the Human Rights Act 1998.

The judgment is not unproblematic, particularly in its failure to take account of the constitutional principle against excessive delegation of legislative power, but the broader question in this context is whether it is necessary for Alexy's theory that there be formally recognised fundamental rights at all. In order for any adjudication to be rational, the judge is required to reconstruct the reasons underlying the rule to be interpreted and applied. If we take the constitution to be the level of competing principle beyond the express rules, resolutions of which explain and justify those rules, then a constitution (of sorts) is an implicit component of all law. Even if one is prepared to take the further step of asserting an inherent judicial duty to refuse to recognise grossly unjust legislation as law, this still only preserves a minimum core of human rights.[19] But this means that the decision to protect certain concrete rights with a special status and by special procedures – that is, the decision to create positive fundamental rights binding on the legislature – is an institutional choice, not a rationally necessary component of a system of law.

A. Types of Convention Rights

Convention rights are primarily defensive rights, and the European Court has been slow to derive protective, procedural and social rights from the Convention. By contrast, the English courts seem to be going down this path quite happily – one might even say thoughtlessly.

The notion that the state has a *protective duty* in respect of Convention rights is very well established. For example, in *R (Javed) v SS for the Home Department*[20] judicial review was granted of the Home Secretary's designation of Pakistan as a safe country of origin for the purposes of asylum law. There was clear evidence that the Pakistani applicants for asylum had been tortured and would be likely to be tortured again. The Government had a duty under Article 3 (freedom from torture) to protect the applicants. To take another example, in *R (A) v Lord Saville of Newdigate*,[21] soldiers who were to give oral evidence at a public inquiry in Londonderry, Northern Ireland, wanted to give their evidence elsewhere, on the grounds that they might be identified and their lives would then be at risk from Irish terrorists. Judicial review was granted on the grounds that the judge chairing the inquiry had failed to take sufficient account of the threat posed to the soldiers' lives.

Procedural rights – in the sense of procedural protection rendered necessary by a substantive right – are not quite so well established. I have already indicated that the specific procedural rights of the Convention are having a big impact. But one of the curiosities of the Human Rights Act is that it omits Article 13 European Convention, the right to an effective remedy, from the list of recognised Convention rights. This may in time drive the judiciary to be more creative in finding procedural aspects of substantive rights. Fascinating in this respect is the judgment of the Court of Appeal in *R (Amin) v SS Home Department*.[22] This case arose from the deaths in custody of two prisoners. One had been killed by a fellow prisoner, who had subsequently been convicted of murder; the other was a suicide. In the case of the former, there had been an internal prison inquiry, but the family wanted a formal public inquiry. In the second case, the jury at the inquest wanted to bring in a verdict of neglect on the part of the prison authorities, but the coroner refused as this would tend to determine a question of criminal liability (although the jury's findings of fact were later published in part by the judge in judicial review proceedings). The Court of Appeal found that there was a procedural duty on the state to investigate any death in which there might be a breach of its (protective) duty under Article 2 European Convention. This duty to investigate would certainly arise whenever a prisoner died in custody. On the facts, the procedural duty had been satisfied.

The European Court of Human Rights has only recognised *social rights in the field of legal aid*,[23] although the right to equality may give rise to other *derivative social rights*.[24] The English courts are already beginning to be more adventurous. In *Lee v Leeds City Council*,[25] the Court of Appeal found no general obligation on public housing authorities under the Human Rights Act to remedy condensation, mildew and mould caused by design defects in the houses they let, but the court stated that in a more serious case, there might well be a breach of Article 8. In *R (Bernard) v Enfield LBC*,[26] the judge held that the failure by a local authority to provide suitable accommodation for a severely disabled woman and her family was a breach of her rights under Article 8 European Convention (right to respect for private and family life, home and correspondence) and awarded her damages as a result. So it seems that in extreme cases, the English courts are going to find social rights under the Convention as well.

Why do the English courts seem to be having so few problems with protective, procedural and social rights? The explanation may well lie, firstly, in the closer relationship between fundamental rights and ordinary law. It is quite normal for ordinary legislation to grant such rights, so the judiciary have few problems in deriving these rights from human rights. Secondly, since the constitution is "decentralised" the same courts interpret fundamental rights as decide ordinary civil and criminal cases. One suspects that the political and economic difficulties, and the potential impact on legislative discretion, surrounding constitutional entitlements do not even register.

B. *Horizontal Effect*

Closely related to the notion of protective rights is, of course, the question of horizontal effect. Here there has been much confusion and doctrinal uncertainty. Most lawyers still assume that Convention rights are really directed towards the actions of legislative and executive bodies. The Human Rights Act states that only public authorities or other bodies in the exercise of public functions act unlawfully if they breach Convention rights. But once it is accepted – as the Act does – that *courts* are public authorities – then the potential for indirect horizontal effect is in place. Since the result of indirect horizontal effect is to create new private law rights and obligations, the only significant absence is a procedural one. There is no cause of action against a private body simply for breach of a constitutional right. Even that point is not as extensive as it sounds. Some lawyers have suggested that where any individual benefits financially from a breach of Convention rights, a claim in unjust enrichment (restitution) might lie.[27] So the only significant constraint is the absence of a tortious action for injunction or damages where one private body violates another's rights.[28]

One area in which everyone knew that the courts were going to get to work at an early stage was the right to privacy. English law remedies for breaches of privacy by private individuals (most notably newspapers) tend to be property-related, either requiring trespass or breach of confidential information. But breach of confidence has proved a fertile ground for judicial development. In *Venables v News Group Newspapers*,[29] the President of the Family Division issued injunctions against newspapers to prevent them from revealing information tending to establish the identity of the two young men who as boys had murdered the toddler James Bulger. Indeed, in this case it was not just their privacy that was at threat. Their lives might also be threatened if their identity and whereabouts became known.[30]

Once one accepts that fundamental rights have horizontal effect, then there will often be a clash of rights. One particular clash of rights (privacy and freedom of expression) is regulated by a detailed provision in the Human Rights Act, which requires the court to have particular regard to the importance of freedom of expression.[31] This came to have practical significance in *Douglas v Hello! Ltd. (no. 1)*.[32] The actors Michael Douglas and Catherine Zeta-Jones had sold the picture rights of their wedding to the OK Magazine. In spite of strict security, Hello! managed to obtain pictures which they intended to publish first. Douglas and Zeta-Jones sought injunctions to prevent the breach of their privacy, but these were denied on the grounds that they had consented in principle to having pictures published. Because of the weight to be given to freedom of expression the court held that they were left to their remedy in damages.

However, clear examples of horizontal effect outside of the realm of privacy rights are, as yet, hard to find. A good example of the difficulties can be found in *Wilson v First County Trust Ltd. (no. 2)*.[33] Wilson had borrowed £5,000 on the security of her BMW car. A provision of the Consumer Credit Act 1974 rendered the agreement unenforceable, because the sum of credit was incorrectly stated on the document as £5,250. If the document had been accurate, the loan and reasonable interest could have been recovered, or the security realised, by court order. The Court of Appeal found the provision of the Act to be contrary to Article 6 European Convention, and also a breach of Article 1 First Protocol (right to property), because it deprived the pawnbroker of a trial to determine the extent to which the agreement was enforceable and the right to recover his money to that extent. This is a situation in which a private right exists, but it is only enforceable to a limited extent. The judgment thus treats the problem as if it is a violation by the state of the creditor's (more extensive) rights. But it could better be cast as a constitutional right to a reasonable return on ones loan from the private individual to whom one has lent the money.

In another interesting case, the Court of Appeal held that the liability of lay rectors to repair the chancel of the local parish church was an unjustified tax in breach of the Convention's right to property.[34] The case was cast as turning on the lawfulness of the discretionary act of a public authority (the Parochial Church Council of an Anglican church). The court entirely overlooked the fact that the Church of England has a property right in play here as well, and that by depriving it of this particular form of income it had deprived it of a property right as well. Again, in the *Wilson* case just referred to, the court entirely omitted to consider the property rights of the debtor in the security she had put up.

However, the courts can get all this completely the other way round. In *RSPCA v AG*[35] the charity sought advice on whether it could amend its membership rules to exclude those who were in favour of hunting with dogs. It was worried that it might be acting in breach of the individual member's freedom of expression. Lightman J held that freedom of expression was not affected, but rather that the society's freedom of association was at stake. This gave it the right to associate with whom it pleased and set membership criteria accordingly. While this part of the judgment is clearly right, the part saying that individual freedom of expression is not relevant is as clearly wrong. There is an unrecognised clash of rights which needs resolving.[36] Similarly on 26 June 2003 the House of Lords reversed the judgment of the Court of Appeal in Wallbank's case[37] on the grounds that the church body was not a public body but was merely enforcing a private property right (albeit a problematic one).

There is thus a general concern about the direction horizontal effect seems to be taking in the UK. The courts seem very unwilling to recognise competing rights. In many cases, because the effect of Convention rights is mediated through the actions of a public authority (often, but not always, a court), the rights of the individual bringing the action get privileged over the rights of the person or body whose behaviour is the subject-matter of the action. The risk of this is that private bodies are held to the same standards as public bodies, which can be detrimental to private liberty. On the other hand, where one has a clearly private body in litigation with another private individual, the majority's right of association does not simply have the effect of trumping the individual's right (which may be correct on the facts and most of the time). It seems to have the effect of preventing the individual right from arising in the first place. In short, the assumed model of human rights is still that of the individual against the state, and the David-and-Goliath mentality seems to creep in to horizontal situations as well.

The difficulties English courts are having in this area demonstrate another way in which the *Theory* is substantively laden. If fundamental rights have the horizontal effect that Alexy suggests they do, this presupposes a rich enough content to these rights such that they can capture the morality of interpersonal "private" relationships as well as the classical political morality of protecting the individual from the over-intrusive or discriminating state. I argue that the common law contains the values with which the Convention needs supplementing to do this work. But if that substantive input is ignored, it might seem preferable, as some have suggested, to restrict the horizontal effect of rights. But the response to this is essentially pragmatic: since some degree of horizontal effect has already crept into the English legal system, the only realistic way forward is to expand the doctrine into one capable of doing all the work it needs to.

C. The General Right to Equality

There are two areas of difficulty with the general right to equality: the grounds of equality and its scope. A general right is general in two senses: it covers all possible grounds of discrimination and it applies in respect of every legal interest. By contrast, the legislation of the last 40 years addressing inequality under English law has focused on specific grounds (race and sex) and specific legal interests (principally employment, housing, education, and provision of goods and services).[38] Article 14 European Convention is completely clear that it is general in respect of the grounds of discrimination,[39] but not so in respect of the scope. As regards scope, discrimination must fall "within the ambit" of another Convention right.[40]

Nevertheless, to remain with the problem of scope, the European Court is reading the ambit test increasingly widely. Social security law is now within the scope of the right to property, whether or not benefits are contributory.[41] Housing law and some aspects of employment law (issues of parental leave) are covered on account of Article 8.[42] All forms of religious discrimination seem to be covered by virtue of Article 9.[43] With a little bit of judicial willingness, there are few cases where one could not find oneself within the ambit of a right, a point which makes political opposition to the ratification of Protocol no. 12 to the European Convention increasingly irrelevant.

The English courts are struggling with the general right to equality. In *Ghaidan v Godin-Mendoza*,[44] the Court of Appeal held that for the purposes of inheriting the protection granted by a statutory tenancy, a homosexual partner was living with the tenant "as his or her wife or husband." The argument was that there was no reason for distinguishing between heterosexual cohabiters and homosexual cohabiters. The reason the court gave was that "sexual orientation is now clearly recognised as an impermissible ground of discrimination." The charitable way to read this is to say that the court is recognising sexual orientation as a special class in which the drawing of distinctions requires particularly strong justification. But one suspects that the court is not treating Article 14 as general. All distinctions require justification, and the mere fact that a distinction is drawn does not necessarily mean that it is impermissibly drawn.

The Court of Appeal got completely confused in *R (S) v Chief Constable of South Yorkshire Police*.[45] This was an attempt by two people who had been charged with criminal offences, but who had been subsequently acquitted or had had their case discontinued, to get the police to destroy their fingerprints and DNA samples. The evidence had been lawfully obtained, but the argument was that once the prosecutions had been dropped or failed, there was no reason to keep the personal data in question. In brief, the Court held that retention was a proportionate response to the need to protect the public from crime and that it did not discriminate unlawfully. It is the reasoning in the Article 14 issue that is most worrying. Lord Woolf CJ starts off by saying that discrimination is not permitted on any ground specified in Article 14. This implies that there are grounds covered by Article 14 and grounds not covered. He then quite rightly goes on to argue that there is an objective reason for distinguishing between people who have been charged with a criminal offence (whose samples may be retained) and people who have never been charged (from whom the police have no power to collect samples). He then goes on to ask whether the discrimination is within the categories referred to in Article 14, and finds that it is not, and that it would be highly undesirable if it were, because this would mean that the distinction could not be drawn, and that the only way of solving the problem would be to take samples from everybody, which would be disproportionate. So Lord Woolf CJ's twofold mistake is to think that Article 14 only covers certain types of distinction (say on grounds of race or sex) and then that it bans those distinctions absolutely. Waller LJ makes a different mistake. He thinks that one has to establish the relevant pool within which there is discrimination. He argues that the relevant pool is all people charged with criminal offences, and that since these are all treated the same way, there is no discrimination. On that basis, there could never be any discrimination at all, because the group being discriminated against are all being treated equally badly as each other. Sedley LJ is a bit better. He recognises that within the group of innocent people, those who have been charged or investigated are being treated differently, but this is acceptable because not all innocent people are the same in respect of potential offending. His only mistake here is to assume that in order to find "any other status" for the purposes of Article 14, one needs to have an involuntary and stigmatic status (which he thinks being accused but not convicted is). However, Sedley LJ then goes on to give the other two judges a lesson in indirect discrimination. The problem is that he has treated this situation not as one of indirect discrimination but direct discrimination. Indirect discrimination does arise in the case: convicted people and innocent accused people are being treated in the same way as regards the retention of their samples, when arguably they should be treated differently. But as Sedley LJ goes on to state, the real complaint was that innocent accused people were being treated differently from innocent unaccused people as regards future access by the police to their personal data. For either group the police should have no access to fingerprint and DNA data. And that is a complaint of direct discrimination.

This was a strong Court of Appeal and it completely mangled the structure of general equality rights. It has, as yet, failed to escape the broad structure of traditional English discrimination law, which makes it unlawful to take account of certain fixed characteristics of people in certain contexts.

D. Proportionality

Proportionality contains two threshold requirements (legitimate end and capable means) and two balancing requirements (least intrusive means necessary and benefit of means to outweigh cost to end). There is a tendency in some of the English case-law, as indeed in the judgments of the European Court of Human Rights, to run the two balancing elements together, but thanks to some sound and influential exposition in the leading practitioners' texts, the courts usually are alive to all relevant questions.

The shift to a proportionality test is significant in English administrative law, which has tended to operate a test of unreasonableness, which leaves considerable discretion as to the choice of means in the hands of the executive. One obvious impact of the Human Rights Act has been to open up to challenge executive acts which are authorised in general. So whereas in the past customs officials might have impounded a car used in illegal smuggling, now they may only do so if that is a proportionate response to the particular offence in question. That at any rate was what the Court of Appeal decided in *Lindsay v Commrs of Customs and Excise*.[46]

The big problem is of course the relationship between proportionality and legislative and executive discretion. This is generally phrased in the UK as a question about the "standard of review," which is unhelpful. To assert that the standard of review is always "correctness" is to be understood as asserting that the court must always take every decision itself – and that would lead to judicial supremacism. But if we follow Alexy's theory, there is a sense in which the standard is always correctness, but firstly that there is a range of correct decisions (structural discretion), and secondly that the court may not be best placed to overturn the judgment of another as to what is or is not correct (epistemic discretion).[47]

R (Daly) v Home Secretary[48] was about the extent to which prison authorities could look at legally privileged correspondence. The House of Lords gave a strong judgment indicating an abandonment of traditional approaches to judicial review and in favour of proportionality as we understand it. Since then there has been considerable debate about the extent to which the courts are obliged to establish for themselves the "primary facts" on which administrative decisions are reached. The cases reveal a variable and context-dependent deference to the expertise of the initial decision-taking body. Thus in *R (Wilkinson) v Broadmoor Hospital*, where the inmate (a criminal) was resisting necessary medical treatment, the Court of Appeal insisted on hearing the medical evidence itself.[49] Other cases simply require the courts to ask whether the factual conclusion reached by the primary decision-taker was one which could be supported by the evidence available to it: a form of "plausibility-review."

In his *Postscript*, Alexy suggests that the degree of court involvement turns on the importance of the interest at stake. This is the "Second Law of Balancing" which is proposed as a solution to the problem of epistemic discretion.[50] The Second Law of Balancing presupposes that courts are exemplars of public reason, and that other decision-taking bodies are imperfect substitutes for courts. This is plausible only under two constraints: firstly, that the "other decision-taking body" is a typical majoritarian legislature, and secondly, that fundamental rights are individual legal rights which need protecting from the legislature. Under these conditions, the court is indeed institutionally the better place to determine the dispute. But the more general principle under which competence is assigned within a well-ordered polity must be one which seeks to optimise *institutional correctness*, not necessarily to optimise the involvement of the court. If it is correct that any political value can form the subject-matter of a constitutional principle, it no longer follows that the court is necessarily the best place to determine how competing principles should be weighed. And if a question of fact is best determined by a non-court body, there is no reason for the court to get more involved the more the constitutional right at stake is infringed. On the contrary, if the question of fact really is better decided elsewhere, the courts should be *less willing* to interfere as the stakes rise. For when they do overturn the decision of the primary fact-finder they will be failing to optimise the principle of institutional correctness.

All this suggests that the problem of epistemic discretion, and its associated problem of the standard of review in the context of proportionality, cannot be resolved without a thorough-going institutional theory of law.

IV. CONCLUSION

I concluded my introduction to *A Theory of Constitutional Rights* by drawing on the well-known distinction in comparative law between centralised and decentralised systems of constitutional review.[51] Broadly speaking, Anglo-American legal systems operate decentralised systems of constitutional review, whereby the constitutionality of law may be raised and determined at any level. Continental systems tend to adopt centralised systems, whereby a special court is established to which such questions may be referred. I must confess to preferring the decentralised model, because it takes the constitution seriously as law, which all courts of law must have regard to. Alexy's conclusion that all law is ultimately constitutional is precisely the approach of the common law systems.[52] The big disadvantage of decentralised review is that – at least in an initial period after major new legislation of constitutional significance – there is great diversity of judicial opinion on a whole range of connected matters. I asked at the start of this chapter what evidence there was that Alexy's model fitted the current developments, or what evidence there was that an alternative model was on offer. What we find, I think, is a mixture of convergence and confusion. But no incompatibility. Over time, English legal doctrine will settle down, and even if at some points one can be a bit gloomy, there is every reason to hope that when it settles down it will have the rational structure that Alexy has so masterfully identified.

NOTES

[1] This chapter was first given at a workshop "Constitutional Rights through Discourse: On Alexy's Theory of Constitutional Rights" held under the auspices of ARENA (Advanced Research on the Europeanisation of the Nation-State) in Oslo, 24–26 April 2003. I am grateful to participants for their insightful comments and stimulating discussion.

[2] Oxford: Oxford University Press, 2002, hereafter TCR.

[3] It should be noted that Alexy does not claim universal applicability for the *Theory*, but develops it in the light of the German Constitution. See TCR, pp. 5–10.

[4] Lord Scarman called for incorporation in an essay in 1974, as did Lord Hailsham, Lord Chancellor from 1970–1974 and 1979–1987, in 1978.

[5] Francesca Klug and Claire O'Brien, "The First Two Years of the Human Rights Act" (2002) *Public Law*, pp. 649–662 at fn. 3.

[6] 1998, chapter 42.

[7] Human Rights Act 1998 (Commencement no. 2) Order 2000/1851.

[8] Klug and O'Brien, *supra*, fn. 5, p. 650.

[9] A.V. Dicey, *An Introduction to the Study of the law of the Constitution*, 10th edn. (ed. E. C. S. Wade), London and New York: MacMillan, 1959, at p. 40.

[10] Sections 3 and 6 respectively.

[11] Section 6(3)(b).

[12] Section 4.

[13] Sections 4(6) and 10.

[14] See Klug and O'Brien, *supra*, fn. 5.

[15] Section 19.

[16] For example, *R v Home Secretary ex parte Khawaja* [1984] AC 74 and other cases cited in my Introduction to the *Theory* at p. xiii.

[17] *R v Secretary of State for Transport ex parte Factortame (no. 2)* [1991] 1 AC 603. It is possible that the British judiciary would not even accept an express departure from European Union law in the absence of a politically negotiated agreement to differ, or withdrawal. The point is not likely to arise in practice.

[18] [2002] 3 WLR 247.

[19] Alexy has argued in defence of the Radbruch Formula elsewhere (see *The Argument from Injustice* (tr. Stanley Paulson and Bonnie Litschewski Paulson), Oxford: Oxford University Press, 2002) and my discussion in a common law context in "Gross Statutory Injustice and the Canadian Head Tax Case" in David Dyzenhaus and Mayo Moran (eds.), forthcoming, on the basis of the forum on "Achieving Human Rights in a Multicultural Society: Reparations, Human Rights and the Limits of Law," Faculty of Law, Toronto, 12–13 April 2003.

[20] [2002] QB 129.

[21] [2002] 1 WLR 505.

[22] [2002] 3 WLR 505.

[23] *Airey v Ireland* (9 October 1979) 3 EHRR 592.

[24] For example, *Willis v UK* (2002) 35 EHRR 21.

[25] [2002] 1 WLR 1488.

[26] [2003] HRLR 4.

[27] See the argument in *Wilson v First County Trust Ltd. (no. 2)* [2002] QB 74.

[28] This is the case in Ireland. See my Introduction, TCR, p. xxxvii and fn. 81.

[29] [2001] Fam 430.

[30] This raises an interesting question which cannot be pursued here about protective duties, horizontal effect and causation. Is it better so say that the newspaper has a horizontal protective duty towards the murderers not to publish information revealing their identity and whereabouts, or to say that the state has a vertical protective duty to the murderers to prevent the papers from revealing information which might risk their lives?

[31] Section 12.

[32] [2001] QB 967.

[33] Note 27 above.

[34] *Aston Cantlow and Wilmcote with Billesley Parochial Church Council v Wallbank* 3 WLR 1323.

[35] [2002] 1 WLR 448.

[36] A rule proposing (e.g.) that members should not use cosmetic products tested on animals makes the potential for clashes of rights more obvious.

[37] See fn. 34.

[38] See (e.g.) Race Relations Act 1976.

[39] "or other status" (French; "sans distinction aucune").

[40] The general approach of the court was set out in the *Belgian Linguistic* Case (1968) 1 EHRR 252.

[41] *Wessels-Bergervoet v Netherlands* 4 June 2002.

[42] See *Van Raalte v Netherlands* (1997) 24 EHRR 14.

[43] *Thlimmenos v Greece* (2000) 31 EHRR 15.

[44] [2003] 2 WLR 478.

[45] [2002] 1 WLR 3223.

[46] [2002] 1 WLR 1766.

[47] See the Postscript to TCR, at pp. 388–425.

[48] [2001] 2 WLR 1622.

[49] [2002] 1 WLR 419.

[50] TCR, p. 418.

[51] TCR, pp. l–li.

[52] Interestingly the Human Rights Act compromises slightly, in that the remedy of a declaration of incompatibility is only available in the High Court and above. See section 4(5).

AGUSTÍN JOSÉ MENÉNDEZ

8. SOME ELEMENTS OF A THEORY OF EUROPEAN FUNDAMENTAL RIGHTS

I. INTRODUCTION

This chapter aims at testing whether and to what extent Alexy's *Theory of Constitutional Rights* can be useful in interpreting and applying the fundamental rights provisions of European Union law, and more specifically, the Charter of Fundamental Rights of the European Union.[1] It is here claimed that Alexy's theory is the best analytical tool with which to determine the authoritative sources of European fundamental rights (section II); to systematize and categorise European fundamental rights norms (section III); to solve conflicts between fundamental rights norms, especially between *fundamental rights and economic freedoms* (section IV); to reveal the *rights structure* implicit in the case law of the European Court of Justice (section V).

It is concluded that by applying Alexy's Structural Theory of Fundamental Rights to Union law, we can determine some of the basic elements of a much needed (structural) theory of European fundamental rights.

II. THE VALIDITY OF FUNDAMENTAL RIGHTS IN UNION LAW: BETWEEN THE COMMON CONSTITUTIONAL TRADITIONS AND THE CHARTER OF RIGHTS

§1: This section aims at two objectives, namely (1) to *understand* the validity basis of constitutional norms in Union law; here it is argued that the ultimate source of legal validity in Union law is to be found in what is common to the core constitutional norms of the Member States, and that this *implies* an explicit connection between *European legal validity* and the *critical reconstruction* of what is common to the national constitutions (§§2–5 and 9) and (2) to give an account of the legal validity of the Charter of Fundamental Rights of the European Union; given that it stands as *the* catalogue of fundamental rights of European Union; it is plausible to claim that it has legal force and legal bite, *but* it has not been formally validated, that is, it has not been *explicitly* enacted as positive European law, as it has not been incorporated to the Treaties (§§6–8).

A. J. Menéndez and E. O. Eriksen (eds.), Arguing Fundamental Rights, 155–184.

A. *The Validity of Constitutional Norms in Union Law*

§2: The basic object of a structural theory of fundamental rights is constituted by the fundamental rights norms of the relevant legal order. Such norms are determined by reference to the authoritative set of fundamental rights provisions contained in the formal, written Constitution.[2] This is so because the *validity of fundamental rights norms* stems from the fact that they have been enacted in the constitution-making process, and consequently, written in the formal constitution. Their validity is thus, first and foremost, *positive*. Thus, we say that all those resident in Italy have a fundamental right to assembly because Article 17 of the Italian Constitution says so. When we go beyond the most obvious reading of positive constitutional rights norms, and we derive further rights from semantically and structurally open-textured fundamental rights provisions,[3] or courts affirm such rights when adjudicating conflicts between fundamental rights norms,[4] there is always an argument built *on the positive enshrinement of fundamental rights norms* through the constitution-making process and reflected in the text of the fundamental norm. To put it differently, the validity of derivate fundamental rights norms is always based on the written, formal constitution.

A major difficulty in building up a structural theory of fundamental rights theory in Community law is that it is far from obvious which is the authoritative positive formulation of European constitutional norms, and even less which is the authoritative procedure of constitution-making. This renders far from self-evident which is the *authoritative set of fundamental rights provisions* in European Community law. In the reminder of this section, I claim that this muddled question can be rendered clearer with the help of Alexy's legal and constitutional theory, and very especially, with the help of his characterisation of legal reasoning as a special case of general practical reasoning.

§3: There is neither one single document, or even a collection of documents, which can be said to be the *formal constitution* of the European Union, or at least, to give formal expression to the *norms which materially speaking* constitute the constitutional framework of the European legal order; nor it is uncontroversial through which law-making process such constitutional norms could be enacted.[5] Still, it is generally admitted that it is possible to reduce European legal norms to a system, grounded and framed by a set of *constitutional norms*, norms which materially, if not formally, will be the constitution of the European Union. To put it differently, the lack of a formal constitution has not been an obstacle to the affirmation, by both European and national courts, of the claim that it is possible to reconstruct the *material constitution of the European legal order*.[6] But if such norms have not been positively established as such, how can we ascertain which are such constitutional norms? And what can be the basis of their legal validity? Why should they bind, after all, European citizens?

§4: The first part of the answer lies with the specific character and purpose of European integration, and of the ensuing legal order. The key observation is that European Community law was not brought about by a *formal European Constitution* which created and structured a new legal order *in one stroke* (in one *constitutional moment*), but by an institutional and procedural structure *which was intended to spell out the implications of the convergence of the national legal orders* in the context of economic integration. Indeed, the Communities were created by what were, formally speaking, *international* treaties.[7] However, it was implicit in the Treaties, and explicit in the political agreement which surrounded them, that the process of integration would be facilitated by the forging of *a European legal order*.[8]

To this, it must be added that such a process was *mandated* by the national constitutions of most of the founding States of the Communities. A systematic reading of the innovative "international" clauses of the post-war constitutions of France (1946), Italy (1947) and Germany (1949) is highly supportive of such a conclusion. On the one hand, the referred constitutions contained innovative provisions enabling the participation of each nation-state in supranational integration processes.[9] On the other hand, there were stipulations in each of the said fundamental laws that ensured the effectiveness of international law within the national legal order.[10] It must be added that a similar debate was opened in the Netherlands in the aftermath of the Second World War, leading to a constitutional amendment in 1953, in view of the ratification of the Treaty which aimed at established the European Defence Community.[11] Finally, the literal text of the Constitution of Luxembourg was not formally amended, but its *Conseil d'État* reconstructed its fundamental law with a similar purpose in mind. When reviewing the constitutionality of the Treaty establishing the Coal and Steel Community, the *Conseil* ruled that Luxembourgois authorities not only could, but actually should, renounce certain sovereign powers if *the pub lic good so required*. In these five cases, we find national constitutional provisions which are properly reconstructed as *mandating integration*. It must be added, in political if not legal terms, that the national *pouvoirs constituents* were highly aware of the fact that the system of sovereign nation-states was plagued by huge democratic shortcomings. The democratic ideal upheld by national constitutions only stood a chance of being realised if some form of supranational community was created in Europe.

§5: So the peculiar configuration of European constitutional law is the result of a choice for a slow but steady process of integration of national legal orders into a supranational one, which was not only legitimate from a democratic standpoint, but actually *mandated* by the very principle of democracy. Still, this does not help us in ascertaining which are the *constitutional norms* of European law, and which can be its validity basis. We should keep in mind that the answer to both questions is determinant for a theory of European fundamental rights, given that fundamental rights are defined by reference to the set of constitutional norms.

Most legal scholars tend to claim that the European material constitution results from a *constitutional reading of the Treaties*, and conclude that the said Treaties are, indeed, the material constitution of the Union. By this, reference is mainly made to the Rome Treaties establishing the European Economic Community (hereafter, TEC) and the Euroatom and the Treaty on European Union, together with the different amending treaties and the treaties through which accession of new member states was effected.[12] This will entail that the *validity of Union constitutional norms* would be *also fully* positive, as the Treaties are a piece of law. It should be noticed that according to such conception, constitutional status is predicated not of *all* the provisions contained in the Treaties, but only of some.

Such a claim is only half way correct. First, the Treaties do not contain all European constitutional provisions. Since *Stauder*[13] *and Internationale*,[14] the European Court of Justice has claimed that the principle of protection of fundamental rights is one of the key constitutional principles of Union law. However, such a principle could neither be found among the provisions of the Treaties in force at the time of the judgments,[15] nor derived from them. The Treaties might contain a good deal of the constitutional provisions in Union law, *but they do not exhaust them*. Indeed, the referred judgments can only be properly understood if we realise that the Court was implicitly affirming some other characterisation of what were the constitutional norms of European law.

Second, it is not obvious how it could be simultaneously affirmed that the Treaties *contain* the constitutional provisions of European law, and that European law is to be regarded as *supreme* over national law (at the very least, when the Union is competent to legislate according to the very Treaties).[16] Affirming both claims at the same time would entail substituting the material constitution of the European Union for the national constitution as the supreme legal norm of each national legal order. But could this be so in the absence of an explicit constitutional decision, and moreover, given that the European process of not only constitution-making but also ordinary law-making are plagued by democratic shortcomings? Would this not entail an involution in democratic terms?

§6: Things are starkly different if we define *the set of constitutional norms* in Union by reference to the core constitutional norms common to the

Member States, which would in turn be partially explicited in the Treaties. On the one hand, such a definition points to a set of constitutional norms which fits more smoothly in the reconstruction of the fundamental norms of Union law undertaken by European and national courts. Decisions such as *Stauder*[17] and *Internationale*[18] can actually be easily explained as rendering explicit what was implicit in the very decision of integrating national legal orders. On the other hand, it offers a more plausible account of the *democratic legitimacy* of the decision to integrate. The new legal order *is* anchored in, and framed by, national constitutional traditions, something which ensures its *constitutional soundness*.[19] The new legal order did not transcend national constitutions, but resulted in their merger or combination within the framework provided by national constitutions themselves (call it, lacking a better expression, *the fusion thesis*).[20] As already hinted, the Treaties must be regarded as specific (but partial) expression of the said common constitutional traditions.[21]

More directly relevant to any theory of European fundamental rights, the *fusion thesis* points to a rather intricate validity basis of Union constitutional norms. Although firmly grounded on positive law, their validity is critically dependent on a *critical comparative reconstruction of the constitutional traditions of the Member States*. European constitutional norms have a positive validity basis *given that, and to the extent that*, they are nothing else but what is *common* to the constitutional norms of the Member States, whose validity basis is, without doubt, a positive one.[22] When the *constitutional traditions* of the Member States diverge,[23] the determination of what *should* be considered as common (or to put it differently, the legal norm which *should be* regarded as the common one) requires *reconstructing* the said traditions through a critical-comparative approach. This calls for considering the different norms in force in each of the national constitutional systems, together with the reasons which underpin each norm and the specific requirements stemming from the *process of integration* (i.e., one should keep in mind that the *common constitutional norm* is intended to further integration). Even if some solutions might be equally acceptable, the *principle of equality before the law*, which can be said to be a structural requirement of any legal order, demands that *only one solution be adopted*. This is reflected in what could be called the *majoritarian comparative approach of the European Court of Justice*, already enunciated by AG Lagrange in 1962:

> the case law of the Court, in so far as it invokes national laws (as it does to a large extent) to define the rules of law relating to the application of the Treaty, is not content to draw on more or less arithmetical "common denominators" between the different national solutions, but chooses from each of the Member States those solutions which, having regard to the objects of the Treaty, appear to be the best or, if one may use the expression, the most progressive. This is the spirit (…) which has guided the Court hitherto.[24]

As a consequence, we can talk of a *positive cum critical* validity basis of European constitutional norms. This can be regarded as a specially intense manifestation of Alexy's special case thesis. This is so to the extent that not only European discourses on derivative constitutional norms, but even on primary European constitutional norms would be indicative of the condition of legal reasoning as a special case of general practical reasoning.

It must be finally added that the *dynamic character* of any legal order aimed at facilitating the integration of different national legal systems makes things (slightly) more complex. As integration advances, the *positive cum critical* mode of validity would tend to be replaced by a *positive* mode of validity. This is mainly the result of two parallel processes. One is the process of Treaty amendment, which has resulted in a progressive specification of the common constitutional traditions, and increasingly, into their *transformation*.[25] Indeed, one of the main arguments put forward by the advocates of the Constitutional Treaty signed in Rome in 2004 (and turned into a dead mouse by French and Dutch citizens in the spring of 2005) was no other than the fact that the Constitutional Treaty would have become the *first formal Constitution of the European Union*, replacing the complex and fragmented constitutional order characteristic of the first 50 years of European integration, and rendering marginal the *positive cum critical* mode of validity. The other is the reading of Union law *in a constitutional key* by the Court of Justice; by doing so, the Court *determines*, in an authoritative way, *what the common constitutional traditions imply in a specific context*. By proclaiming authoritatively what are the results of critical comparative analysis of the common constitutional traditions, the Court fully positives the mode of validity of the ensuing norms. Indeed, the clearest example of this jurisprudential specification of the common constitutional traditions is the elaboration of a catalogue of fundamental rights in Union law.[26]

§7: This places us in a position to ascertain which are the fundamental rights norms in Union law, and also of explaining which is the basis of their validity. Once we have clarified the peculiar characteristic of European constitutional law, it comes as no surprise that the founding treaties of the European Communities did not contain any specific reference to the protection of fundamental rights,[27] and that no catalogue of fundamental rights has been *formally* incorporated into the Treaties. And still, the progressive consolidation of the Communities and of their legal order, together with different political developments (more on this in a moment), rendered unavoidable the explicitation of European *fundamental rights norms*.[28] When deciding *Stauder* and *Internationale*, the Court of Justice can be said to have reacted to the diffused and latent will among European leaders and citizens to stress the *rights identity of the* Union in the late 1960s.[29] This was closely related to the perspectives of enlargement of the Communities after the departure of De Gaulle, the need of differentiation vis-à-vis the Eastern bloc, especially after the invasion of Czechoslovakia by Soviet troops, and the projection of a positive social image after the crisis of legitimacy scenified in the Paris spring of 1968. Indeed, the *economic object* of the three Communities was heavily criticised, and indeed exposed as alleged evidence of the fact that the Communities were the Trojan horse of "Americanisation."[30]

§8: Still, the *positive cum critical* mode of validity of European fundamental rights norms grants the European Court of Justice a great deal of leeway in determining which are to be considered European *fundamental rights* and in which relationship they stand to each other. In contrast to what is the case with national constitutional courts operating under a written catalogue of rights (under a predominantly positive mode of validity), the Court determines not only *derivate constitutional rules*, but also the very identity of the fundamental rights norms.[31] This opens the way to the exponential growth of what is considered as a matter of fundamental rights, something which might devalue the currency of fundamental rights, and actually weaken their protection.[32]

The elaboration of a Charter of Fundamental Rights of the European Union was intended to solve such problems. The Charter was written as if it would become the *authoritative* restatement of the *common constitutional traditions of the Member States* on what concerns the protection of fundamental rights. To put it differently, it was intended as the detailed and articulated expression of the "principle of fundamental rights protection" affirmed by the Court, from which the *positive cum critical* validity of European constitutional rights norms stems.[33]

Still, the fact is that the Charter has not been *formally* incorporated into the primary law of the Community.[34] After it was elaborated by the Convention of representatives of national and European institutions in 2000, national governments, who have a constitutional veto power in Union law, limited themselves to *solemnly proclaim the Charter*, without formally transforming it into positive law. The Charter was then included as Part II of the Constitutional Treaty signed in Rome in 2004, but, as just said, French and Dutch citizens turned the Treaty a dead mouse.

This, however, does not deprive the Charter of *legal value* and *legal bite*. This is so for three reasons, indirectly related to the mode of validity of European constitutional norms. First, the Charter *consolidates* already existing law. The Charter does not bring about fundamental rights, but merely produces an authoritative catalogue of such rights, as comprised in the common constitutional traditions of Member States.[35] Second, the institutions of the

Union act as if the Charter was legally binding upon them. Since its proclamation, the Council, the Commission and the Parliament make continuous reference to the Charter in order to ground their decisions and resolutions. This implies that the lack of formal incorporation does not result in a different attitude towards the Charter.[36] Third, the Court of First Instance of the Union, the Advocates General of the Court of Justice and some national constitutional courts have invoked repeatedly the Charter as a relevant legal source in the justification of their decisions.[37] To this it must be added that the *Charter-making process* has had considerable symbolic and political effects. It has acted as one of the major spurs to the process of *explicit constitution-making* of the Union, within which the Charter might be formally incorporated into the primary law of the Union.[38]

The *consolidation* of the common constitutional traditions in the Charter does not necessarily imply that the validity basis of European fundamental rights norms has changed. As long as Union law *remains a law of integration*, the *common constitutional traditions* will remain an essential part of the *constitutional law of the Union*,[39] and thus, the validity basis of European constitutional norms would keep on revealing with special intensity the fact that legal reasoning is a special case of general practical reasoning (or what is the same, the validity basis will remain clearly a *positive cum critical* one).

§9: On such a basis, we can come to two main conclusions. First, that the ascertainment of the validity of Union constitutional norms is a complex one. The central role played by the constitutional traditions common to the Member States implies that European constitutional norms result from the *critical comparative* reconstruction of what is common to the national constitutional traditions of the Member States. This intriguing feature reveals very clearly the *openness* of legal argumentation to *general practical arguments*, as established in Alexy's *special case thesis*. While in national constitutional orders this comes to the fore when considering the validity basis of derivative constitutional rights norms, the peculiarity of European Union law is that this is also the case on what concerns all constitutional rights norms, given that there is not such a thing as a formal, written constitution, but indeed a multiplicity of national written constitutions which collectively play a similar role. Second, the Charter of Fundamental Rights is the document which comes closer to being an authoritative set of the fundamental rights norms of Union law. However, its legal value derives not from its having being *positively enacted through a constitution-making process*, but from the fact that it consolidates existing law. This implies a further reaffirmation of the peculiar mode of validity of European constitutional norms.

III. A TYPOLOGY OF EUROPEAN FUNDAMENTAL RIGHTS NORMS: FUNDAMENTAL RIGHTS, ORDINARY RIGHTS AND COLLECTIVE GOODS

§10: Any theory of fundamental rights presupposes a distinction between *constitutional* and *non-fundamental rights*, if the category of fundamental rights is to be *distinctive*, and not merely coextensive with the category of legal rights. In its turn, such a distinction presupposes *the bifurcation* of the principle of legality in two: on the one hand, the Constitution; on the other hand, statutes.[40] Such a distinction comes hand in hand with the establishment of a hierarchical relationship between the constitution and ordinary statutes.[41] This is at the very basis of the idea of fundamental rights as *binding to the legislature*, that is, as norms which frame the action of the legislature *in substantive terms* to the extent that "they incorporate decisions about the basic normative structure of state and society."[42] A further necessary distinction to be drawn is that between *individual fundamental rights* and *collective goods*.[43] Fundamental rights norms might express both of them.[44] The main difference between the two lies in the non-distributive character of collective goods,[45] which has direct implications over the *legal means of enforceability* of the respect of the said collective goods.

§11: These basic distinctions established in Alexy's structural theory of fundamental rights allow us to establish the basis of a systematization of the provisions of the Charter of Fundamental Rights, given that:

we can distinguish between what are *properly speaking* fundamental rights, because they mandate certain contents to the legislature (§12), and those rights which are ordinary rights, because their content is left in the hands of *the European or the national legislatures* (§13);

we can distinguish between *fundamental rights* which are formulated as *individual rights* and fundamental rights which are formulated as *collective goods* (§14).

§12: A good deal of the provisions of the Charter can be reconstructed as containing fundamental rights norms, that is, norms that provide rights of the individuals against the legislature (either European or national).[46] Clear examples are Article 7 (the right to privacy) or Article 39, section 1 (the right to vote in European elections).

As it is also well-established, the characterisation of a right as fundamental does not imply that ordinary legislators cannot *outwork or limit* such a right.[47] Moreover, there are cases in which the proper way of ensuring a fundamental right is to *make it positive*.[48] Limitation is best captured by a discursive theory of fundamental rights, which openly acknowledges that "constitutional protection always depends on a relationship between a reason for constitutional protection and some relevant contrary reason."[49] This is the proper interpretation of the reference, part of the common constitutional traditions of Member States, to the *essence* of fundamental rights and freedoms.[50] Thus, Article 51, section 1, first sentence of the Charter, which provides that "[a]ny limitation on the exercise of the rights and freedoms recognised by this Charter must be provided for by law and *respect the essence of those rights and freedoms*" is to be interpreted consequently.

It is in such a light that we have to interpret references such as the one contained in Article 3, section 2, first sentence (right of the patients to informed consent before being subject to medical or biological treatment). The referred provision affirms the right "according to the procedures laid down by law." Such a reference does not imply full discretion to the ordinary legislator, but must be interpreted as referring to the scope of the fundamental right limit (the "essence" of the right).[51]

§13: It is doubtful whether certain provisions of the Charter might be considered as *fundamental* in that sense. This is the result of the interplay of Article 51 of the Charter and of a series of clauses that habilitate national legislatures to determine the substantive content of some rights mentioned in the Charter. Many provisions contained in the Charter end up in one of the following style clauses: "under the conditions established by national laws and practices,"[52] "in accordance with the national laws governing the exercise of such freedom and right,"[53] "in accordance with the general principles common to the laws of Member States"[54] or "in accordance with Community law and national law and practices."[55] Such clauses do not seem very different from the usual limiting clauses character of constitutional texts, especially those which habilitate the legislature *in general terms* to limit fundamental rights. A typical case is that of those limiting clauses which mandate the legislature to respect the *essence* of the right when proceeding to its regulation, to which we have just made mention.[56] This is complicated by the *division of competencies* between the Union and its Member States. To the extent that such style clauses reflect a lack of competence of the Union as law stands, they constitute a reiteration of the basic principle contained in Article 51, namely, that the Charter should not be read as expanding the competencies of the Union to the detriment of the Member States. This might be taken to mean that the fundamental legal provisions qualified by such style clauses cannot be read as imposing constraints on national legislators different from those stemming from the respective national constitutional law. But were that so, those legal provisions would not be binding upon national legislatures; in institutional terms, they would not add anything to the arguments which individuals could make before *national* courts in order to have legislation set aside in the name of fundamental rights.

However, such is a hasty conclusion. If one takes seriously the idea that any fundamental right limit must come hand in hand with a protected scope of a given right, one is led to proceed in two steps. First, the competence of the Union should be determined. In those areas in which the Union does not have *any competence title*, it is pretty obvious that the Charter of Fundamental Rights cannot be said to be applicable. Article 51 of the Charter precludes that the Charter is applicable (at the very least, in legal terms)[57] to *purely internal situations*. However, it must be kept in mind that the number of those *purely internal situations* is extremely reduced, to the extent that it can be quite rightly affirmed that there is no area of national competence which is completely free from the influence of Community law, at the very least through the so-called *horizontal effect of some of the basic Community principles* (in themselves, closely associated to the fundamental principles contained in the Charter).[58] Second, in those areas where some Community competence title is established, the fundamental rights provisions of the Charter of Fundamental Rights should be applicable both *as norms*, that is, to the extent that they give rise to concrete *rules*, but also, and perhaps mainly, as *reasons for other norms*. In controversial cases, the underlying principles should be taken into account, and weighted and balanced against the other relevant principles. This will be considered in more detail in the next section (§§16ff).

§14: Finally, not all fundamental legal provisions give rise to *fundamental* rights. We can find provisions that require public institutions to achieve a certain objective or goal, but without giving rise to any subjective fundamental position,[59] that is, without assigning individuals rights against the legislature. Such provisions have been referred as "policy clauses," meaning something rather equivalent to what Alexy might term[60] as "collective goods" or as provisions affirming principles supported by collective goods, which do not necessarily give rise to subjective individual rights.[61] This does not rule out, but rather renders more likely, that there would be *conflicts between individual fundamental rights and collective goods*.[62] But more on this in the next section.

Examples from the Charter are: Article 11, section 2 ("the freedom and pluralism of the media shall be respected"), Article 25 (rights of the elderly to lead a life of dignity and independence and to participate in social and cultural life), Article 26 (protection of the disabled), Article 37 ("a high level of environmental protection and the improvement of the quality of the environment must be integrated into the policies of the Union and ensured in accordance with the principle of sustainable development") or Article 38 ("Union policies shall ensure a high level of consumer protection").

The same argument made in relation to *rights of dubious fundamental nature* (§13) can be repeated here. To the extent that the *collective good provision* is coupled with a style clause that reiterates the division of competencies between the Union and its member states, the bite of the collective good is limited unless some competence claim of the Union can be established.

IV. WEIGHING AND BALANCING FUNDAMENTAL RIGHTS AGAINST ECONOMIC FREEDOMS

§15: *A Theory of Constitutional Rights* draws a basic distinction between rules and principles. Such a distinction is closely connected to the *special case thesis*, that is, to the idea that law is a special case of practical reasoning. Rules are *definitive reasons for action*, while principles are *prima facie reasons for action*, or optimization commands.[63] Prima facie reasons for action can only be turned into definitive reasons for action through an argumentative process, in which they are weighted and balanced against other prima facie reasons *according to the principle of proportionality in a large sense.*[64] Principles reflect the *argumentative* character of law, as they are closely connected to the *ideal dimension of law*. To quote Alexy:

> For a participant, the legal system is not only a system of norms qua results or products, but also a system of procedures or processes, and so, from a participant's perspective, the reasons taken into account in a procedure- here, the process of making a decision and justifying it- belong to the procedure and thereby to the legal system[65]

Thus, legal positivism contributes the basic insight that the integrative role of law in modern societies is dependent in its being mostly composed of uncontroversial action *rules*.[66] But this is not incompatible with the recognition of the central *argumentative* features of law, of its *being a mixture of principles and rules*.

The characterization of legal systems as a combination of principles and rules requires distinguishing between *fundamental rights as rules*[67] (as specific substantive reasons for action, which given the institutional character of law, can become reasons for *legal remedies*[68]) and *fundamental rights as principles,* thus, *as reasons for other norms.*[69] Such a distinction renders clear that the relevance of fundamental rights is not limited to the rules which might be derived in a rather straightforward way from the literal tenor of the fundamental rights provisions, that fundamental rights have a wider normative impact in the whole legal system.

The characterization of legal systems as a combination of rules and principles, which implies the distinction between *fundamental rights norms and fundamental rights* principles, and the *principle of proportionality in a large sense* as the criterion to weight and balance conflicting *fundamental rights principles* are of much help in interpreting and applying Union fundamental rights provisions, and especially, the provisions of the Charter of Fundamental Rights. This allows us to realize that:

Fundamental rights provisions might give expression to *both* a fundamental right rule and a fundamental right principle (§16)
Fundamental rights provisions which fell beyond the scope of competence of the Union have a value as *principles* which frame Union law as a *whole* (§17)
The most transparent and accountable way of solving a conflict between *fundamental rights* is to adjudicate through a judgment of proportionality (§18)

§16: Consider Article 2, Section 2 of the Charter of Fundamental Rights, which states that "No one shall be condemned to the death penalty, or executed." Its level of specifity allows us to derive a fundamental rights rule of the kind "Death penalty is not allowed." However, together with some other Charter provisions (such as Article 1) it could be so constructed as to derive from it a fundamental right principle concerning the constitutionally acceptable types of punishment (a principle interdicting dignity-infringing penalties, not far from what other legal systems refer as the interdiction of cruel and unusual punishment). The strength of such an argument could be reinforced by the consideration of similar national constitutional provisions concerning types of punishment.

§17: As *prima facie reasons for action,* fundamental rights can be seen as argumentative cards that habilitate the individual to keep the balance of power between constitutional and ordinary legislator, by means of having resort to the intricacies of the checks and balances imposed upon the ordinary political process. This insight allows us to put in the right perspective the value of some of the provisions of the Charter, specifically those in which reference is made to fundamental rights whose substantive content falls beyond the scope of competence of the European Union.

This is the case of Article 2, just referred, but also and mainly of socio-economic rights (rights to solidarity).The fact that they refer to substantive contents which fall beyond the scope of competence of the Union might incline us to think that the only reason to include them in the Charter is purely rhetorical.

However, they are legally relevant *as reasons for other legal norms*. In that regard, the *explicit affirmation of such rights in the Charter* can have an impact on the trend towards a slow but steady reconsideration of the proper balance between the four basic Community economic freedoms and social goals (more on this, in a minute).[70] In this sense, the said rights can be *interpreted as the canon of exceptions* to the full realization of the four economic freedoms which Member States can invoke. In that sense, the affirmation of a good deal of the socio-economic rights in the Charter does not result in the affirmation of *individual socio-economic rights*, but it *widens* the political room within which

Member States can *further the realization of socio-economic rights through national legislation*, even if in conflict with the four economic freedoms.

§18: There are two quite related implications of the affirmation of socio-economic rights in the charter: (1) it renders more likely that *conflicts* between fundamental rights would not be *simply decided* , but argued explicitly as a matter of *weighing* and balancing the conflicting rights; (2) it is likely to result in a greater weight being assigned to socio-economic rights *vis-à-vis* economic freedoms, in line with what has just been argued in §16.

Explicit weighing and balancing. Elements of "balancing" of economic freedoms against social principles can already be found in the judgment of the Court in the famous case *Cassis de Dijon*. The Court argued that in the absence of common rules, obstacles to free movement of goods within the Community must be accepted "in so far as those provisions may be recognised as being necessary in order to satisfy mandatory requirements relating in particular to the effectiveness of fiscal supervision, the protection of public health, the fairness of commercial transactions and the defence of the consumer."[71] Two clear recent examples of "unwritten" exceptions to the economic freedoms can be found in *Bachman* and *Albany*. The first case dealt with the right to deduct from the Income Tax base pension fund contributions. Belgian tax law made such a possibility conditional upon the amounts being paid to an undertaking established in Belgium or to the Belgian establishment of a foreign insurance undertaking. Such a measure seemed to run against the free movement of workers (and also against the freedom to provide services). The impossibility of deducting pension plan contributions made to non-Belgian financial institutions made it more costly to workers to move in or out of Belgium. It also sheltered Belgian pension plans from the potential higher competitiveness of foreign undertakings. However, the Court of Justice was receptive to the Belgian argument that the "cohesion of the tax system" could be read as a further legitimate exception to the referred economic freedoms.[72] A general social goal, such as the safeguard of the "cohesion of the tax system" was given priority to "market" freedoms. *Albany* concerned the issue of compulsory affiliation to a sectorial fund intended to top up the basic pension under Dutch law. In this case, the plaintiff operated a textile business. Under Dutch law, social agents can agree on the establishment of a compulsory sectorial pension fund, which had been done in the textile industry. The plaintiff was affiliated with the said fund. But following changes in Dutch pension law, the company requested to be allowed to discontinue its affiliation with the fund. The company had decided to substitute the compulsory pension fund contributions for affiliation with a private insurance company. After being denied such exemption, the company challenged before Dutch courts its compulsory affiliation with the fund. It argued that the establishment of such kind of compulsory funds by social agents was in breach of the Community's competition rules because it prevented private companies from offering private pension fund schemes. It also argued that Dutch provisions ran against the freedom of establishment and the freedom to provide services. The Court concluded that, even if a compulsory pension fund should be considered as an undertaking for the purposes of Article TEC 85, this kind of arrangement did not fall within the scope of Treaty provisions on competition law. This finding was based on the argument that the goals of the EC Treaty go beyond "a system ensuring that competition in the internal market is not distorted." They include the laying out of "a policy in the social sphere" and the promotion "throughout the Community of a harmonious and balanced development of economic activities" and "a high level of employment and social protection."[73]

The Charter of Rights is quite likely to reinforce this trend. The solemn proclamation of the Charter of Fundamental Rights might become a major symbolic act in the development of Community law. The process of debating and drafting a bill of rights of the Community legal order points towards the *constitutionalisation* of the European legal order.[74] This has major formal and substantial consequences. In formal terms, the ultimate affirmation of fundamental rights as the most fundamental provisions of the legal order, as the provisions which bind all the public institutions of the European legal order and the European citizens.[75] In substantial terms,[76] the Charter affirms the *political* character of the European Union, and makes it clear that the most basic societal choices concern not so much the shape of the economy, but the shape of societal relationships. Indeed, this seems to be the line of reasoning adopted by AG Jacobs in *Eugen Schmidberger Internationale Transporte Planzüge v Republik Österreich*.[77] The case concerns the balance to be struck between the basic economic freedoms and the freedoms of expression and assembly, as stated in Articles 11 and 12 of the Charter. A legal demonstration in Austria had resulted in a serious distortion of road traffic between Italy and Northern Europe. An Austrian entrepreneur claimed damages to the Austrian authorities. He argued that the authorities were to be held responsible. By granting the permission to demonstrate, they would have infringed on the freedom of movement of goods. With extensive reference to the Charter, the Advocate General claims that there is a need for a proper *weighing* and balancing of economic freedoms and fundamental rights. The outcome of such a balancing exercise cannot be predetermined once and for all, but must be undertaken with reference to each specific case. In this concrete instance, AG Jacobs argues that preference should be given to the freedoms of expression and assembly.[78]

Increased weight to socio-economic rights. The European Court of Justice has, in cases of conflict, become increasingly inclined to give more weight to social principles to the detriment of the four economic freedoms. The Charter is likely to reinforce this trend. In fact, the most innovative feature of the Charter might not be the series of statements on social rights, but the affirmation of *solidarity* as one of the founding values of the Union. The second paragraph of the Preamble introduces an authoritative statement of the founding values of the Union, which are said to be human freedom, dignity, equality and *solidarity*. *Solidarity* is the title of the referred chapter IV, something which opens up for a systemic interpretation of Community law in the light of such a value. The Charter enumerates several rights to solidarity, although the realisation of some of these is not within the actual field of competence of the Union. The overlapping effect of Article 51 and the Charter clauses that refer to national constitutional law rule out that any competence accrues to the Union. The affirmation of such rights, coupled with the decision not to give "fundamental" status to the four economic freedoms,[79] reinforces the argument that European integration is not only about negative integration or market-making, but also about market-redressing. All these features of the Charter render possible to grant more weight to social values when interpreting the provisions of Community law. Thus, the set of rights included in chapter IV of the Charter, under the heading "solidarity," could be constructed so as to provide support to Member States when claiming exceptions to the four economic freedoms in order to further goals of a socio-economic character.[80] It is not implausible to claim that this could become the trend.[81]

The Opinion of AG Geelhoed in *American Tobacco* points in this direction. The AG revisits the relationship between economic freedoms and social goals in Community law. She finds that at its present stage of development, Community law does not aim exclusively at the creation of a single market, but also includes other legitimate goals of Community action, such as the protection of public health. The Union's competence basis might still be related to the fostering of the basic economic freedoms,[82] but this does not mean that the *actual exercise* of Community competences is exclusively aimed at market-making.[83] AG Geelhoed adds that some of the social goals constitute basic preconditions for a single market. This prompts her to hint at a radical change in legal reasoning. Instead of focusing in a first step on whether a given national provision distorts the common market, and only in a second step on whether such a measure can be justified by reference to some legitimate public goal, some paragraphs of the text invite a direct weighing and balancing of principles.[84] Were this to be later developed by other Advocates General and by the Court, it would advance the *constitutionalisation* of Community law, in the sense of rendering the framework of legal reasoning closer to what is characteristic of national constitutional laws.[85]

V. THE HIDDEN (AND UNEXPLOITED) EGALITARIAN POTENTIAL OF UNION LAW: FACTUAL EQUALITY

§19: *A Theory* offers a neat distinction between principles of legal and factual equality, which are usually portrayed as antagonistic even within national constitutional traditions.

On the one hand, legal equality, or equality before the law, is concerned with *the evaluation of state action* itself, without considering its transformative impact or potentiality upon *social reality*, so to say. On the other hand, factual equality is concerned with the *factual consequences of state* action.[86] This distinction has at least a double merit. First, that it is clear and not confusing, as it is not infrequently the case with distinctions between *equality before the law* and *equality through the law*. Second, that it might reveal the *egalitarian* potential of what are usually regarded as *arguments of equality before the law*.

Indeed, it will be argued in this section that *with such a distinction in mind*, we can observe that the jurisprudence of the Court of Justice on the principle of non-discrimination on the grounds of nationality might have occasionally undermined the achievement of *social equality* and *contributed to develop the argumentative skills* needed in order to further *social equality* (§20-21) that this can be further proved by considering the jurisprudence of the Court on the *principle of equal treatment of men and women concerning payment and working conditions* (§22).

§20: The principle of *non-discrimination on the grounds of nationality*, enshrined in Article 7 TEC (now Article 12 TEC) has played a major role in the process of European integration. In economic terms, it has been invoked once and again in order to challenge national laws, regulations or practices which were regarded as obstacles to *the forging of a common market* of goods, labour, services and capital, as mandated by the Treaties. In legal terms, it has rendered *suspicious* any differential treatment based on nationality.[87] In practical terms, it can be said to have *shifted* the burden of proof against norms which discriminate between nationals and non-nationals. The combination of the thickening of Community secondary norms which *harmonized or approximated national* laws with the jurisprudential reading of the principle of non-discrimination on the grounds of nationality has had the combined effect of placing all European residents under the same laws. Not only *all residents in the Union* are subject to the same norms *within each legal order*, but such laws *become one* under the harmonizing effect of Union law.

Market-making and legal order-making were thus based in the *black-listing* of the distinction between nationals and non-nationals. This was, according to the preamble of the Treaties, done in the name of achieving the objectives of the Treaties, which were *both economic and social*, as stems very clearly from the Preamble of the Treaties and from the (original text) of Articles 2 and 3 TEC. However, the shifting of the burden of proof against measures which had *the effect of discriminating between nationals and non-nationals* had the effect of leaving without effect many legal norms which were intended to further factual equality within Member States. Indeed, the differential treatment of nationals and non-nationals could be the *unintended effect* of a measure which foremostly aimed at the entrenching of a given model of *social insurance* or of *labour relationships* which aimed at transforming reality in an egalitarian sense.[88] The almost unconditional way in which the Court of Justice applied the principle of non-discrimination on the grounds of nationality is one of the main bases on which it has been claimed that Union law is inspired by a neo-liberal or economicist vision of the relationships between politics and markets.

§21: This picture is rendered more nuanced if we consider a paradoxical feature of community law. Union law was structured since its very inception as *the law of integration*, to paraphrase the title of Pescatore's famous book.[89] This explains the marked teleological character of the Treaties themselves, and also of the jurisprudence of the European Court of Justice.[90]

This teleological character of the Community legal order has made unavoidable that the European Court of Justice has applied the principle of non discrimination on grounds of nationality with a concern not only for *legal*, but also *factual* equality. The question in the case law of the Court is whether Europeans are equal before the law, but in doing so the Court checks whether the *factual equality* of European residents has been infringed by the national statutes. Consequently, community law is one of the legal systems where legal argumentation with reference to factual equality is more frequent, and where this kind of argument has been more perfected.

Consider the following three cases in which the Court went beyond formal equality by means of reviewing the correctness of the *legal construction of difference by national legal orders* in each concrete case.

The Spirits case.[91] In a series of cases, the Court of Justice developed the concepts of "competing markets" in order to test whether national tax provisions resulted in a discrimination against imported products. In most cases, the national tax provisions were either aimed at one specific product (which happened to be imported)[92] or did make some reference to the national or imported character of the goods. In the *Spirits* case, the Court was confronted with a piece of French legislation which established different tax liabilities for spirits on the formally neutral criterion of whether they were based on wine or fruit, or whether they were based on grain. It was the case that nationally manufactured liquours were in most cases based on wine or fruit, and enjoyed *de facto* a lower level of taxation. Given that both liquors based on wines and fruits, and liquors based on cereals, could be regarded as, if not similar products, at least competing products, the "protective nature of the tax system" was deemed to be clear.[93]

The Feldain case.[94] A special tax on cars, relative to the power of the engine (basically calculated by reference to the amount of energy consumed, cylinder capability) had been established in France. The tax was calculated according to a given formula. What it is interesting for our present purposes is to notice that the formula resulted in a more than proportional increase of the tax due as the power of the car increased.

Such a formula seemed to be completely ecumenical from the standpoint of nationality. The power of the car, and not its nationality, were the relevant variables considered when calculating the tax liability. However, it was called to the attention of the Court that the formula resulted in special heavy tax liabilities for those cars exceeding a certain power. Such power was barely coincidental with the maximum power of cars manufactured in France. Thus, the set of cars upon which a heavy and more than proportional tax liability was imposed were *imported cars*. It was clear that the measure was not discriminatory towards *imported cars* with similar power to *French manufactured cars*, but it discriminated *against* a set of cars which *were all imported*. On such a basis, the Court came to the conclusion that this piece of French tax law was in breach of the principle of non-discrimination on the basis of nationality.[95]

The Biehl case.[96] It is well-established that the different treatment of tax purposes of residents and non-residents is justified, provided that such differentiation is based on the different objective nature of the two situations. This is especially relevant on what concerns personal income taxation. It is well-established that the right to a certain set of tax benefits associated with the assessment of the global ability to pay tax should only be granted in the state of residency of the taxpayer, while those tax systems where income accrues without the taxpayer being resident are legitimately entitled to tax the income accrued in their jurisdiction in a more *flat manner*. The case at hand related to the different treatment of residents and non-residents under an specific provision of Luxembourg income tax law. It was established that withheld tax in excess of the final tax liability could not be restituted to all those who were not resident in the territory of the Grand Duchy of Luxembourg during the entire fiscal year. In formal terms, the provision did not make any reference to nationality. The relevant criterion was *residence*, as such a non-suspicious criterion. In fact, Luxembourgeois citizens shifting their residence to other member states or third countries will be denied the right to claim tax withheld in excess of their final tax liability for the said fiscal year. However, the Court came to the conclusion that the provision was in breach of Community law. It was an instance of covert discrimination. The apparently neutral formula operated in practice to the discrimination of non nationals, to the extent that they are *much more likely* to be the ones not able to claim the repayment of the overpaid tax.[97]

§22: This entails that, whatever the present shape and consequences of the arguments, the concepts and strategies of argumentation developed with reference to *economic freedoms* could be applied to the furthering of social values.

This can be proved by means of considering the jurisprudence of the Court of Justice on what concerns the Community provisions on gender equality. The original Article 119 of the Treaty of the European Economic Community established the basic principle of equal pay for equal work. Despite such interdiction, strict formal equality would not interdict different pay for work which is formally different, but to which the same value is attached,[98] or the establishment of job classification schemes that would isolate men and women, and allow for the application of different pay rates.[99]

The Rinner-Kühn case.[100] German legislation established as a general principle that employers should provide workers with up to 6 weeks of sick pay. Part-time employees working up to 10 hours a week were not granted such a benefit. The plaintiff was a woman working for ten hours a week for a German company. She argued that the proportion of women falling under the excluded category was disproportionately high. Therefore, the exclusion amounted to a *de facto* discrimination contrary to Article 119 TEC. The Court accepted the line of argument of the plaintiff. Characteristically, it left to the national court to proceed to the definitive weighing and balancing of the principle of non-discrimination against other competing principles (aims of social policy; the measure being suitable and requisite for attaining that aim).[101]

The Dekker case.[102] The plaintiff was selected as the most suitable candidate for a job, but was finally not offered the job on account of the fact that she was three months pregnant, and the company insurer will not reimburse the benefits the company was liable to during her maternity leave. Even if the decision could be based on a formally non-discriminative rule, the Court found that this was *de facto* a case of discrimination on the basis of sex. The fact that pregnancy affects women only is not a reason not to consider whether the measure is or not discriminatory of women.[103] Resort to a criterion which can only be applied to women in order to justify the refusal of an appointment is to be regarded as an instance of discrimination on the basis of sex.

§23: In brief, the European Court of Justice has applied what formally are principles of *formal equality*, that is *equality before the law*, in ways which render them close to *principles of factual equality*. The very nature of Union law as the *law of European economic and legal integration* has forced the European Court of Justice to develop the argumentative skills needed in order to *contest the criteria of legal differentiation established by national legal orders*, something which renders effective the goals of *market-making* and *legal order-making*.

This allows us to conclude that, quite paradoxically, a legal system which has fostered *negative economic integration* and, as such, has created considerable difficulties for national provisions aiming at the protection of very basic social goals and values, has develop argumentative skills which lay the ground for the eventual pursuit of factual equality.

VI. CONCLUSIONS

This chapter aimed at testing whether Alexy's *A Theory of Constitutional Rights* could be applied beyond German constitutional law, more specifically, to European Community Law.

It was argued that the solemn proclamation of the Charter of Fundamental Rights must be regarded as providing the authoritative standpoint from which to construct a theory of European Fundamental Rights. Such a theory should pay preferential attention to the case law of the European Court of Justice, but also to the jurisprudence of national constitutional courts, as essential elements of the *national constitutional traditions*.

It was claimed that clarity is achieved by distinguishing between provisions establishing fundamental rights and collective goods norms, and that the specific interplay of certain *limiting clauses* and the limitation of the competence of the Union renders dubious the fundamental nature of certain provisions of the Charter. However, it was argued that such clauses do not fully eliminate the *binding* nature of the provisions, to the extent that one can derive from then principles which would apply where some competence basis of the Union can be established. Moreover, the *Theory of Constitutional Rights* allows us realising the legal value of some of the provisions of the Charter which establish fundamental rights which fall mainly or fully beyond the sphere of competence of the Union. By means of distinguishing between the value of fundamental rights *as norms* and fundamental rights *as reasons for other norms*, it was argued that provisions such as many of those stating *rights to solidarity* must be considered as establishing principles which should be considered in the sphere of competence of the Union. This was illustrated by considering the impact that the Charter might have in the reconsideration of the weight of some economic freedoms, now to be interpreted as specific formulations of more general fundamental rights.

Finally, *A Theory* provides the perspective from which to realise that even if the Communities have not been attributed a competence on social issues, and even if the substantive content of Community law provisions, coupled with its *position of supremacy* to national law in its areas of competence, the case-law of the European Court of Justice might provide interesting clues as to how to realize rights to solidarity in the European legal order. The Court of Justice has tended to consider arguments not only of formal but also of factual equality when considering the basic economic rights at the heart of the common market. This was illustrated by reference both to the principle of non-discrimination on the basis of nationality and the principle of non-discrimination on the basis of sex.

NOTES

1 OJ C 364, of 18.12.2000, at pp. 1–22.

2 TCR, p. 30: "Fundamental rights norms are those norms which are expressed by provisions relating to fundamental rights, and fundamental rights provisions are those statements, and only those statements, contained in the text of the Basic Law."

3 TCR, pp. 33–38.

4 TCR, pp. 54–56.

5 The European Communities were established as international organizations through what were formally international treaties. This was so despite the obvious political purposes pursued through the "ever closer union" of the six founding Member States, the so-called Little Europe. A first constitutional draft was elaborated within the context of the negotiation of the Treaties establishing the frustrated Defence and Political Communities in 1953 (cf. Richard T. Griffiths, *Europe's First Constitution*, London: Kogan Page, 2001). But such a text was never ratified, and never entered into force. Since its members were first directly elected by European citizens in 1979, the European Parliament has tried twice to turn itself into an *Assemblée Constituent* (in 1984, with the Spinelli project: OJ C 77, of 19.03.1984, pp. 53ff; and in 1994, the Hermann project: OJ C 61, of 10.02.1994, pp. 155ff). It has failed to do so. A new moment was signalled in 2001, and led to the elaboration of a Draft Constitutional Treaty for the European Union. The rejection of the proposal by French and Dutch voters in the spring of 2005 rendered extremely improbable that the draft will ever enter into force. But a new consitutional process is likely any time in the future. (see Erik Oddvar Eriksen, John Erik Fossum and Agustín José Menéndez, *Developing a Constitution for Europe*, London: Routledge, 2004).

6 The German Constitutional Court in 22 BVerfGE 293 at 296. The European Court of Justice in Case 294/83, *Parti écologiste "Les Verts" v European Parliament*, judgment of 23 April 1986, [1986] ECR 1357, paragraph 23: "the European Economic Community is a Community based on the rule of law, inasmuch as neither its Member States nor its institutions can avoid a review of whether the measures adopted by them are in conformity with the basic constitutional charter, the Treaty." This move have already been advocated back in 1955 by Advocate General Lagrange, who in case 8/55 argued that the Treaty of the European Coal and Steel Community should be regarded as "the Charter of the Community from the material point of view (…) even though concluded in the form of a Treaty."

7 By the founding Treaties of the Communities, reference is made to the Treaty of Paris of 1951 (Treaty establish the European Coal and Steel Community) and the Rome Treaties (the Treaty establishing the European Economic Community and the Treaty establishing the European Community of Atomic Energy).

8 This idea of a European legal order which went beyond the Treaties is enshrined in (at least) two key provisions of the Treaties. First, the Treaties assign to the European Court of Justice

the power to review the legality of European and national measures within the scope of application of the Treaties (Article 162 TEC, now Article 220 TEC). This implies a clear reference to a European legal order which goes beyond the Treaties themselves, to the extent that the standard of review was legality and not just the provisions of the Treaties. Second, an autonomous law-making procedure is established (Article 189 TEC, now Article 249 TEC). It leads to directly applicable and effective legal provisions (characteristics which were clearly proper of regulations, and which would partially be assigned to directives later on) (cf. Case 26/62 *Van Gend en Loos*, [1963] ECR 1 and Case 41/74, *Van Duyn v Home Office*, [1974] ECR 1337;). The European Court of Justice could review the legality of both regulations and directives in certain cases (Article 173 TEC, now Article 230 TEC). What is relevant here is that the yardstick of review was again defined by reference to legality, and thus, pointed to a European legal order which went beyond the Treaties.

9 Cf. Article 27 of the French Constitution; Article 11 of the Italian Constitution; and Article 24 of the German Constitution.

10 Cf. Articles 26 and 28 of the French Constitution; Article 10 of the Italian Constitution; and Article 24 of the German Constitution.

11 Cf. Jonkheer HF van Panhuys, "The Netherlands Constitution and International Law," 47 (1953) *American Journal of International Law*, pp. 537–558. Article 65 of the Dutch Constitution as thus amended affirmed the primacy of international law within the national legal order, while Article 67 enabled the conferral of legislative, administrative and jurisdictional powers to "organisations based on international law." Article 63 went so far as stating that "the contents of the agreement may deviate from certain provisions of the Constitution," subject to the double condition that the "development of the international legal order requires this" and that "the agreement is approved by a two-thirds majority in both parliamentary chambers."

12 Major instance of Treaty-making and Treaty amendment are the Paris Treaty of 1951 establishing the European Coal and Steel Community, the Rome Treaties of 1957 establishing the European Economic Community and EUROATOM, the Single European Act of 1986, The Maastricht Treaty of 1991, and the Treaties of Amsterdam of 1996 and Nice of 2000. Minor Treaty amendments include the Saar Treaty of 1956, the Convention on Certain Institutions Common to the European Communities of 1957, the Merger Treaty of 1965 and the Budget Treaties of 1970 and 1975.

13 Case 29/69, *Stauder* [1969] ECR 419.

14 Case 11/70, *Internationale*, [1970] ECR 1125.

15 Indeed, no reference to the protection of fundamental rights was enshrined in the text of the Treaties until the Single Act of 1985 (and in a clearer, less ambiguous manner, until the Treaty of Maastricht of 1991).

16 Case 6/64, *Costa v Enel*, [1964] ECR 585.

17 *Supra*, fn. 13, at paragraph 7: "Interpreted in this way, the provision at issue contains nothing capable of prejudicing the fundamental rights enshrined in the general principles of Community law protected by the Court".

18 *Supra*, fn. 14.

19 On this, see Catherine Richmond, "Preserving the Identity Crisis: Autonomy, System and Sovereignty in European law," 16 (1997) *Law and Philosophy*, pp. 377–420; Neil D. MacCormick, *Questioning Sovereignty. Law, State and Nation in the European Union*, Oxford: Oxford University Press, 1999, especially chapters 6 and 7.

20 Maurizio Fioravanti and Stefanno Mannoni, "Il modelo costituzionale europeo. Tradizione e prospettive," in G. Bonacchi (ed.), *Una Costituzione senza stato*, Bologna: Il Mulino,

2001, pp. 23–70 and Jürgen Habermas, "Constitutional Democracy," 29 (2001b) *Political Theory*, pp. 766–781. And what was common among the national legal orders would complement the specific legal provisions contained in the Treaties and in the secondary law of the Union. Indeed, the judges of the European Court of Justice, who were jurists of the six Member States learned in national legal orders (and, in some cases, international law), could only put flesh in the bones of the Treaty by means of a constant reference to what was common in the national legal orders of the six, by means of a critical comparative approach of the six national legal orders. See, among others, Koen Lenaerts, "Le droit comparé dans le travail du juge communitaire," 37 (2001) *Revue Trimestrelle du Droit Européen*, pp. 487–528.

21 The consolidation of the Communities and the thickening of secondary European law (due to the accrual of new competences to the Communities, and due to the growth of the number of regulations and directives in force, of the *acquis communitaire*) resulted in two parallel processes of constitutionalisation. On the one hand, Community law was increasingly interpreted in a constitutional key, not only by the European Court of Justice, but also by national courts. On the other hand, the process of Treaty amendment was increasingly permeated by a constitution-making logic, even if not framed in constitutional terms. Thus, even if constitutionalisation might have originally been strongly motivated by a coherent reading of the Treaties by the European Court of Justice and national courts, soon it was closely connected to a discussion on the legitimacy basis of the European Union. Paradoxically, the very success of constitutional law without constitutional politics rendered the assessment of Union law by reference to democratic standards an issue, and a pressing one for that matter.

22 In this regard, some doubts could arise concerning the *source of validity* of British constitutional law. On this, see Cristoph Möllers, "The politics of law and the law of politics: two constitutional traditions in Europe," in Eriksen, Fossum and Menéndez (eds.), *supra*, fn. 5, pp. 129–139.

23 Even if the divergence is a rather benign one, assuming that national solutions are basically *equivalent*, the principle of equality before European law would require Union law *to opt for one single solution*, and thus, to choose among solutions which are potentially equally valid.

24 Case 14/61, *Hoogovens v High Authority*, [1962] ECR 253, at pp. 283–284.

25 This *innovation* on the common constitutional traditions is in itself an indicator of the *constitutionalisation* of the process of Treaty amendment. See John Erik Fossum and Agustín José Menéndez, *The Constitution's Gift*, 11 (2005) *European Law Journal*, pp. 380–420.

26 Cf. Koen Lenaerts, Piet Van Nuffel and Robert Bray, *Constitutional Law of the European Union*, London: Sweet and Maxwell, 1999, at pp. 548ff.

27 Article 6 TEC contained a clause on prohibition of discrimination on the grounds of nationality, and Article 119 TEC stated the principle of equal pay for equal work for men and women.

28 Pierre Pescatore, "Les Droits de l'Homme et l'Integration Européenne," 4 (1968) *Cahiers de droit européen*, pp. 629–673.

29 The usual narrative on the matter goes that the thickening of Community secondary law (regulations and directives), when coupled with the explicit affirmation of the supremacy of Community norms,[29] created a serious risk of conflict between Community secondary norms and national fundamental rights provisions. In *Stauder* and *Internationale*, the Court would have *internalised* the said tension by affirming that the principle of fundamental rights protection, even if unwritten, was one of the founding principles of the new legal order. This standard interpretation attributes *strategic motivations* to the Court of Justice.

However, if the *common constitutional traditions* are taken seriously as the very constitutional foundation of Community law, then the judgment of the Court does not need to be interpreted exclusively as a clever strategic move.

[30] Cf., for example, the block-buster of the late 60s, Jean Jacques Servan-Schreiber, *Le Défi Américain*, Paris: Denöel, 1967.

[31] Thus, fundamental rights argumentation in Community law was not tied down to an authoritative text of fundamental rights provisions. This rendered fundamental rights argumentation in Community law rather peculiar, and implied that one of the three basic constrains of such argumentation (TCR, pp. 371ff) was absent.

[32] It is far from obvious that rights are better protected when there are more fundamental rights. See TCR, pp. 350–1 and 365ff. The key question is not the "level of protection" of rights, but the balance which is struck between different rights.

[33] On such a basis, the Charter could be said to be a fragment of the (formal) constitution of the European Union. The situation in Community law would be therefore not so different from that prevailing in the British legal system at present. The British legal system lacks a formal constitution. However, the Human Rights Act, which incorporates the European Convention of Human Rights, can be interpreted as a piece of a formal constitution (On the constitutional materials of the United Kingdom, see Neil D. MacCormick, "Does the United Kingdom have a Constitution? Reflections on MacCormick v Lord Advocate," 29 (1978) *Northern Ireland Legal Quarterly*, pp. 1–20. See the judgment on *John MacDonald MacCormick v Lord Advocate*, 1953 S.C. 396 [Court of Session]. The background to the case is explained in an extremely entertaining way by John MacCormick, *The Flag in the Wind*, London: Wackburg, 1950).

[34] If the Draft Treaty establishing the Constitution will be turned into a constitution in a formal sense, the Charter will be *formally* incorporated into Union law. The Charter, as drafted by the Charter Convention but with some amendments, constitutes Part II of the Draft Treaty. See "Draft Treaty establishing a Constitution for the European Union," OJ C 169, of 18 July 2003, pp. 1–105.

[35] Agustín J. Menéndez, "Finalité through rights" in Erik O. Eriksen, John E. Fossum and Agustín J. Menéndez, *The Chartering of Europe. The European Charter of Fundamental Rights and its constitutional implications*, Nomos: Baden-Baden, 2003, pp. 30–47, pp. 41ff.

[36] Agustín J. Menéndez, "Chartering Europe", 40 (2002) *Journal of Common Market Studies*, pp. 471–490, pp. 475–476.

[37] Menéndez, *supra*, fn. 35, pp. 41ff.

[38] See, for example, Declaration 23 annexed to the Treaty of Nice, OJ C 80, of 10.3.2001, at pp. 85–86. See especially paragraphs 4 to 7 of the said Declaration. Cf. also the collection of speeches related to the signalling of a constitutional moment in Mark Leonard (ed.), *The Future Shape of Europe*, Brussels: Foreign Policy Centre. See also Lionel Jospin, *Ma Vision de l'Europe et de la mondialisation*, Paris: Plon, 2001. It must be added that the Constitutional Treaty was not easy to characterise as the result of a genuine constitutional moment. On this, see Agustín José Menéndez, "Between Laeken and the Deep Blue Sea," 10 (2005) *European Public Law*, pp. 105–144.

[39] This was reflected in the (now defunct) Constitutional Treaty of the European Union. Together with the adoption of the Charter as Part II of the Constitutional Treaty, Article 9.3 read: "Fundamental rights, as guaranteed by the European Convention for the Protection of Human Rights and Fundamental Freedoms, and as they result from the constitutional traditions common to the Member States, shall constitute general principles of the Union's law."

40 The democratic principle is not only connected to communicative action and deliberation, but also to concrete mechanisms of decision-making. The role of law as a complement of morality, taking care of the basic shortcomings of the latter, justifies constraining deliberation to fit worldly constraints. However, this renders very real the danger of a legitimacy gap of legislation, as not all those affected would have a real chance of participating in deliberation and decision-making. This partial heteronomous character of ordinary legislation can be mediated by a dual conception of democracy, which distinguishes different modes of legitimacy.

Detailed implications vary across different constitutional systems, but in all of those falling upon the model of democratic constitutionalism, some form of constitutional dualism is relevant. This presupposes that the constitution is a differentiated form of law, it is in a relevant sense the higher law of the land. The dual (or even more plural) character of the sources of law is clearly linked to a complex understanding of the democratic principle of legitimacy. One finds legal norms supported by the full mode of legitimacy (the constitution), and ordinary laws which are based on a more viable type of legitimacy, and which are constrained in their contents and impact by the higher law. The archetypical kind of higher law is fundamental rights provisions. Equipped with such rights, the citizen is given claims that, at the same time, protect the values (individualistic and collective) lying behind the rights and that allow her to put in motion institutional mechanisms that alter the balance of power design in the constitution itself. Non-majoritarian institutions step in the way of ordinary statutes and either set it aside or create obstacles for their implementation in the name of the Constitution. Judicial review of legislation based on the infringement of fundamental rights and independent institutions in charge of ensuring the monitoring of rights (of the type of ombudsmen) are characteristic remedies associated to fundamental rights.

41 See, for example, TCR, p. 349. Rivers, Translator's Introduction, p. xix.

42 TCR, p. 350.

43 TCR, pp. 65–66, 80–81 and 188. See especially p. 65, fn. 79: "That a principle relates to such collective interests means that it requires the creation or maintenance of states of affairs which satisfy certain criteria, broader than the enforcement or satisfaction of individual rights, to the greatest extent legally and factually possible." See also Robert Alexy, "Individual Rights and Collective Goods," in Carlos Santiago Nino (ed.), *Rights*, Aldershot: Dartmouth, 1992b, pp. 163–181.

44 ATC, p. 80.

45 Ibid., pp. 167–168.

46 As it is typical of fundamental rights proper, the rights established by the Charter of Fundamental Rights constitute an institutional embodiment of substantive moral claims, but they are also given the form of normative reasons against the action of the legislature, which give rise to reasons for the enforceability of the right.

47 On the concept of fundamental rights limits, see TCR, pp. 181ff. A criticism of the idea of the "inalienable core" in TCR, pp. 192ff.

48 This can be affirmed without qualifications about rights to entitlements in the wide sense or to positive state action, within which a distinction can be established between rights to protection, rights to organisation and procedure and rights to entitlements in the narrow sense. TCR, chapter 9, especially pp. 296–297 for the three-fold distinction.

49 TCR, p. 209.

50 Similar implications have other style clauses such as "in accordance with the Treaty establishing the European community."

51 On "laws of infringement," see TCR 199.

52 Article 35 (health care).

53 Article 9 (right to marry and found a family), Article 10 (right to conscientious objection), Article 14, section 3 (freedom to found educational establishments).

54 Article 41, section 3 (right to good administration; making good damages), Article 45, section 2 (free movement of nationals of third countries).

55 Article 16 (freedom to conduct a business), Article 27 (workers' right to information and consultation with the undertaking), Article 28 (right to collective bargaining), Article 30 (protection in the event of unjustified dismissal), Article 34, sections 1, 2 and 3 (social security and social assistance).

56 §13.

57 I do not consider here the *political* effect that the existence of two systems of fundamental rights might have in some cases.

58 This is a clear conclusion established in the debates of the working group on competencies in the Laeken Convention. This is accepted even by those who are more skeptical of any expansion of the competencies of the Union. See the Conclusions of the Working Group II of the Laeken Convention, on the Charter of Fundamental Rights and the eventual accession of the Union to the European Convention of Human Rights. CONV 354/02, available at http://register.consilium.eu.int/pdf/en/02/cv00/00354en2.pdf.

59 CHARTE 4414/00, submitted by the representative of the Spanish government, Mr. Rodríguez-Bereijo, seems to have heavily influenced the drafting of social rights. The three-folded typology between fundamental rights, ordinary rights and policy clauses proposed there. But see also *For a Europe of civil and Social Rights*, Report by the Comité des sages (Brussels, European Commission, 1996), pp. 51ff. ("Rights in the form of objectives to be achieved").

60 Although I am not completely sure that such terminological use if congenial to Alexy's approach. Cf. TCR, p. 112, dealing with Ihering's protectionist import duty.

61 Alexy, *supra*, fn. 43, p. 167 states that collective goods are non distributive goods. Within the Charter of the European Union, the said provisions make reference to the protection of non-distributive goods in legal terms. See also p. 176: "There might occasionally be good grounds to endow the individual with rights in such a way that he would be able to enforce collective goods either for himself or as an advocate of the community. However, this situation cannot be generalised. As a rule, more persuasive grounds exist in favour of establishing only collective modes of enforcement of collective goods, as we see in the political process of a democratic system." See also TCR, p. 65: "That a principle relates to such collective interests means that it requires the creation or maintenance of a state of affairs which satisfy certain criteria, broader than the enforcement or satisfaction of individual rights, to the greatest extent legally and factually possible."

62 See Alexy, *supra*, fn. 43, pp. 174ff.

63 TCR, p. 47.

64 TCR, p. 51, pp. 66ff.

65 Cf. Alexy, *The Argument from Injustice*, Oxford: Oxford University Press, 2002b, at p. 73.

66 Herbert L A Hart, "The Concept of Law and The Concept of Law," Oxford: Oxford University Press, 1961, p. 135. See also Neil MacCormick, *Legal Reasoning and Legal Theory*, Oxford: Oxford University Press, 1978, p. 241. See also "The Concept of Law and 'The Concept of Law'," 14 (1994) *Oxford Journal of Legal Studies*, pp. 1–23.

67 TCR, p. 59: "Rules are definitive reasons."

68 Alexy, *supra*, fn. 61, at p. 166.

69 TCR, p. 59: "[T]he position taken here is that rules and principles are reasons for norms" and Francisco Laporta, "Sobre el concepto de derechos humanos" 4 *Doxa* (1987), pp. 23–46.

[70] Cf. Álvaro Castro Oliveira, "Workers and other Persons: Step-by-step from movement to citizenship-Case Law 1995–2001," 39 (2002) *Common Market Law Review*, pp. 77–122; Siofra O'Leary and José Fernández Martín, "Judicially Created Exceptions to the free provision of services," 11 (2000) *European Business Law Review*, pp. 347–362; Leonor Moral Soriano, "How proportionate should anti-competitive State intervention be?," 28 (2003) *European Law Review*, pp. 112–123.

[71] See Case 120/78, *Rewe v Bundesmonopolverwaltung für Branntwein* [1979] ECR 649, par. 8.

[72] See Case C-204/90, *Hanns Martin Bachmann v Belgian State*, [1992] ECR I-249, par. 21–23; Case C-300/900, *Commission v Belgium*, [1992] ECR I-305, par. 14–16, 20–22.

[73] Case C-67/96, *Albany International BV v Stichting Bedrijfspensionenfonds Textielindustrie*, [1999] ECR I-5751. See par. 54 of the judgment.

[74] Eriksen, Fossum, Menéndez, *supra*, fn. 35.

[75] TCR, p. 349.

[76] TCR, p. 350.

[77] Case C-112/00, [2003] ECR I-5659 Opinion delivered on July 11, 2002.

[78] See the comment of Cristopher Brown, 40 (2003) *Common Market Law Review*, pp. 1499–1510.

[79] They are only referred to in the Preamble. Some of such freedoms can be subsumed in some provisions of the Charter. Thus, Article 16 (freedom to conduct a business) can be seen as encompassing the freedom of establishment. However, the right is formulated at a higher level of abstraction.

[80] See Olivier De Schutter: "La contribution de la Charte des droits fondamentaux de l'Union européenne à la garantie des droits sociaux dans l'ordre juridique communautaire," 12 (2001) *Revue Universelle des Droits de L'Homme*, pp. 33–47 and see Agustín José Menéndez, "Sinews of Peace" 16 (2003b) *Ratio Juris*, pp. 374–398. The representative of the British government in the Laeken Convention, Mr. Hain, proceed to slightly twist this argument, claiming that the inclusion of social and economic rights in the Charter, without sufficiently strong horizontal clauses, gave rise to the risk of "our domestic legislation being disregarded on social matters." See the verbatim reports of the Plenary meeting of the Convention, of 3 October 2002. Available at http://www.europarl.eu.int/europe2004/textes/verbatim_021003.htm.

[81] The only serious obstacle to such a *use* of rights to solidarity is the restrictive literal tenor of Article 51, section 1, which states that Member States are bound by the Charter "when they are implementing Union law." Such a wording is too narrow, as it was well-settled in the jurisprudence of the European Court of Justice that Member States were bound by "European" fundamental rights standards when they invoked an exception to the market freedoms. However, such an objection can be overcome with two further arguments. First, Article 51, section 1 can be read as determining the "compulsory" scope of the Charter. It could not be read as precluding a Member State from invoking it even in an area where it is not bound by it. Even less so from invoking it *vis-à-vis* Community institutions, which are bound by the Charter *in all cases*. Second, the literal tenor of the provision should be interpreted as providing a succinct formulation of positive law at the time of codification. Thus, the scope of the Charter should overlap with the scope of fundamental rights protection established by the Court of Justice. Therefore, "implementing" must be interpreted as comprising also those cases in which Member States claim an exception to the economic freedoms. Some authors have pointed to the formulation of Article 49, section 1 as evidence to the contrary. See the critical remarks of Weiler in a discussion which took place at Harvard.

Available at http://www.jeanmonnetprogram.org/wwwboard/seminar01/Vitorino_Discussion.rtf. He finds the drafting of the Charter poor as reference is only made to "implementing Union law."

82 Par. 100: "The issue boils down to the following: if a (potential) barrier to trade arises, the Community must be in a position to act. Such action must, as I construe the *biotechnology* judgment, consist in the removal of those barriers. Article 95 EC creates the power to do so."

83 Par. 106: "In other words, the realisation of the internal market may mean that a particular public interest – such as here public health – is dealt with at the level of the European Union. In this, *the interest of the internal market is not yet the principal objective of a Community measure*. The realisation of the internal market simply determines the level at which another public interest is safeguarded" (my emphasis).

84 Par. 229: "The value of this public interest [public health] is so great that, in the legislature's assessment other matters of interest, such as the freedom of market participants, must be made subsidiary to it."

85 A similar theoretical approach seems to be followed by Moral Soriano, *supra*, fn. 87, at pp. 112–123.

86 TCR, p. 276.

87 See, among others, Alan Dashwood and Siofra O'Leary (eds.), *The Principle of Equal Treatment in EC Law*, London: Sweet and Maxwell, 1997 and Gillian More, "The Principle of Equal Treatment: From Market Unifier to Fundamental Right" in Paul Craig and Gráinne de Búrca, *The Evolution of EU Law*, Oxford: Oxford University Press, 1999, pp. 517–553.

88 See, for example, in Case C-72/91, Sloman Neptun, [1993] ECR I-887, especially par. 25ff the Court was ready to claim that the decision of a sectorial authority to refuse a German shipping company the right to engage a radio office and five seafarers under conditions which were less protective of the social rights of workers than German legislation was contrary to the Treaties, while at the same time considering that the social objectives proclaimed by the same Treaties were not to be realized through its jurisprudence, but through legislation. See especially par. 25ff of the judgment. See De Schutter, *supra*, fn. 80 and "La garanzia dei diritti e principi sociali nella 'Carta dei diritti fondamentali' " in Gustavo Zagrebelsky, Sergio Dellavalle and Jörg Luther (eds.), *Diritti e Costituzione nell'Unione Europea*, Bari and Roma: Laterza, 2003, pp. 192–220.

89 Pierre Pescatore, *The Law of Integration: Emergence of a new phenomenon in international relations, based on the experience of the European Communities*, Leiden: Sithoff, 1974.

90 Joxerramón Bengoetxea, *The Legal Reasoning of the European Court of Justice*, Oxford: Oxford University Press, 1993.

91 Case 168/78, *Commission v France*, [1980] ECR 347.

92 Case 27/67, *Fink Frucht GmbH v Haupotzollamt München-Landsbergerstrasse* [1968] ECR 327, which referred to Italian sweet pepper liquor, which was charged a tax at the border. Such tax was not found to be discriminatory because it did not result in a higher tax burden on the said liquor, but was *merely charged at the border*. And Case 45/75, *Rewe-Zentrale v Hauptzollamt Ladau-Pfalz*, [1976] ECR 181 the Court established the concept of similar products as those which "have similar characteristics and meet the same needs from the point of view of consumers."

93 Section 41 of the judgment.

94 Case 433/85, *Feldain v Directeur des Services Fiscaux*, [1987] ECR 3536. This case was a more sophisticated version of Case 112/84, *Humblot v Directeur des Services Fiscaux*, [1985] ECR 1367. In *Humblot*, tax liability was calculated according to a two-fold formula, which rendered more obvious the cover discrimination on the basis of nationality.

[95] Par. 20: "A system of road tax in which one tax band comprises more power ratings for tax purposes than the others, with the result that the normal progression of the tax is restricted in such a way as to afford an advantage to top-of-the-range cars of domestic manufacture, and in which the power rating for tax purposes is calculated in a manner which places vehicles imported from other member states at a disadvantage has a discriminatory or protective effect within the meaning of Article 95 of the treaty."

[96] C-175/88 *Biehl*, [1990] ECR I-1779.

[97] On a side remark, it might be said that this judgments stressed the fact that the Court seemed to have been more concerned about the potential tax penalty deriving from a higher tax liability (a case which will occur in case that the taxpayer will not work during the rest of the year) than with the potential tax benefit which could derive for him.

[98] See, for example, case 109/88, *Handels og Kontorfunktionærernes Forbund i Danmark v Dansk Arbejdsgiverforening, acting on behalf of Danfoss*, [1989] ECR 3199.

[99] See, for example, case 61/81, *Commission v United Kingdom*, [1982] ECR 2601, par. 8.

[100] Case 171/88, *Rinner-Kühn v FWW Spezial-Gebäudereinigung GmbH*, [1989] ECR 2743.

[101] Par. 14 of the judgment.

[102] Case C-177/88, *Dekker v Stichting Vormingscentrum voor Jong Volwassenen*, [1990] ECR I-3941.

[103] Par. 17 of the judgment.

PART V

BIBLIOGRAPHY OF ROBERT ALEXY

9. THE WORK OF ROBERT ALEXY

MONOGRAPHIES

1. *Theorie der juristischen Argumentation*, Frankfurt/M. 1978; New edition Frankfurt/M. 1983; 4th printing, Frankfurt/M. 2001.

   Translation into English by Ruth Adler and Neil MacCormick: *A Theory of Legal Argumentation*, Clarendon Press, Oxford 1989.

   Translation into Spanish by Manuel Atienza and Isabel Espejo: *Teoría de la argumentación jurídica*, Centro de Estudios Constitucionales, Madrid 1989.

   Translation into Italian by Massimo La Torre: *Teoria dell'argomentazione giuridica*, Giuffrè editore, Milan 1998.

   Translation into Portugese by Zilda Hutchinson Schild Silva: *Teoria da Argumentação Jurídica*, Landy, São Paulo 2001.

   Translation into Chinese by Shu Guoying, Fazhi Verlag, Beijing 2002.

2. *Theorie der Grundrechte*, Baden-Baden 1985; New edition, Frankfurt/M. 1986; 3rd printing, Frankfurt/M. 1996.

   Translation into Spanish by Ernesto Garzón Valdés: *Teoría de los derechos fundamentales*, Centro de Estudios Constitucionales, Madrid 1993; New edition, Madrid 1997; 2nd printing Madrid 2001.

   Translation into English by Julian Rivers: *A Theory of Constitutional Rights*, Oxford University Press, Oxford 2002.

3. *Begriff und Geltung des Rechts*, Freiburg/München 1992; 2nd printing, Freiburg/München 1994; New edition, Freiburg/München 2002.

   Translation into Spanish by Jorge M. Seña: *El concepto y la validez del derecho*, Gedisa, Barcelona 1994; 2nd printing, Barcelona 1997.

   Translation into Italian by Fabio Fiore: *Concetto e validità del diritto*, Einaudi, Turin 1997.

   Translation into Korean by Zoonil Yi, Kiran, Seoul 2000.

   Translation into English by Bonnie Litschewski Paulson and Stanley L. Paulson: *The Argument from Injustice. A Reply to Legal Positivism*, Clarendon Press, Oxford 2002.

A. J. Menéndez and E. O. Eriksen (eds.), Arguing Fundamental Rights, 187–202.

4. *Mauerschützen. Zum Verhältnis von Recht, Moral und Strafbarkeit*, Hamburg 1993; also published in: R. Alexy/H.-J. Koch/L. Kuhlen/H. Rüßmann, *Elemente einer juristischen Begründungslehre*, Baden-Baden 2003, pp. 469–492.

5. *Der Beschluß des Bundesverfassungsgerichts zu den Tötungen an der innerdeutschen Grenze vom 24. Oktober 1996*, Hamburg 1997

   Translation into Spanish by A. Daniel Oliver-Lalana: *Derecho injusto, retroactividad y principio de legalidad penal. La doctrina del Tribunal Constitucional Federal alemán sobre los homicidios cometidos por los centinelas del Muro de Berlín*, in: *Doxa* 23 (2000), pp. 197–230.

6. *Põhiõigused Eesti põhiseaduses (Die Grundrechte der estnischen Verfassung;* Translation into Estonian by Madis Ernits and Pille Vinkel), Tartu 2001.

COLLECTIONS OF ARTICLES

1. *Derecho y razón práctica*, Mexico 1993.
2. *Recht, Vernunft, Diskurs. Studien zur Rechtsphilosophie*, Frankfurt/M. 1995.
3. *Teoría del discurso y derechos humanos* (introduction and translation by Luis Villar Borda), Bogotá 1995.
4. *La pretensión de corrección del derecho. La polémica Alexy/Bulygin sobre la relatión entre derecho y moral* (co-authored with Eugenio Bulygin; introduction and translation by Paula Gaido), Bogotá 2001.
5. *Tres escritos sobre los derechos fundamentales y la teoría de los principios* (introduction and translation by Carlos Bernal Pulido), Bogotá 2003.

EDITED BOOKS

1. W. Krawietz and R. Alexy (eds.), *Metatheorie juristischer Argumentation*, Berlin 1983.
2. R. Alexy, R. Dreier and U. Neumann (eds.), *Rechts- und Sozialphilosophie in Deutschland heute, Archiv für Rechts- und Sozialphilosophie*, Volume 44 (1991).
3. R. Alexy and R. Dreier (eds.), *Rechtssystem und praktische Vernunft. Verhandlungen des 15. Weltkongresses der Internationalen Vereinigung für Rechts- und Sozialphilosophie (IVR) in Göttingen, August 1991*, Bd. 1, *Archiv für Rechts- und Sozialphilosophie*, Volume 51 (1993).
4. A. Aarnio, R. Alexy and G. Bergholtz (eds.), *Justice, Morality and Society.* Homage/Festschrift to Aleksander Peczenik, Lund 1997.

5. R. Alexy and J. Laux (eds.), *50Jahre Grundgesetz. Tagung der Rechtswissenschaftlichen Fakultät der Christian-Albrechts-Universität und des Vereins Kieler Doctores Iuris e. V.*, Baden-Baden 2000.
6. R. Alexy, L. H. Meyer, S.L. Paulson, and G. Sprenger (eds.), *Neukantianismus und Rechtsphilosophie*, Baden-Baden 2002.
7. R. Alexy, H.-J. Koch, L. Kuhlen and H. Rüßmann, *Elemente einer juristischen Begründungslehre*, Baden-Baden 2003.

ARTICLES AND CHAPTERS IN BOOKS

1. 'Eine Theorie des praktischen Diskurses', in: W. Oelmüller (ed.), *Normenbegründung – Normendurchsetzung, Materialien zur Normendiskussion*, Bd. 2, Paderborn 1978, pp. 22–58.

   Translation into English by David Frisby: 'A Theory of Practical Discourse', in: S. Benhabib/F. Dallmayr (eds.), *The Communicative Ethics Controversy*, Massachusetts Institute of Technology Press, Cambridge, Mass./London 1990, pp. 151–190.
2. 'Zum Begriff des Rechtsprinzips', in: *Rechtstheorie*, Beiheft 1 (1979), pp. 59–87; further published in: R. Alexy, *Recht, Vernunft, Diskurs. Studien zur Rechtsphilosophie*, Frankfurt/M. 1995, pp. 177–212.
3. 'R. M. Hares Regeln des moralischen Argumentierens und L. Nelsons Abwägungsgesetz', in: *Vernunft, Erkenntnis, Sittlichkeit. Internationales philosophisches Symposion aus Anlaß des 50. Todestages von Leonard Nelson*, edited by P. Schröder, Hamburg 1979, pp. 95–122.
4. 'Aarnio, Perelman und Wittgenstein. Einige Bemerkungen zu Aulis Aarnios Begriff der Rationalität der juristischen Argumentation', in: A. Peczenik/J. Uu-sitalo (eds.), *Reasoning on Legal Reasoning*, Vammala/Finnland 1979, pp. 121–137.
5. 'Die logische Analyse juristischer Entscheidungen', in: *Archiv für Rechts- und Sozialphilosophie*, Vol. 14 (1980), pp. 181–212; further published in: R. Alexy,

   Recht, Vernunft, Diskurs. Studien zur Rechtsphilosophie, Frankfurt/M. 1995, pp. 13–51; R. Alexy/H.-J. Koch/L. Kuhlen/H. Rüßmann, *Elemente einer juristischen Begründungslehre*, Baden-Baden 2003, pp. 9–35.
6. 'Teleologische Auslegung und Gesetzesbindung', in: *Loccumer Protokolle* 31 (1980), pp. 143–151.
7. 'Die Idee einer prozeduralen Theorie der juristischen Argumentation' in: *Rechtstheorie*, Volume 2 (1981), pp. 177–188; further published in: R. Alexy, *Recht, Vernunft, Diskurs. Studien zur Rechtsphilosophie*, Frankfurt/M. 1995, pp. 94–108.

   Translation into Spanish by Carlos de Santiago: 'La idea de una teoría procesal de la argumentación jurídica', in: E. Garzón Valdés (ed.), *Derecho y filosofía*,

Barcelona/Caracas 1985, pp. 43–57; further published in: R. Alexy, *Derecho y razón práctica*, Mexico 1993, pp. 59–73.

8. 'The Foundation of Legal Reasoning' (with A. Aarnio/A. Peczenik), in: *Rechtstheorie* 12 (1981), pp. 133–158 (Part I), pp. 257–279 (Part II), pp. 423–448 (Part III); further published in: *The International Library of Essays in Law & Legal Theory, Schools, Bd. 5.1: Legal Reasoning*, edited by A. Aarnio/ N. MacCormick, Aldershot/ Hongkong/ Singapur/ Sidney 1992, pp. 15–40, 233–281.

   German Version: 'Grundlagen der juristischen Argumentation', in: W. Krawietz/R. Alexy (eds.), *Metatheorie juristischer Argumentation*, Berlin 1983, pp. 9–87.

   Translation into Italian by Riccardo Guastini: 'I fondamenti del ragionamento giuridico', in: P. Comanducci/ R. Guastini (eds.), *L'analisi del ragionamento giuridico*, Turin 1987, pp. 121–187.

9. 'Juristische Argumentation und praktische Vernunft', in: *Jahrbuch der Akademie der Wissenschaften in Göttingen 1982*, pp. 29–32.

10. 'Das Gebot der Rücksichtnahme im baurechtlichen Nachbarschutz', in: *DÖV* (1984), pp. 953–963.

11. 'Rechtsregeln und Rechtsprinzipien', in: *Archiv für Rechts- und Sozialphilosophie*, Volume (1985), pp. 13–29; further published in: R. Alexy/H.-J. Koch/ L. Kuhlen/H. Rüßmann, *Elemente einer juristischen Begründungslehre*, Baden-Baden 2003, pp. 217–233.

12. 'Ermessensfehler', in: *JZ* (1986), pp. 701–716; further published in: R. Alexy/ H.-J. Koch/L. Kuhlen/H. Rüßmann, *Elemente einer juristischen Begründungslehre*, Baden-Baden 2003, pp. 251–286.

    Translation into Portuguese by Luís Afonso Heck: 'Vícios no exercício do poder discricionário', in: *Revista dos tribunais* 89/779 (2000), pp. 11–46.

13. 'Teorija diskursa i pravni sistem', in: *Filozofska istrazivanja* 20 (1987), pp. 185–194 (Translation into Croatian by Maja Uzelac).

    German Version: 'Diskurstheorie und Rechtssystem', in: *Synthesis philosophica* 5 (1988), pp. 299–310.

14. 'Artikel: Argumentation, Argumentationstheorie', in: *Ergänzbares Lex ikon des Rechts*, 2/30 (1987), pp. 1–4.

15. 'Rechtssystem und praktische Vernunft', in: *Rechtstheorie* 18 (1987), pp. 405–419; further published in: R. Alexy, *Recht, Vernunft, Diskurs. Studien zur Rechtsphilosophie*, Frankfurt/M. 1995, pp. 213–231.

    Translation into Spanish by Jorge M. Seña: 'Sistema juridico y razon práctica', in: R. Alexy, *El concepto y la validez del derecho*, Barcelona 1994, pp. 159–177.

16. 'Legal Expert Systems and Legal Theory', in: H. Fiedler/F. Haft/R. Traunmüller (eds.), *Expert Systems in Law – Impacts on Legal Theory and Computer Law*, Tübingen 1988, pp. 67–74.

17. 'Idée et structure d'un système du droit rationnel', in: *Archives de philosophie du droit* 33 (1988), pp. 22–38 (Translation into French by Ingrid Dwars).

German Version: 'Idee und Struktur eines vernünftigen Rechtssys-tem's, in R. Alexy/R. Dreier/U. Neumann (eds.) *Rechts- und Sozialphilosophie in Deutschland heute, Archiv für Rechts- und Sozialphilosophie*, Volume 44 (1991), pp. 30–44.

18. 'Sistema jurídico, principios juricos y razón práctica, in: *Doxa* 5 (1988), pp. 139–151 (Translation into Spanish by Manuel Atienza); further published in: R. Alexy, *Derecho y razón práctica*, Mexiko 1993, pp. 9–22.

Translation into Finnish: 'Oikeusjärjestelmä, oikeusperiaate ja käytännölli-nen järki', in: *Lakimies* 1989, pp. 618–633.

19. 'Probleme der Diskurstheorie', in: *Zeitschrift für philosophische Forschung* 43 (1989), pp. 81–93: further published in: R. Alexy, *Recht, Vernunft, Diskurs. Studien zur Rechtsphilosophie*, Frankfurt/M. 1995, pp. 109–126. Translation into English: 'Problems of Discourse Theory', in: *Crítica* 20 (1988), pp. 43–65.

Translation into Spanish: 'Problemas de la teoría del discurso', in: *Congreso Internacional Extraordinario de Filosofía 1987, Bd. 1*, edited by Universität Cordoba, Cordoba/Argentina o. J., pp. 59–70. Translation into Portuguese by João Mauricio Adeodato: 'Problemas da Teoria do Discurso', in: *Anuário do Mestrado em Direito* 5 (1992), pp. 87–105.

20. 'Individuelle Rechte und kollektive Güter', in: *Internationales Jahrbuch für Rechtsphilosophie und Gesetzgebung*, edited by O. Weinberger, Vol. 1 (1989), pp. 49–70; further published in: R. Alexy, *Recht, Vernunft, Diskurs. Studien zur Rechtsphilosophie*, Frankfurt/M. 1995, pp. 232–261. Translation into English by Ruth Adler: 'Individual Rights and Collective Goods', in: *The International Library of Essays in Law & Legal Theory, Schools, Bd. 8: Rights*, edited by Carlos Nino, Aldershot/ Hongkong/Singapore/Sidney 1992, pp. 163–181.

Translation into Spanish by Jorge M. Seña: 'Derechos individuales y bienes colectivos', in: R. Alexy, *El concepto y la validez del derecho*, Barcelona 1994, pp. 179–208.

21. 'Begriff und Möglichkeit der Wirtschaftsethik', in: F. U. Pappi (ed.), *Wirtschaftsethik*, Christiana Albertina Sonderheft, Kiel 1989, pp. 9–20.

22. 'Zur Kritik des Rechtspositivismus', in: *Archiv für Rechts- und Sozialphilosophie*, Vol. 37 (1990), pp. 9–26.

Translation into English: 'On Necessary Relations Between Law and Morality', in: *Ratio Juris* 2 (1989), pp. 167–183.

Translation into Spanish by Pablo Larrañaga: 'Sobre las relaciones necesarias entre el derecho y la moral', in: R. Alexy, *Derecho y razón práctica*, Mexico 1993, pp. 37–58; further published in: Rodolfo Vázquez (ed.), *Derecho y moral. Ensayos sobre en debate contemporáneo*, Barcelona 1998, pp. 115–137.

23. 'Juristische Begründung, System und Kohärenz', in: *Rechtsdogmatik und praktische Vernunft, Symposion zum 80. Geburtstag von Franz Wieacker*, edited by O. Behrends/M. Dießelhorst/R. Dreier, Göttingen 1990, pp. 95–107.

24. 'The Concept of Jurisprudence' (with Ralf Dreier), in: *Ratio Juris* 3 (1990), pp. 1–13; further published in: *Indian Socio-Legal Journal* 8 (1992), pp. 1–10.

25. 'The Concept of Coherence and Its Significance for Discursive Rationality' (with Aleksander Peczenik), in: *Ratio Juris* 3 (1990), pp. 130–147.

26. 'Die immanente Moral des Grundgesetzes', in: F. Bydlinski/T. Mayer-Maly (eds), *Rechtsethik und Rechtspraxis, Veröffentlichungen des Internationalen Forschungszentrums für Grundfragen der Wissenschaften Salzburg, N. F. Bd. 42*, Innsbruck/Wien 1990, pp. 97–117.

27. 'Problems of Discursive Rationality in Law', in: *Archiv für Rechts- und Sozialphilosophie*, Vol. 42 (1990), pp. 174–179.

28. 'Grundrechte als subjektive Rechte und als objektive Normen', in: *Der Staat* 29 (1990), pp. 49–68; further published in: R. Alexy, *Recht, Vernunft, Diskurs. Studien zur Rechtsphilosophie*, Frankfurt/M. 1995, pp. 262–287.

Translation into Japanese by Go Koyama in: *Meijo Law Review* 43 (1994), pp. 179–193; 44 (1994), pp. 321–341

Translation into Chinese by Ming-Shiou Cherng in: *The Constitutional Review* 24 (1999), pp. 83–98.

Translation into Korean by Hyo-Jeon Kim, in: *Constitutional Law* 6 (2000), pp. 301–325; further published in: Hyo-Jeon Kim (ed.), *Zum Verständnis der deutschen Grundrechtstheorie*, Seoul 2004, pp. 351–376.

29. 'Antwort auf einige Kritiker', in: R. Alexy, *Theorie der juristischen Argumentation*, 2nd printing, Frankfurt/M. 1991, pp. 399–435.

30. 'Statutory Interpretation in the Federal Republic of Germany' (with Ralf Dreier), in: D. N. MacCormick/R. S. Summers (eds.), *Interpreting Statutes, A Comparative Study*, Aldershot/Brookfield/Hongkong/ Singapore/Sydney 1991, pp. 73–121.

31. 'Fortwirkungen nationalsozialistischer Denkweisen in Rechtslehre und Rechtsprechung nach 1945?', in; F. J. Säcker (ed.), *Recht und Rechtslehre im Nationalsozialismus*, Baden-Baden 1992, pp. 219–226.

32. 'Rights, Legal Reasoning and Rational Discourse', in: *Ratio Juris* 5 (1992), pp. 143–152.

    Translation into Spanish by Pablo Larrañaga: 'Derechos, razonamiento jurídico y discurso racional', in: R. Alexy, *Derecho y razón práctica*, Mexico 1993, pp. 23–35; further published in: *Isonomía* 1 (1994), pp. 37–49.
    Translation into Chinese by Ji Tao, in: *Zhejiang University Law Review* 2003, pp. 83–90.

33. 'Zur Verteidigung eines nichtpositivistischen Rechtsbegriffs', in: *Öffentliche oder private Moral? Festschrift für Ernesto Garzón Valdés*, edited by W. Krawietz/G. H. v. Wright, Berlin 1992, pp. 85–108.

    Translation into Polish by Lech Morawski: 'Wobronie niepozytywistycznej koncepcji prawa', in: *Panstwo i prawo* 48 (1993), pp. 34–49.

34. 'Eine diskurstheoretische Konzeption der praktischen Vernunft', in: R. Alexy/ R. Dreier (eds.), *Rechtssystem und praktische Vernunft, Archiv für Rechts- und Sozialphilosophie*, Vol. 51 (1993), pp. 11–29.

    Translation into English by Ruth Adler and Neil MacCormick: 'A Discourse-Theoretical Conception of Practical Reason', in: *Ratio Juris* 5 (1992), pp. 231–251.

    Translation into Spanish by Jorge M. Seña: 'Una concepción teórico-discursiva de la razón práctica', in: R. Alexy, *El concepto y la validez del derecho*, Barcelona 1994, pp. 131–157.

35. 'Normenbegründung und Normanwendung', in: *Rechtsnorm und Rechtswirklichkeit. Festschrift für Werner Krawietz*, edited by A. Aarnio/S. L. Paulson/ O. Weinberger/G. H. v. Wright/D. Wyduckel, Berlin 1993, pp. 3–17; further published in: R. Alexy, *Recht, Vernunft, Diskurs. Studien zur Rechtsphilosophie*, Frankfurt/M. 1995, pp. 52–70.

    Translation into English: 'Justification and Application of Norms', in: *Ratio Juris* 6 (1993), pp. 157–170.

36. 'Walter Ulbrichts Rechtsbegriff', in J. Eckert (ed.), *Die Babelsberger Konferenz vom 2./3. April 1958*, Baden-Baden 1993, pp. 191–202; Reprinted in: *Recht und Politik* 29 (1993), pp. 207–212.

37. 'Legal Argumentation as Rational Discourse', in: *Rivista internazionale di filosofia del diritto* 70 (1993), pp. 165–178.

    Translation into Italian by Giovanni Sartor: 'L'argomentazione giuridica come discorso razionale', in: *Informatica e diritto* 3 (1994), pp. 5–20.

    Translation into Spanish by Luis Villar Borda: 'Interpretación jurídica y discurso racional', in: R. Alexy, *Teoría del discurso y derechos humanos*, Bogotá 1995, pp. 35–61

    German Version: 'Die juristische Argumentation als rationaler Diskurs', in: *Facetten der Wahrheit. Festschrift für Meinolf Wewel*, edited by E. G. Valdés/

R. Zimmerling, Freiburg/München 1995, pp. 361–378; further published in: R. Alexy/ H.-J. Koch/L. Kuhlen/H. Rüßmann, *Elemente einer juristischen Begründungslehre*, Baden-Baden, pp. 113–122.

38. 'Ota Weinbergers Kritik der diskurstheoretischen Deutung juristischer Rationalität', in: P. Koller/W. Krawietz/P. Strasser (eds.), *Institution und Recht, Rechtstheorie*, Vol. 14 (1994), pp. 143–157.

39. 'A Definition of Law', in: *Prescriptive Formality and Normative Rationality in Modern Legal Systems*. Homage to S. Summers, edited by W. Krawietz/D. N. MacCormick/G. H. v. Wright, Berlin 1994, pp. 101–107.

40. 'Basic Rights and Democracy in Jürgen Habermas's Procedural Paradigm of the Law', in: *Ratio Juris* 7 (1994), pp. 227–238.

    German Version: 'Grundrechte und Demokratie in Jürgen Habermas's prozeduralem Rechtsparadigma', in: *Gerechtigkeit und Geschichte. Beiträge eines Symposions zum 65. Geburtstag von Malte Dießelhorst*, edited by O. Behrends/ R. Dreier, Göttingen 1996, pp. 78–89.

41. 'Juristische Interpretation', in: R. Alexy, *Recht, Vernunft, Diskurs. Studien zur Rechtsphilosophie*, Frankfurt/M. 1995, pp. 71–92.

    Translation into Italian: 'Interpretazione giuridica', in: *Enciclopedia delle scienze sociali*, edited by Istituto della enciclopedia italiana, Vol. 5, Rome 1996, pp. 64–71.

42. 'Diskurstheorie und Menschenrechte', in: R. Alexy, *Recht, Vernunft, Diskurs. Studien zur Rechtsphilosophie*, Frankfurt/M. 1995, pp. 127–164.

    Translation into Spanish by Luis Villar Borda: 'Teoría del discurso y derechos humanos', in: R. Alexy, *Teoría del discurso y derechos humanos*, Bogotá 1995, pp. 63–138.

    Translation into English: 'Discourse Theory and Human Rights', in: *Ratio Juris* 9 (1996), pp. 209–235; *Archiv für Rechts- und Sozialphilosophie*, Vol. 67 (1997), pp. 81–104; further published in: João Lopes Alves (ed.), *Ética e o Futuro da Democracia*, Lisabon 1998, pp. 133–142; *Indian Socio-Legal Journal* 25 (1999), pp. 53–58.

43. 'Jürgen Habermas' Theorie des juristischen Diskurses', in: R. Alexy, *Recht, Vernunft, Diskurs. Studien zur Rechtsphilosophie*, Frankfurt/M. 1995, pp. 165–174.

    Translation into English: 'Jürgen Habermas's Theory of Legal Discourse', in: *Cardozo Law Review* 17 (1996), pp. 1027–1034; further published in: M. Rosenfeld/A. Arato (eds.), *Habermas on Law and Democracy*, Berkeley/Los Angeles/London 1998, pp. 226–233.

44. 'Law, Discourse, and Time', in: *Archiv für Rechts- und Sozialphilosophie*, Vol. 64 (1995), pp. 101–110.

Translation into French by François Boudreault: 'Droit, discours et temps', in: *Temps et droit. Le droit a-t-il pour vocation de durer?*, edited by F. Ost/M. van Hoecke, Brussels 1998, pp. 15–29.

Translation into Chinese by Chueh-an Yen: 'Regeln und Formen des allgemeinen praktischen und des juristischen Diskurses', from: *Theorie der juristischen Argumentation*, 4th printing., Frankfurt/M. 2001 (No. 1), pp. 361–367, in: *National Chengchi Law Review* 53 (1995), pp. 41–44.

45. 'Grundgesetz und Diskurstheorie', in: W. Brugger (ed.), *Legitimation des Grundgesetzes aus Sicht von Rechtsphilosophie und Gesellschaftstheorie*, Baden-Baden 1996, pp. 343–360.

46. 'John Rawls' Theorie der Grundfreiheiten', in: *Zur Idee des politischen Liberalismus. John Rawls in der Diskussion*, edited by Philosophischen Gesellschaft Bad Homburg and W. Hinsch, Frankfurt/M. 1997, pp. 263–303.

Translation into Italian by Anna Castelli and Fabrizio Sciacca: 'La teoria delle libertà fondamentali di John Rawls', in: Fabrizio Sciacca (ed.), *Libertà fondamentali in John Rawls*, Milan 2002, pp. 1–36.

47. 'Bulygins Kritik des Richtigkeitsarguments', in: *Normative Systems in Legal and Moral Theory*. Homage to Carlos E. Alchourrón and Eugenio Bulygin, edited by E. Garzón Valdés/W. Krawietz/G. H. v. Wright/R. Zimmerling, Berlin 1997, pp. 235–250.

Translation into Spanish by Paula Gaido: 'La crítica de Bulygin al argumento de la corrección', in: Robert Alexy/Eugenio Bulygin, *La pretensión de corrección del derecho. La polemica Alexy /Bulygin sobre la relación entre derecho y moral*, Bogotá 2001, pp. 53–84.

48. 'Carlos Santiago Ninos Begründung der Menschenrechte', in: *Staatsphilosophie und Rechtspolitik*. Homage to Martin Kriele, edited by B. Ziemske/Th. Langheid/H. Wilms/G. Haverkate, München 1997, pp. 187–217.

49. 'Precedent in the Federal Republik of Germany' (with Ralf Dreier), in: D. N. MacCormick/R. S. Summers (eds.), *Interpreting Precedents. A Comparative Study*, Aldershot/Brookfield USA/Singapore/Sydney 1997, pp. 17–64.

50. 'Grundrechte im demokratischen Verfassungsstaat', in: *Justice, Morality and Society*. Homage to Aleksander Peczenik, edited by A. Aarnio/R. Alexy/G. Bergholtz, Lund 1997, pp. 27–42; further published in: W. Deppert/D. Mielke/ W. Theobald (eds), *Mensch und Wirtschaft. Interdisziplinäre Beiträge zur Wirtschafts- und Unternehmensethik*, Leipzig 2001, pp. 15–31.

Translation into Japanese by Koichi Aoyagi in: *Yokohama Law Review* 5 (1997), pp. 193–223.

Translation into Chinese by Ming-Shiou Cherng in: *Law Review of Central Police University* 5 (2000), pp. 427–441.

Translation into Spanish by Alfonso García Figueroa: 'Los derechos fundamentales en el Estado constitucional democrático', in: Miguel Carbonell (ed.), *Neoconstitucionalismo(s)*, Madrid 2003, pp. 31–47.

51. 'Giustizia come correttezza', in: *Ragion pratica* 9 (1997), pp. 103–113 (Translation into Italian by Bruno Celano).

52. 'Güter- und Übelabwägung, Rechtlich; Norm/Normen, Rechtlich; Prinzipien, Rechtlich', in: *Lexikon der Bioethik*, edited by W. Korff/L. Beck/P. Mikat, Gütersloh 1998, Bd. 2, pp. 181–182; pp. 777–779; Bd. 3, pp. 66–67.

53. 'Coherence and Argumentation or the Genuine Twin Criterialess Super Criterion', in: A. Aarnio/R. Alexy/A. Peczenik/W. Rabinowicz/J. Wolenski, *On Coherence Theory of Law*, Lund 1998, pp. 41–49.

54. 'Die Institutionalisierung der Menschenrechte im demokratischen Verfassungsstaat', in: S. Gosepath/G. Lohmann (eds.), *Philosophie der Menschenrechte*, Frankfurt/M. 1998, pp. 244–264.

Translation into Spanish by María Cecilia Añaños Meza: 'La institucionalización de los derechos humanos en el Estado constitucional democrático', in: *Derechos y libertades* 8 (2000), pp. 21–41.

55. 'Law and Correctness', in: M. D. A. Freeman (ed.), *Legal Theory at the End of the Millennium*, Oxford 1998 *(Current Legal Problems* 51 (1998)), pp. 205–221.

German Version: 'Recht und Richtigkeit', in: *The Reasonable as Rational? On Legal Argumentation and Justification.* Homage to Aulis Aarnio, edited by W. Krawietz/R. S. Summers/O. Weinberger/G. H. v. Wright, Berlin 2000, pp. 3–19.

56. 'A Defence of Radbruch's Formula', in: D. Dyzenhaus (ed.), *Recrafting the Rule of Law: The Limits of Legal Order*, Oxford/ Portland, Oregon 1999, pp. 15–39; further published in: *Lloyd's Introduction to Jurisprudence*, 7th edn., edited by M.D.A. Friedman, London 2001, pp. 374–391.

Transaltion into Bulgarian (with minor revisions) by Stanislava Drumeba: 'Granuzite me nemoralnoto prabo', in: Ivaylo Znepolski/Heinz Wisman (eds.), *Okolo Habermas. Normatifnosta b modernite obschestba i idejata sa cprabedlibocma*, Sofia 2000, pp. 45–90.

Translation into Spanish by José Antonio Seoane: 'Una defensa de la fórmula de Radbruch', in: *Anuario da Facultade de Dereito da Universidade da Coruña* 5 (2001), pp. 75–95.

57. 'My Philosophy of Law: The Institutionalisation of Reason', in: L. J. Wintgens (ed.), *The Law in Philosophical Perspectives. My Philosophy of Law*, Dordrecht/ Boston/London 1999, pp. 23–45.

Translation into Spanish by José Antonio Seoane: 'La institucionalización de la razón', in: *Persona y Derecho* 43 (2000), pp. 217–249.

58. 'Notizen zu einer Diskurstheorie des Rechts und (Diskussion mit K. Günther/R. Zaczyk/R. Zippelius) Rechtsdiskurs und Rechtssubjekt', in: P. Siller/B. Keller (eds.), *Rechtsphilosophische Kontroversen der Gegenwart*, Baden-Baden 1999, pp. 49–50, 65–73.

59. 'Direitos Fundamentais no Estado Constitucional Democrático. Para a relação entre direitos do homem, direitos fundamentais, democracia e jurisdição constitucional', in: *Revista da Faculdade de Direito da Universidade Federal do Rio Grande do Sul* 16 (1999), pp. 203–214 (Translation into Portuguese by Luís Afonso Heck); further published in: *Revista de direito administrativo* 217 (1999), pp. 55–66.

60. 'Grundrechte', in: *Enzyklopädie Philosophie*, edited by H. J. Sandkühler, Hamburg 1999, Bd. 1, pp. 525–529.

    Translation into Spanish by Carlos Bernal Pulido: 'Los derechos fundamentales', in: R. Alexy, *Tres escritos sobre los derechos fundamentales y la teoría de los principios*, Bogotá 2003, pp. 19–39.

61. 'The Special Case Thesis', in: *Ratio Juris* 12 (1999), pp. 374–384.

    Translation into Spanish by Isabel Lifante: 'La tesis del caso especial', in: *Isegoría* 21 (1999), pp. 23–35.

62. 'Colisão de Direitos Fundamentais e Realização de Direitos Fundamentais no Estado de Direito Democrático', in: *Revista da Faculdade de Direito da Universidade Federal do Rio Grande do Sul* 17 (1999), pp. 267–279 (Translation into Portuguese by Luís Afonso Heck); further published in: *Revista de direito administrativo* 217 (1999) pp. 67–79.

    German Version: 'Kollision und Abwägung als Grundprobleme der Grundrechtsdogmatik', in: *World Constitutional Law Review*, Korean Branch of International Association of Constitutional Law (ed.) 6 (2001), pp. 181–207; further published in: M. La Torre/A. Spadaro (eds.), *La ragionevolezza nel diritto*, Turin 2002, pp. 9–26.

    Translation into Estonian by Madis Ernits: 'Kollisioon ja kaalumine kui põhiõiguste dogmaatika põhiprobleemid', in: *Juridica* 9 (2001), pp. 5–13.

    Translation into Italian by Massimo La Torre: 'Collisione e bilanciamento quale problema di base della dogmatica dei diritti fondamentali', in: M. La Torre/A. Spadaro (eds.), *La ragionevolezza nel diritto*, Turin 2002, pp. 27–44.

63. 'Einleitung: 50Jahre Grundgesetz', in: R. Alexy/J. Laux (eds.), *50Jahre Grundgesetz. Tagung der Rechtswissenschaftlichen Fakultät der Christian- Albrechts-Universität und des Vereins Kieler Doctores Iuris e. V.*, Baden-Baden 2000, pp. 9–13.

64. 'Zur Struktur der Rechtsprinzipien', in: B. Schilcher/P. Koller/B.-C. Funk (eds.), *Regeln, Prinzipien und Elemente im System des Rechts*, Wien 2000, pp. 31–52.

Translation into English: 'On the Structure of Legal Principles', in: *Ratio Juris* 13 (2000), pp. 294–304.

Translation into Spanish by Carlos Bernal Pulido: 'Sobre la estructura de los principios jurídicos', in: R. Alexy, *Tres escritos sobre los derechos fundamentales y la teoría de los principios*, Bogotá 2003, pp. 93–137.

65. 'On the Thesis of a Necessary Connection between Law and Morality: Bulygin's Critique', in: *Ratio Juris* 13 (2000), pp. 138–147.

Translation into Spanish by Paula Gaido: 'Sobre la tesis de una conexión necesaria entre derecho y moral: la crítica de Bulygin', in: Robert Alexy/Eugenio Bulygin, *La pretensión de corrección del derecho. La polémica Alexy /Bulygin sobre la relación entre derecho y moral*, Bogotá 2001, pp. 95–115.

66. 'Grundrecht und Status' (Reprint of Ch. 5 of: *Theorie der Grundrechte*, 3rd printing, Frankfurt/M. 1996 (No. 2)), in: S. L. Paulson/M. Schulte (eds.), *Georg Jellinek. Beiträge zu Leben und Werk*, Tübingen 2000, pp. 209–225.

67. 'Grundrechtsnorm und Grundrecht', in: *Rechtstheorie*, Vol. 13 (2000), pp. 101–115.

68. 'Die Abwägung in der Rechtsanwendung', in: *Jahresbericht des Institutes für Rechtswissenschaft an der Meiji Gakuin Universität Tokio* 17 (2001), pp. 69–83.

69. Translation into Chinese by Shu Guoying: 'Einleitung und Tafel der erarbeiteten Regeln und Formen', from: *Theorie der juristischen Argumentation, 4th* printing, Frankfurt/M. 2001, pp. 17–49, 361–367 (English title: 'Problematic and developmental orientation of the theories of legal argumentation'), in: *Archives for Legal Philosophy and Legal Sociology* (China University of Politics and Law, Beijing) 2001, pp. 78–115.

70. 'Law and Morality: A Continental-European Perspective', in: *International Encyclopedia of the Social & Behavioral Sciences*, edited by N. J. Smelser/P. B. Bates, Bd. 12, Amsterdam/Paris/New York/Oxford/ Shannon/Singapore/Tokyo 2001, pp. 8465–8469.

German Version: 'Recht und Moral', in: *Marburger Jahrbuch Theologie* 14 (2002), pp. 83–92.

71. Verfassungsrecht und einfaches Recht – (Verfassungsgerichtsbarkeit und Fachgerichtsbarkeit), in: *VVDStRL* 61 (2002), pp. 7–33.

Translation into Portuguese by Luís Afonso Heck: 'Direito constitucional e direito ordinário. Jurisdição constitucional e jurisdição especializada', in:

Revista dos tribunais 91/799 (2002), pp. 33–51; new printing: *Revista dos tribunais* 92/809 (2003), pp. 54–73.

Translation into Spanish by Carlos Bernal Pulido: 'Derecho constitucional y derecho ordinario. – Jurisdicción constitucional y jurisdicción ordinaria', in: R. Alexy, *Tres escritos sobre los derechos fundamentales y la teoría de los principios*, Bogotá 2003, pp. 41–92.

72. 'Zur Entwicklung der Menschen- und Grundrechte in Deutschland', in: *Christiana Albertina* 54 (2002), pp. 6–18.

73. 'Postscript', in: R. Alexy, *A Theory of Constitutional Rights*, translation by Julian Rivers, Oxford 2002, pp. 388–425.

Translation into Spanish by Carlos Bernal Pulido: 'Epílogo a la Teoría de los Derechos Fundamentales', in: *Revista Española de Derecho Constitutional* 22 (2002), pp. 13–64.

74. 'Hans Kelsens Begriff des relativen Apriori', in: R. Alexy/L. H. Meyer/S. L. Paulson/ G. Sprenger (eds.), *Neukantianismus und Rechtsphilosophie*, Baden-Baden 2002, pp. 179–202.

75. 'Grundrechte, Abwägung und Rationalität', in: *Ars Interpretandi. Yearbook of Legal Hermeneutics* 7 (2002), pp. 113–125.

Translation into Italian by Damiano Canale: 'Diritti fondamentali, bilanciamento e razionalità', in: *Ars Interpretandi. Annuario di ermeneutica giuridica, 7* (2002), pp. 131–144.

English Version: 'Constitutional Rights, Balancing, and Rationality', in: *Ratio Juris* 16 (2003), pp. 131–140.

Translation into Spanish by David García Pazos and Alberto Oehling de los Reyes: 'Derechos fundamentales, ponderación y racionalidad', in: F. F. Segado (ed.), *The Spanish Constitution in the European Constitutional Context. La Constitución Española en el Contexto Constitucional Europeo*, Madrid 2003, pp. 1505–1514.

76. 'Ragionevolezza im Verfassungsrecht. Acht Diskussionsbemerkungen', in: M. La Torre/A. Spadaro (eds.), *La ragionevolezza nel diritto*, Turin 2002, pp. 143–150.

Translation into Italian by Massimo La Torre: 'Ragionevolezza nel Diritto costituzionale. Otto osservazioni sulla discussione', in: M. La Torre/A. Spadaro (eds.), *La ragionevolezza nel diritto*, Turin 2002, pp. 151–157.

77. 'Die Gewichtsformel', in: *Gedächtnisschrift für Jürgen Sonnenschein*, edited by J. Jickeli/P. Kreutz/D. Reuter, Berlin 2003, pp. 771–792.

Translation into Korean by Jong-Sup Chong and Zin-Wan Park, in: *Seoul Law Journal* 44(3) (2003), pp. 327–355.

78. 'The Nature of Arguments about the Nature of Law', in: L. H. Meyer/ S. L. Paulson/T. W. Pogge (eds.), *Rights, Culture, and the Law. Themes from the Legal and Political Philosophy of Joseph Raz*, Oxford 2003, pp. 3–16.

79. 'The Nature of Legal Philosophy', in: Associations 7 (2003), pp. 63–75; further published in: *Ratio Juris* 17 (2004), pp. 156–167.

80. 'On Balancing and Subsumption. A Structural Comparison', in: *Ratio Juris* 16 (2003), pp. 433–449.

81. 'Menschenrechte ohne Metaphysik?', in: *Deutsche Zeitschrift für Philosophie* 52 (2004), pp. 15–24.

REVIEWS

1. H. J. Koch, 'Unbestimmte Rechtsbegriffe und Ermessen-sermächtigungen im Verwaltungsrecht', Frankfurt/M. 1979, in: *Archiv fürRechts- und Sozialphilosophie* 66 (1980), pp. 297–300.

2. D. Neil MacCormick, 'Legal Reasoning and Legal Theory, Oxford 1978', in: *Rechtstheorie* 11 (1980), pp. 120–128.

3. Kaufmann/W. Hassemer (eds.), 'Einführung in Rechtsphilosophie und Rechtstheorie der Gegenwart', 4th Edition, Heidelberg 1985, in: *Jura* 1988, pp. 168.

4. H. Dreier, 'Dimensionen der Grundrechte', Hannover 1993, in: *Archiv des öffentlichen Rechts* 121 (1996), pp. 155–158.

   Translation into Spanish: *Diálogo científico* 6 (1997), pp. 49–52.

5. H. Prakken, 'Logical Tools for Modelling Argument. A Study of Defeasible Reasoning in Law', Dordrecht/Boston/London 1997, in: *Argumentation* 14 (2000), pp. 66–72.

OTHER PIECES

1. 'Entrevista a Robert Alexy. Antworten auf Fragen Manuel Atienzas', in: *Doxa* 24 (2001), pp. 671–687; further published in: *Diálogo científico* 12 (2003), pp. 173–190.
2. 'Gustav Radbruch (1878–1949)', in: *Christiana Albertina* 58 (2004), pp. 47–51.

ELECTRONIC PUBLICATIONS

1. 'Data und die Menschenrechte – Positronisches Gehirn und doppeltriadischer Personenbegriff', contribution tor "Ringvorlesung des Instituts für Neuere Deutsche Literatur und Medien zur Erforschung von Populärkultur am Beispiel von STAR TREK", 8 February 2000, University of Kiel.

TABLE OF CASES

EUROPEAN COURT OF JUSTICE

8/55	*Fédération Charbonnière de Belgique v High Authority of the European Coal and Steel Community*, [1955] ECR 291
14/61	*Hoogovens v High Authority*, [1962] ECR 253
26/62	*Van Gend en Loos*, [1963] ECR 1
6/64	*Costa v Enel*, [1964] ECR 585
27/67	*Fink Frucht GmbH v Haupotzollamt München-Landsbergerstrasse* [1968] ECR 327
29/69	*Stauder* [1969] ECR 419
11/70	*Internationale*, [1970] ECR 1125
41/74	*Van Duyn v Home Office*, [1974] ECR 1337
45/75	*Rewe-Zentrale v Hauptzollamt Ladau-Pfalz*, 1976 [ECR] 181
120/78	*Rewe v Bundesmonopolverwaltung für Branntwein* [1979] ECR 649
168/78	*Commission v France*, [1980] ECR 347
61/81	*Commission v United Kingdom*, [1982] ECR 2601
294/83	*'Les Verts' v European Parliament*, judgment of 23 April 1986, [1986] ECR 1357
112/84	*Humblot v Directeur des Services Fiscaux*, [1985] ECR 1367
433/85	*Feldain v Directeur des Services Fiscaux*, [1987] ECR 3536
109/88	*Handels og Kontorfunktionærernes Forbund i Danmark v Dansk Arbejdsgiverforening, acting on behalf of Danfoss*, [1989] ECR 3199
171/88	*Rinner-Kühn v FWW Spezial-Gebäudereinigung GmbH*, [1989] ECR 2743
C-175/88	*Biehl*, [1990] ECR I-1779
C-177/88	*Dekker v Stichting Vormingscentrum voor Jong Volwassenen*, [1990] ECR I-3941
C-204/90	*Hanns Martin Bachmann v Belgian State*, [1992] ECR I-249
C-300/90	*Commission v Belgium*, [1992] ECR I-305
C-72/91	*Sloman Neptun*, [1993] ECR I-887
C-67/96	*Albany* [1999] ECR I-5751
C-112/00	*Schmidberger* [2003] ECR I-5659

EUROPEAN COURT OF HUMAN RIGHTS

Belgian Linguistic Case (no 2) (1968) 1 EHRR 252
Airey v Ireland (1979) 3 EHRR 592
See *Van Raalte v Netherlands* (1997) 24 EHRR 14
Thlimmenos v Greece (2000) 31 EHRR 15
Willis v UK (2002) 35 EHRR 21
Wessels-Bergervoet v Netherlands (2004) 38 EHRR 793

A. J. Menéndez and E. O. Eriksen (eds.), Arguing Fundamental Rights, 203–206.

GERMANY

6 BVerfG 32	*Elfes*
7 BVerfG 198	*Lüth*
22 BVerfG 293	*European Community Regulations*
30 BVerfG 59	
30 BVerfG 173	*Mephisto*
30 BVerfG 296	
39 BVerfG 1	
43 BVerfG 130	
43 BVerfG 142	
46 BVerfG 160	*Schleyer*
49 BVerfG 89	*Atomic Energy Act*
53 BVerfG 30	
54 BVerfG 143	
54 BVerfG 263	
61 BVerfG 1	
64 BVerfG 301	
80 BVerfG 137	
86 BVerfG 1	
88 BVerfG 203	
89 BVerfG 1	
89 BVerfG 214	
99 BVerfG 19	
95 BVerfG 173	
103 BVerfG 89	
47 BAG 363	

IRELAND

Meskell v Coras Iompair Eireann [1973] I.R. 121

UNITED KINGDOM

John MacDonald MacCormick v Lord Advocate [1953] SC 396
R v Home Secretary ex parte Khawaja [1984] AC 74
R v Secretary of State for Transport ex parte Factortame (no. 2), [1991] 1 AC 603
Venables v News Group Newspapers [2001] Fam 430
Douglas v Hello! Ltd. (no. 1) [2001] QB 967
R (Daly) v Home Secretary, [2001] 2 WLR 1622
Aston Cantlow and Wilmcote v Wallbank, [2001] 3 WLR 1323
Wilson v First County Trust Ltd. (no. 2) [2002] QB 74
R (Javed) v SS for the Home Department [2002] QB 129
R (Wilkinson) v Broadmoor Hospital [2002] 1 WLR 419
RSPCA v AG [2002] 1 WLR 448
R (A) v Lord Saville of Newdigate [2002] 1 WLR 505
Lee v Leeds City Council [2002] 1 WLR 1488
Lindsay v Commrs of Customs and Excise [2002] 1 WLR 1766

R (S) v Chief Constable of South Yorkshire Police, [2002] 1 WLR 3223
Thoburn v Sunderland City Council, [2002] 3 WLR 247
R (Amin) v SS Home Department, [2002] 3 WLR 505
R (Bernard) v Enfield LBC [2003] HRLR 4
Ghaidan v Godin-Mendoza, [2003] 2 WLR 478

UNITED STATES

Campbell Soup Co. v Wentz, [1948] 172 F.2d 80, 3rd Circ.

BIBLIOGRAPHY

Ackerman, Bruce. 1998. *We the People: Transformations*, Cambridge (MA): Harvard University Press.
Alejandro, Roberto. 1996. "What is Political about Rawls' Political Liberalism?," 58 *The Journal of Politics*, pp. 1–24.
Alexy, Robert. 1981. "Die Idee einer prozeduralen Theorie der juristischen Argumentation," 2 *Rechtstheorie*, pp. 177–188.
———. 1986. *Theorie der Grundrechte*, Frankfurt am Main: Suhrkamp.
———. 1989. *A Theory of Legal Argumentation. The Theory of Rational Discourse as Theory of Legal Justification*, Oxford: Oxford University Press.
———. 1992a. "A Discourse-Theoretical Conception of Practical Reason," in 5 *Ratio Juris*, pp. 231–251.
———. 1992b. "Individual Rights and Collective Goods," in Carlos Santiago Nino (ed.), *Rights*, Dartmouth: Aldershot, pp. 163–181.
———. 1993. "Justification and Application of Norms," 6 *Ratio Juris*, pp.157–170.
———. 1995. *Recht, Vernunft, Diskurs*, Frankfurt am Main: Suhrkamp.
———.1996a. "Jürgen Habermas Theory of Legal Discourse," 17 *Cardozo Law Review*, pp. 1027–1034. (also published in Michel Rosenfeld and Andrew Arato (eds.), *Habermas on Law and Democracy: Critical Exchanges*, Berkeley, University of California Press, 1998, pp. 226–233).
———. 1996b. "Discourse Theory and Human Rights," in 9 *Ratio Juris*, pp. 209–235.
———. 1998a. "Law and Correctness," in Michael Freeman (ed.), *Legal Theory at the End of the Millennium*, Oxford: Oxford University Press, pp. 205–222.
———. 1998b. "Die Institutionalisierung der Menschenrechte im demokratischen Verfassungsstaat," in Stefan Gosepath and Georg Lohmann (eds.), *Philosophie der Menschenrechte*, Frankfurt: Suhrkamp, pp. 246–254.
———. 1999a. "Grundrechte," in Hans Jörg Sandkühler (ed.), *Enzyklopädie Philosophie*, vol. 1, Hamburg: Felix Meiner, pp. 525–529.
———. 1999b. "The Special Case Thesis," 12 *Ratio Juris*, pp. 374–384.
———. 2000. "On the structure of legal principles," 13 *Ratio Juris*, pp. 294–304.
———. 2002a. *A Theory of Constitutional Rights*, Oxford: Oxford University Press, (English translation of *Theorie der Grundrechte*. Frankfurt am Main: Suhrkamp, 1986).
———. 2002b. *The Argument from Injustice. A reply to legal positivism*, Oxford: Oxford University Press.
———. 2003a. "Fundamental rights, Balancing, and Rationality," 16 *Ratio Juris*, pp. 131–140.
———. 2003b. "Die Gewichtsformel," in Joachim Jickeli, Peter Kreutz and Dieter Reuter (eds.), *Gedächtnisschrift für Jürgen Sonnenschein*, Berlin: De Gruyter, pp. 771–792.

A. J. Menéndez and E. O. Eriksen (eds.), Arguing Fundamental Rights, 207–214.

———. 2003c. "On Balancing and Subsumption. A Structural Comparison," 16 *Ratio Juris*, pp. 433–449.

Apel, Karl Otto. 1998. *Auseinander-setzungen in Erprobung des transzendental-pragmatischen Ansatzes*, Frankfurt: Suhrkamp.

Aquinas, Thomas. 1978. *Summa Theologica*, Chicago (IL): Encyclopedia Britannica.

Arai-Takahashi, Yukati. 2002. *The Margin of Appreciation Doctrine and the Principle of Proportionality in the Jurisprudence of the European Court of Human Rights*, Antwerp and New York (NY): Intersentia.

Austin, John. 1995. *The Province of Jurisprudence Determined*, Cambridge (MA): Cambridge University Press.

Barro, Robert. 1997. *Determinants of Economic Growth*, Cambridge (MA): The MIT Press.

Barry, Brian. 1991. *Democracy and Power*, Oxford: Oxford University Press.

Bengoetxea, Joxerramón. 1993. *The Legal Reasoning of the European Court of Justice*, Oxford: Oxford University Press.

Benhabib, Seyla. 2002. *The Claims of Culture. Equality and Diversity in a Global Era*, Princeton (NJ): Princeton University Press.

Bernal Pulido, Carlos. 2003. *El principio de proporcionalidad y los derechos fundamentales*, Madrid: Centro de Estudios Políticos y Constitucionales.

Böckenförde, Ernest Wolfgang. 2000. *Recht, Staat, Freiheit*, Frankfurt: Suhrkamp.

Bohman, James. 1991. *New Philosophy of Social Science: Problems of Interderminacy*, Cambridge (MA): The MIT Press.

———. 1998. "Survey Article: The Coming of Age of Deliberative Democracy," 6 *The Journal of Political Philosophy*, pp. 400–425.

Brandom, Robert B. 2000. *Articulating Reasons*, Cambridge (MA) and London: Harvard University Press.

Brown, Cristopher. 2003. "Comment to Schmidberger," 40 *Common Market Law Review*, pp. 1499–1510.

Brunkhorst, Hauke, Wolfgang Köhler and Matthias Lutz-Bachmann (eds.). 1999. *Recht auf Menschrechte*, Frankfurt: Suhrkamp.

Buchanan, James M. 1975. *The Limits of Liberty*, Chicago and London: Chicago University Press.

Bulygin, Eugenio. 2000. "Alexy's Thesis of the Necessary Connection Between Law and Morality", 13 *Ratio Juris*, pp. 133–137.

Dahl, Robert A. 1989. *Democracy and its Critics*, New Haven (CT): Yale University Press.

Dashwood, Alan and Siofra O'Leary (eds.). 1997. *The Principle of Equal Treatment in EC Law*, London: Sweet and Maxwell.

De Schutter, Olivier. 2001. "La contribution de la Charte des droits fondamentaux de l'Union européenne à la garantie des droits sociaux dans l'ordre juridique communautaire," 12 *Revue Universelle des Droits de L'Homme*, pp. 33–47.

———. 2003. "La garanzia dei diritti e principi sociali nella "Carta dei diritti fondamentali" in Gustavo Zagrebelsky, Sergio Dellavalle, and Jörg Luther (eds.), *Diritti e Costituzione nell' Unione Europea*, Bari and Roma: Laterza, pp. 192–220.

Dershowitz, Alan. 1989. "Is it necessary to apply physical pressure to terrorists and to lie about it," 23 *Israel Law Review*, pp. 192–200.

———. 2002. *Why Terrorism Works*, New Haven (CT): Yale University Press.

———. 2004. "The Torture Warrant: A rejoinder to professor Strauss," 48 *New York School Law Review*, pp. 275–94.

Dicey, Albert Venn. 1959. *An Introduction to the Study of the Law of the Constitution*, (10th edn.) Emlyn Capel Stewart Wade (ed.), London and New York: MacMillan.

Dworkin, Ronald. 1977. *Taking Rights Seriously*, London: Duckworth.

———. 1981. "What is Equality? Part 2: Equality of Resources," 10 *Philosophy and Public Affairs*, pp. 283–345.

———. 1986. *Law's Empire*, Cambridge (MA): Harvard University Press.

———. 1996. *Freedom's Law*, Cambridge (MA): Harvard University Press.

Dyzenhaus, David. 2004. *The Unity of Public Law*, Oxford: Hart Publishers.

Eriksen, Erik Oddvar. 2001. *Demokratiets sorte hull*, Oslo: Abstrakt Forlag.

Eriksen, Erik Oddvar, and Jarle Weigård. 2003. *Understanding Habermas. Communicative Action and Deliberative Democracy*, London: Continuum.

Eriksen, Erik Oddvar, John Erik Fossum, and Agustín José Menéndez (eds.). 2003. *The Chartering of Europe*, Baden-Baden: Nomos.

———. 2004. *Developing a Constitution for Europe*, London: Routledge.

Estlund, David. 1993. "Who's Afraid of Deliberative Democracy? On the Strategic/Deliberative Dichotomy in Recent Constitutional Jurisprudence" 71 *Texas Law Review*, pp. 1437–1477.

———. 1997. "Beyond Fairness and Deliberation: The Epistemic Dimension of Democratic Authority," in James Bohman and William Rehg (eds.), *Deliberative Democracy*, Cambridge (MA): The MIT Press, pp. 173–204.

Ewald, François. 1986. *L'Etat providence*, Paris: Grasset.

Feldamn, David. 2002. *Civil Liberties and Human Rights in England and Wales*, Oxford: Oxford University Press.

Fioravanti, Maurizio and Stefanno Mannoni, 2001. "Il modelo costituzionale europeo. Tradizione e prospettive," in G. Bonacchi (ed.), *Una Costituzione senza stato*, Bologna: Il Mulino, pp. 23–70.

Fiss, Owen. 1986. "The Death of Law," 72 *Cornell Law Review*, pp. 1–16.

Forst, Rainer. 1994. *Kontexte der Gerechtigkeit*, Frankfurt: Suhrkamp.

———. 1999a. "Die Rechtfertigung der Gerechtigkeit. Rawls' Politischer Liberalismus und Habermas' Diskursteorie in der Diskussion," in Hauke Brunkhorst and Peter Niesen (eds.), *Das Recht der Republik*, Frankfurt: Suhrkamp.

———. 1999b. "The Basic Right to Justification: Toward a Constructivist Conception of Human Rights," 6 *Constellations*, pp. 35–60.

———. 2001. "The Rule of Reasons. Three Models of Deliberative Democracy," 14 *Ratio Juris*, pp. 345–378.

Forsthoff, Ernst. 1974. "Grundrechte," in Joachim Ritter (ed.), *Historisches Wörterbuch der Philosophie*, vol. 3, Basel and Stuttgart: Schwabe, pp. 922–923.

Fossum, John Erik, and Agustín José Menéndez, 2005. "The Constitution's Gift," 11 *European Law Journal*, pp. 380–420.

Gaus, Gerald F. 1997. "Reason, Justification and Consensus: Why Democracy Can't Have it All," in James Bohman and William Rehg (eds.), *Deliberative Democracy*, Cambridge (MA): The MIT Press, pp. 205–42.

Gauthier, David. 1986. *Morals by Agreement*, Oxford: Oxford University Press, 1986.

Gearty, Connor. 2003. *Principles of Human Rights Adjudication*, Oxford: Oxford University Press.

Goldford, Dennis J. 2005. *The American Constitution and the Debate on Originalism*, Cambridge (MA): Cambridge University Press.

Gosepath, Stefan. 1995. "The Place of Equality in Habermas and Dworkin's Theories of Justice" 3 *European Journal of Philosophy*, pp. 21–35.

———. 2001. "Democracy out of Reason. Comment on Rainer Forst's 'The rule of Reasons,'" 14 *Ratio Juris*, pp. 379–389.

Greenberg, Karen J. (ed.). 2005. *The Torture Debate in America*, Cambridge (MA): Cambridge University Press.

Griffiths, Richard T. 2001. *Europe's First Constitution*, London: Kogan Page.

Gril, Peter. 1998. *Die Möglichkeit praktischer Erkenntnis aus der Sicht der Diskursteorie*, Berlin: Duncker and Humbolt.

Günther, Klaus. 1989. "A Normative Conception of Coherence for a Discursive Theory of Legal Justification," 2 *Ratio Juris*, pp. 155–166.

———. 1993a. "Critical Remarks on Robert Alexy's 'Special-Case Thesis'" 6 *Ratio Juris*, pp. 143–156.

———. 1993b. *The Sense of Appropriateness: Application Discourses in Morality and Law*, Albany (NY): State University of New York Press.

———. 1999. "Welchen Personenbegriff braucht die Diskurstheorie des Rechts?," in Hauke Brunkhorst and Peter Niesen (eds.), *Das Recht der Republik*, Frankfurt: Suhrkamp, pp. 83–104.

Gutmann, Amy and Dennis Thompson. 1996. *Democracy and Disagreement*, Cambridge (MA): Harvard University Press.

———. 2002. "Deliberative Democracy Beyond Process," 10 *The Journal of Political Philosophy*, pp. 153–174.

Habermas, Jürgen. 1988. "Law and Morality," 8 *Tanner Lectures on Human Values*, pp. 217–279.

———. 1990. *Moral Consciousness and Communicative Action*, Cambridge (MA): The MIT Press.

———. 1992. *Faktizität und Geltung*, Frankfurt am Main: Suhrkamp.

———. 1995. "Om förhållandet mellan politik, rätt och moral," in Erik Oddvar Eriksen and Anders Molander (eds.), *Habermas: Diskurs, rätt och demokrati*, Gothenburg: Daidalos.

———. 1996a. *Between Facts and Norms*, Cambridge (MA): The MIT Press (English translation of *Faktizität und Geltung*, Frankfurt am Main: Suhrkamp, 1992).

———. 1996b. "Reply to symposium participants," 17 *Cardozo Law Review*, pp. 1477–1557, reprinted in Michel Rosenfeld and Andrew Arato (eds.), *Habermas on Law and Democracy*, Berkeley, Los Angeles, and London: California University Press, 1998, pp. 381–452.

———. 1998. *The Inclusion of the Other: Studies in Political Theory*, Cambridge (MA): The MIT Press, 1998.

———. 1999a. "A short Reply," 12 *Ratio Juris*, pp. 445–453.

———. 1999b. *Wahrheit und Rechtferdigung*, Frankfurt: Suhrkamp.

———. 2001a. "Why does Europe need a Constitution?," 11 (second series) *New Left Review*, pp. 5–26.

———. 2001b, "Constitutional Democracy", 29 *Political Theory*, pp. 766–81.

———. 2003. *Truth and Justification*, Cambridge (MA): The MIT Press (English translation of *Wahrheit und Rechtferdigung*, Frankfurt: Suhrkamp, 1999).

Hager, Johannes. 1994. "Grundrechte im Privatrecht," 49 *Juristenzeitung*, pp. 373–383.

Hart, Herbert. L. A. 1961. *The Concept of Law*, Oxford: Oxford University Press.

Hayek, Friedrick A. *Law.* 1982. *Legislation, and Liberty*, One-volume edition, London: Routledge & Kegan Paul.

Hervey, Tamara and Jeff Kenner (eds.). 2003. *Economic and Social Rights under the EU Charter*, Oxford: Hart Publishers.

Hirschl, Ran. 2004. *Towards Juristocracy*, Cambridge (MA): Harvard University Press.

Höffe, Otfried. 1996. *Vernunft und Recht. Bausteine zu einem interkulturellen Rechtsdiskurs*, Frankfurt: Suhrkamp.

Hohfeld, Wesley Newcomb. 1919. *Fundamental Legal Concepts as applied in Judicial Reasoning*, New Haven: Yale University Press [originally the book was published in two parts in the *Yale Law Journal*, vol. 23 (1913), pp. 16–59 and vol. 26 (1917), pp. 710–770].

Holmes, Stephen and Cass Sunstein. 1999. *The Cost of Rights. Why Liberty depends on taxes*, New York (NY): Norton.

Honig, Bonnie. 2001. "Dead Rights, Live Futures. A reply to Habermas's 'Constitutional Democracy,'" 29 *Political Theory*, pp. 792–805.

Honoré, Tony. 1993. "The Dependence of Morality on Law," 13 *Oxford Journal of Legal Studies*, pp. 1–17.

———. 2002. "The Necessary Connection between law and morality," 22 *Oxford Journal of Legal Studies*, pp. 489–495.

Jellinek, Georg. 1914. *Allgemeine Staatslehre*, Berlin: O. Häring.

Jospin, Lionel. 2001. *Ma Vision de l'Europe et de la mondialisation*, Paris: Plon.

Jowell, Jeffrey and Jonathan Cooper. 2003. *Delivering Rights: How the Human Rights Act is Working and for Whom*, Oxford: Hart Publishers.

Kalinowski, Georges. 1972. *La Logique des normes*, Paris: Presses Universitaires de France.

Kelsen, Hans. 1967. *Pure Theory of Law*, Berkeley and Los Angeles: University of California Press.

———. 1997. *Introduction to the Problems of Legal Theory*, Oxford: Oxford University Press.

Klug, Francesca and Claire O'Brien. 2002. "The First Two Years of the Human Rights Act" *Public Law*, pp. 649–662.

Kumm, Mattias. 2004. "Fundamental rights as Principles: On the Structure and Domain of Constitutional Justice," 2 *International Journal of Constitutional Law*, pp. 574–96.

Laband, Paul. 1911. *Das Staatsrecht des Deutschen Reiches*, vol. 2, Tübingen: Mohr.

Laporta, Francisco. 1987. "Sobre el concepto de derechos humanos" 4 *Doxa*, pp. 23–46.

Lasser, Mitch. 2004. *Judicial Deliberations: A Comparative Analysis of Transparency and Legitimacy*, New York (NY): Oxford University Press.

La Torre, Massimo. 2002. "Theories of Legal Argumentation and Concepts of Law. An Approximation," 15 *Ratio Juris*, pp. 377–402.

Lenaerts, Koen. 2001. "Le droit comparé dans le travail du juge communitaire," 37 *Revue Trimestrelle du Droit Européen*, pp. 487–528.

Lenaerts, Koen, Piet Van Nuffel, and Robert Bray. 1999. *Constitutional Law of the European Union*, London: Sweet and Maxwell.

Leonard, Mark (ed.). 2001. *The Future Shape of Europe*, Brussels: Foreign Policy Centre.

Levison, Sanford (ed.). 2004. *Torture: A Collection*, New York (NY): Oxford University Press.

Luhmann, Niklas. 1995. *Das Recht der Gesellschaft*, Frankfurt am Main: Suhrkamp.

MacCormick, John. 1950. *The Flag in the Wind*, London: Wackburg.

MacCormick, Neil D. 1978a. "Does the United Kingdom have a Constitution? Reflections on MacCormick v Lord Advocate," 29 *Northern Ireland Legal Quarterly*, pp. 1–20.

———. 1978b. *Legal Reasoning and Legal Theory*, Oxford: Oxford University Press.

———. 1994. "The Concept of Law and 'The Concept of Law'," 14 *Oxford Journal of Legal Studies*, pp. 1–23.

———. 1999. *Questioning Sovereignty. Law, State and Nation in the European Union*, Oxford: Oxford University Press.

MacCormick, Neil and Ota Weinberger. 1997. *An Institutional Theory of Law, New Approaches to Legal Positivism*, Dordrecht: Kluwer.

Markesinis, Basil M. 1999. "Privacy, Freedom of Expression and the Horizontal Effect of the Human Rights Bill: Lessons from Germany," 115 *Law Quarterly Review*, pp. 47–88.
Maus, Ingeborg. 1989. "Die Trennung von Recht und Moral als Begrenzung des Rechts," 20 *Rechtstheorie*, pp. 191–210.
———. 1996. "Liberties and Popular Sovereignty: On Jürgen Habermas's Reconstruction of the System of Rights," 17 *Cardozo Law Review*, pp. 825–882.
Menéndez, Agustín José. 2001. *Justifying Taxes*. Dordrecht: Kluwer.
———. 2002. "Chartering Europe," 40 *Journal of Common Market Studies*, pp. 471–90.
———. 2003a. "Finalité through rights" in Erik O. Eriksen, John E. Fossum, and Agustín J. Menéndez (eds.), *The Chartering of Europe. The European Charter of Fundamental Rights and its Constitutional Implications*, Nomos: Baden-Baden, pp. 30–47.
———. 2003b. "Sinews of Peace" 16 *Ratio Juris*, pp. 374–398.
———. 2005. "Between Laeken and the Deep Blue Sea," 10 *European Public Law*, pp. 105–144.
Michelman, Frank I. 1997. "How can the People ever make the Laws? A Critique of Deliberative Democracy," in James Bohman and William Rehg (eds.), *Deliberative Democracy*, Cambridge (MA): The MIT Press, pp. 145–171.
Moher, Andrew. 2004. "The Lesser of Two evils. An argument for judicially sanctioned torture in a post-9/11 world," 26 *Thomas Jefferson Law Review*, pp. 469–489.
Möllers, Cristoph. 2004. "The politics of law and the law of politics: two constitutional traditions in Europe," in Eriksen, Fossum and Menéndez (eds.), *Developing a Constitution for Europe*, London: Routledge, pp. 129–139.
Moral Soriano, Leonor. 2003. "How proportionate should anti-competitive State intervention be?," 28 *European Law Review*, pp. 112–123.
More, Gillian. 1999. "The Principle of Equal Treatment: From Market Unifier to Fundamental Right" in Paul Craig and Gráinne de Búrca (eds.), *The Evolution of EU Law*, Oxford: Oxford University Press, pp. 517–553.
Nelson, Leonard. 1972. "Kritik der praktischen Vernunft," in Paul Bernays et. al., *Gesammelte Schriften, 4* (eds.) *Vorlesungen über die Grundlagen der Etik*, Hamburg: Felix Meiner Verlag.
O'Leary, Siofra and José Fernández Martín. 2000. "Judicially Created Exceptions to the free provision of services," 11 *European Business Law Review*, pp. 347–362.
Oliveira, Álvaro Castro. 2002. "Workers and other Persons: Step-by-step from movement to citizenship-Case Law 1995–2001," 39 *Common Market Law Review*, pp. 77–122.
Palandt, Otto. 2003. *Bürgerliches Gesetzbuch*, Munich: Beck (62nd edn).
Van Panhuys, Jonkheer HF. 1953. "The Netherlands Constitution and International Law," 47 *American Journal of International Law*, pp. 537–558.
Patzig, Günther. 2002. "Can Moral Norms be Rationally Justified?," 41 *Angewandte Chemie. International Edition*, pp. 3553–3558.
Pavlakos, George. 1998. "The Special Case Thesis. An Assessment of R. Alexy's Discursive Theory of Law," 11 *Ratio Juris*, pp. 126–154.
———. 1999. "Persons and Norms: On the normative groundwork of Discourse-Ethics" 85 *Archiv für Rechts- und Sozialphilosophie*, pp.1–22.
Peers, Steve and Angela Ward (eds.). 2004. *The EU Charter of Fundamental Rights*, Oxford: Hart Publishers.
Pescatore, Pierre. 1968. "Les droits de l'homme et l'intégration européenne," 4 *Cahiers du Droit Européen*, pp. 629–670.
———. 1970. "Fundamental Rights and Freedoms in the System of the European Communities," 18 *American Journal of Comparative Law*, pp. 343–351.

———. 1974. *The Law of Integration: Emergence of a New Phenomenon in International Relations, Based on the Experience of the European Communities*, Leiden: Sithoff.

Pettit, Phillip. 1997. *Republicanism: A Theory of Freedom and Government*, Oxford: Oxford University Press.

Pitzner, Rainer and Michael Ronellenfitsch. 1996. *Das Assessorexam im Öffentlichen Recht*, Neuwied: Werner Verlag, (9th edn).

Pröpper, Igno M.A.M. 1993. "Argumentation and Power in Evaluation-Research and in its Utilization in the Policy Making Process," in Rene von Schomberg (ed.), *Science, Politics and Morality. Scientific Uncertainty and Decision Making*, Dordrecht: Kluwer Academic Publishers.

Raabe, Marius. 1998. *Grundrechte und Erkenntnis*, Baden-Baden: Nomos.

Radbruch, Gustav. 1980. "Five Minutes of Legal Philosophy," in Joel Feinberg and Hyman Gross (eds.), *Philosophy of Law*, Belmont, California: Wadsworth, (translated by Stanley L. Paulson), pp. 103–104 (a new translation, by Bonnie Litschewski and Stanley L. Paulson in 26 (2006) *Oxford Journal of Legal Studies*, pp. 13–15).

Rawls, John. 1971. *A Theory of Justice*, Cambridge (MA): Harvard University Press.

———. 1993. *Political Liberalism*, New York (NY): Columbia University Press.

———. 1995. "Reply to Habermas," 92 *The Journal of Philosophy*, pp. 132–180.

———. 1997. "The Idea of Public Reason Revisited," 64 *The University of Chicago Law Review*, pp. 765–807.

———. 1999. *The Law of Peoples*, Cambridge (MA): Harvard University Press.

———. 1999a. *A Theory of Justice* (revised edition), Cambridge (MA): Harvard University Press.

———. 1999b. *The Law of the Peoples*, Cambridge (MA): Harvard University Press.

Raz, Joseph. 1986. *The Morality of Freedom*, Oxford: Oxford University Press.

Richmond, Catherine. 1997. "Preserving the Identity Crisis: Autonomy, System and Sovereignty in European law," 16 *Law and Philosophy*, pp. 377–420.

Rivers, Julian. 2002. "A Theory of Constitutional Rights and the British Constitution" in Robert Alexy, *A Theory of Constitutional Rights*, Oxford: Oxford University Press, xvii-li.

———. 2005. "Gross Statutory Injustice and the Canadian Head Tax Case" in David Dyzenhaus and Mayo Moran (eds.), *Calling power to account*, Toronto: Toronto University Press.

Rosenfeld, Michael and Andrew Arato (eds.), 1998. *Habermas on Law and Democracy: Critical Exchanges*, Berkeley: University of California Press.

Roth, Kenneth, Minky Worden, and Amy D. Bernstein (eds.). 2005. *Torture. Does it Make us Safer? Is it Ever OK? A Human Rights Perspective*, New York (NY): New Press.

Schlink, Bernhard. 2001. "Der Grundsatz der Verhältnismässigkeit," in Peter Badura and Horst Dreier (eds.), *Festschrift 50 Jahre Bundesverfassungsgericht*, vol. 2, Tübingen: Mohr Siebeck, pp. 445–465.

Schmitt, Carl. 1933. "Weiterentwicklung des totalen Staates in Deutschland" 9:2 *Europäische Revue*, pp. 65–70.

———. 1970. *Verfassungslehre*, Berlin: Duncker and Humblot.

———. 1994. *Positionen und Begriffe im Kampf mit Weimar-Genf-Versailles 1929–39*, (3rd edn), Berlin: Duncker and Humblot.

Servan-Schreiber, Jean Jacques. 1967. *Le Défi Américain*, Paris: Denöel.

Singer, Marcus S. 1958. "Moral Rules and Principles," in A. I. Melden (ed.), *Essays in Moral Philosophy*, Seattle: University of Washington Press.

Starck, Christian. 1996. "Verfassungsgerichtsbarkeit und Fachgerichte," 51 *Juristenzeitung*, pp. 1033–1042.

Tribe, Lawrence. 2000. *American Constitutional Law*, vol. 1, New York: Foundation Press (3rd edn).

Tuori, Karlo. 2002. *Critical Legal Positivism*, Aldershot: Ashgate.

Tyler, Tom R. 1990. *Why People Obey the Law*, New Haven (CT): Yale University Press.

Waldron, Jeremy. 1999. *Law and Disagreement*, Oxford: Oxford University Press.

Weiler, Joseph. 1986. "Eurocracy and Distrust: Some Questions Concerning the Role of the European Court of Justice in the Protection of Fundamental Human Rights within the Legal Order of the European Communities," 61 *Washington Law Review*, pp. 1103–1142.

Weithman, Paul J. 1995. "Contractualist Liberalism and Deliberative Democracy," 24 *Philosophy & Public* Affairs, pp. 314–343.

Wellmer, Albert. 1986. *Ethik und Dialog*, Frankfurt: Suhrkamp.

Whitty, Noel, Thérèse Murphy, and Stephen Livingstone. 2001. *Civil Liberties Law: The Human Rights Act Era*, Oxford: Oxford University Press.

Von Wright, Georg Henrik. 1963. *The Logic of Preference*, Edinburgh: Edinburgh University Press.

Wittgenstein, Ludwig. 1978. *Philosophical Investigations*, Oxford: Basil Blackwell.

Wróblewski, Jerzy. 1992. *The Judicial Application of Law*, Dordrecht: Kluwer.

Yoo, John. 2004a. "The Status of Soldiers and Terrorists under the Geneva Convention," 3 *Chinese Journal of International Law*, pp. 135–150.

———. 2004b. "Transferring Terrorists," 79 *Notre Dame Law Review*, pp.1183–1236.

———. 2005a. "Letter regarding the 'views of our Office concerning the legality under international law of interrogation methods to be used on captured al Qaeda operatives,' " in Karen J. Greenberg and Joshua L. Dratel (eds.), *The Torture Papers*, New York (NY): Cambridge University Press, pp. 218–222.

———. 2005b. *The Powers of War and Peace*, Chicago (IL): Chicago University Press.

Zagrebelsky, Gustavo, Sergio Dellavalle and Jörg Luther (eds.). 2003. *Diritti e Costituzione nell'Unione Europea*, Bari and Roma: Laterza.

NAME INDEX

(The indexes of names and subjects have been compiled by
Flavia Carbonell and Raúl Letelier)

SUBJECT INDEX

Law and Philosophy Library

1. E. Bulygin, J.-L. Gardies and I. Niiniluoto (eds.): *Man, Law and Modern Forms of Life.* With an Introduction by M.D. Bayles. 1985 ISBN 90-277-1869-5
2. W. Sadurski: *Giving Desert Its Due.* Social Justice and Legal Theory. 1985 ISBN 90-277-1941-1
3. N. MacCormick and O.Weinberger: *An Institutional Theory of Law.* New Approaches to Legal Positivism. 1986 ISBN 90-277-2079-7
4. A. Aarnio: *The Rational as Reasonable.* A Treatise on Legal Justification. 1987 ISBN 90-277-2276-5
5. M.D. Bayles: *Principles of Law.* A Normative Analysis. 1987 ISBN 90-277-2412-1; Pb: 90-277-2413-X
6. A. Soeteman: *Logic in Law.* Remarks on Logic and Rationality in Normative Reasoning, Especially in Law. 1989 ISBN 0-7923-0042-4
7. C.T. Sistare: *Responsibility and Criminal Liability.* 1989 ISBN 0-7923-0396-2
8. A. Peczenik: *On Law and Reason.* 1989 ISBN 0-7923-0444-6
9. W. Sadurski: *Moral Pluralism and Legal Neutrality.* 1990 ISBN 0-7923-0565-5
10. M.D. Bayles: *Procedural Justice.* Allocating to Individuals. 1990 ISBN 0-7923-0567-1
11. P. Nerhot (ed.). *Law, Interpretation and Reality.* Essays in Epistemology, Hermeneutics and Jurisprudence. 1990 ISBN 0-7923-0593-0
12. A.W. Norrie: *Law, Ideology and Punishment.* Retrieval and Critique of the Liberal Ideal of Criminal Justice. 1991 ISBN 0-7923-1013-6
13. P. Nerhot (ed.): *Legal Knowledge and Analogy.* Fragments of Legal Epistemology, Hermeneutics and Linguistics. 1991 ISBN 0-7923-1065-9
14. O. Weinberger: *Law, Institution and Legal Politics.* Fundamental Problems of Legal Theory and Social Philosophy. 1991 ISBN 0-7923-1143-4
15. J. Wróblewski: *The Judicial Application of Law.* Edited by Z. Bańkowski and N. MacCormick. 1992 ISBN 0-7923-1569-3
16. T. Wilhelmsson: *Critical Studies in Private Law.* A Treatise on Need-Rational Principles in Modern Law. 1992 ISBN 0-7923-1659-2
17. M.D. Bayles: *Hart's Legal Philosophy.* An Examination. 1992 ISBN 0-7923-1981-8
18. D.W.P. Ruiter: *Institutional Legal Facts.* Legal Powers and their Effects. 1993 ISBN 0-7923-2441-2
19. J. Schonsheck: *On Criminalization.* An Essay in the Philosophy of the Criminal Law. 1994 ISBN 0-7923-2663-6
20. R.P. Malloy and J. Evensky (eds.): *Adam Smith and the Philosophy of Law and Economics.* 1994 ISBN 0-7923-2796-9
21. Z. Bańkowski, I. White and U. Hahn (eds.): *Informatics and the Foundations of Legal Reasoning.* 1995 ISBN 0-7923-3455-8
22. E. Lagerspetz: *The Opposite Mirrors.* An Essay on the Conventionalist Theory of Institutions. 1995 ISBN 0-7923-3325-X

Law and Philosophy Library

23. M. van Hees: *Rights and Decisions.* Formal Models of Law and Liberalism. 1995 ISBN 0-7923-3754-9
24. B. Anderson: *"Discovery" in Legal Decision-Making*. 1996 ISBN 0-7923-3981-9
25. S. Urbina: *Reason, Democracy, Society.* A Study on the Basis of Legal Thinking. 1996 ISBN 0-7923-4262-3
26. E. Attwooll: *The Tapestry of the Law.* Scotland, Legal Culture and Legal Theory. 1997 ISBN 0-7923-4310-7
27. J.C. Hage: *Reasoning with Rules.* An Essay on Legal Reasoning and Its Underlying Logic. 1997 ISBN 0-7923-4325-5
28. R.A. Hillman: *The Richness of Contract Law.* An Analysis and Critique of Contemporary Theories of Contract Law. 1997 ISBN 0-7923-4336-0; 0-7923-5063-4 (Pb)
29. C. Wellman: *An Approach to Rights.* Studies in the Philosophy of Law and Morals. 1997 ISBN 0-7923-4467-7
30. B. van Roermund: *Law, Narrative and Reality.* An Essay in Intercepting Politics. 1997 ISBN 0-7923-4621-1
31. I. Ward: *Kantianism, Postmodernism and Critical Legal Thought.* 1997 ISBN 0-7923-4745-5
32. H. Prakken: *Logical Tools for Modelling Legal Argument.* A Study of Defeasible Reasoning in Law. 1997 ISBN 0-7923-4776-5
33. T. May: *Autonomy, Authority and Moral Responsibility.* 1998 ISBN 0-7923-4851-6
34. M. Atienza and J.R. Manero: *A Theory of Legal Sentences.* 1998 ISBN 0-7923-4856-7
35. E.A. Christodoulidis: *Law and Reflexive Politics.* 1998 ISBN 0-7923-4954-7
36. L.M.M. Royakkers: *Extending Deontic Logic for the Formalisation of Legal Rules.* 1998 ISBN 0-7923-4982-2
37. J.J. Moreso: *Legal Indeterminacy and Constitutional Interpretation.* 1998 ISBN 0-7923-5156-8
38. W. Sadurski: *Freedom of Speech and Its Limits.* 1999 ISBN 0-7923-5523-7
39. J. Wolenski (ed.): *Kazimierz Opalek Selected Papers in Legal Philosophy.* 1999 ISBN 0-7923-5732-9
40. H.P. Visser 't Hooft: *Justice to Future Generations and the Environment.* 1999 ISBN 0-7923-5756-6
41. L.J. Wintgens (ed.): *The Law in Philosophical Perspectives.* My Philosophy of Law. 1999 ISBN 0-7923-5796-5
42. A.R. Lodder: *DiaLaw.* On Legal Justification and Dialogical Models of Argumentation. 1999 ISBN 0-7923-5830-9
43. C. Redondo: *Reasons for Action and the Law.* 1999 ISBN 0-7923-5912-7
44. M. Friedman, L. May, K. Parsons and J. Stiff (eds.): *Rights and Reason.* Essays in Honor of Carl Wellman. 2000 ISBN 0-7923-6198-9

Law and Philosophy Library

45. G.C. Christie: *The Notion of an Ideal Audience in Legal Argument*. 2000 ISBN 0-7923-6283-7
46. R.S. Summers: *Essays in Legal Theory*. 2000 ISBN 0-7923-6367-1
47. M. van Hees: *Legal Reductionism and Freedom*. 2000 ISBN 0-7923-6491-0
48. R. Gargarella: *The Scepter of Reason*. Public Discussion and Political Radicalism in the Origins of Constitutionalism. 2000 ISBN 0-7923-6508-9
49. M. Iglesias Vila: *Facing Judicial Discretion*. Legal Knowledge and Right Answers Revisited. 2001 ISBN 0-7923-6778-2
50. M. Kiikeri: *Comparative Legal Reasoning and European Law*. 2001 ISBN 0-7923-6884-3
51. A.J. Menéndez: *Justifying Taxes*. Some Elements for a General Theory of Democratic Tax Law. 2001 ISBN 0-7923-7052-X
52. W.E. Conklin: *The Invisible Origins of Legal Positivism*. A Re-Reading of a Tradition. 2001 ISBN 0-7923-7101-1
53. Z. Bańkowski: *Living Lawfully*. Love in Law and Law in Love. 2001 ISBN 0-7923-7180-1
54. A.N. Shytov: *Conscience and Love in Making Judicial Decisions*. 2001 ISBN 1-4020-0168-1
55. D.W.P. Ruiter: *Legal Institutions*. 2001 ISBN 1-4020-0186-X

Volumes 56–63 were published by Kluwer Law International.

56. G. den Hartogh: *Mutual Expectations*. A Conventionalist Theory of Law. 2002 ISBN 90-411-1796-2
57. W.L. Robison (ed.): *The Legal Essays of Michael Bayles*. 2002 ISBN 90-411-1835-7
58. U. Bindreiter: *Why Grundnorm?* A Treatise on the Implications of Kelsen's Doctrine. 2002 ISBN 90-411-1867-5
59. S. Urbina: *Legal Method and the Rule of Law*. 2002 ISBN 90-411-1870-5
60. M. Baurmann: *The Market of Virtue*. Morality and Commitment in a Liberal Society. 2002 ISBN 90-411-1874-8
61. G. Zanetti: *Political Friendship and the Good Life*. Two Liberal Arguments against Perfectionism. 2002 ISBN 90-411-1881-0
62. W. Sadurski (ed.): *Constitutional Justice, East and West*. 2002 ISBN 90-411-1883-7
63. S. Taekema: *The Concept of Ideals in Legal Theory*. 2003 ISBN 90-411-1971-X
64. J. Raitio: *The Principle of Legal Certainty in EC Law*. 2003 ISBN 1-4020-1217-9
65. E. Santoro: *Autonomy, Freedom and Rights*. A Critique of Liberal Subjectivity. 2003 ISBN 1-4020-1404-X
66. S. Eng: *Analysis of Dis/agreement – with particular reference to Law and Legal Theory*. 2003 ISBN 1-4020-1490-2

Law and Philosophy Library

67. D. González Lagier: *The Paradoxes of Action*. (Human Action, Law and Philosophy). 2003 ISBN Hb-1-4020-1661-1
68. R. Zimmerling: *Influence and Power*. Variations on a Messy Theme. 2004 ISBN Hb-1-4020-2986-1
69. A. Stranieri and J. Zeleznikow (eds.): *Knowledge Discovery from Legal Databases*. 2005 ISBN 1-4020-3036-3
70. J. Hage: *Studies in Legal Logic*. 2005 ISBN 1-4020-3517-9
71. C. Wellman: *Medical Law and Moral Rights*. 2005 ISBN 1-4020-3751-1
72. T. Meisels: *Territorial Rights*. 2005 ISBN 1-4020-3822-4
73. G.W. Rainbolt: *The Concept of Rights*. 2005 ISBN 1-4020-3976-X
74. O. Ezra: *Moral Dilemmas in Real Life*. Current Issues in Applied Ethics. 2006 ISBN 1-4020-4103-9
75. N.T. Casals: *Group Rights as Human Rights*. A Liberal Approach to Multiculturalism. 2006 ISBN 1-4020-4208-6
76. C. Michelon Jr.: *Being Apart from Reasons*. The Role of Reasons in Public and Private Moral Decision-Making. 2006 ISBN 1-4020-4282-5
77. A.J. Menéndez and E.O. Eriksen (eds.): *Arguing Fundamental Rights*. 2006 ISBN 1-4020-4918-8